Learning to Teach
in the Digital Age

Colin Lankshear and Michele Knobel
General Editors

Vol. 78

The New Literacies and Digital Epistemologies series
is part of the Peter Lang Education list.
Every volume is peer reviewed and meets
the highest quality standards for content and production.

PETER LANG
New York • Bern • Frankfurt • Berlin
Brussels • Vienna • Oxford • Warsaw

Sean Justice

Learning to Teach in the Digital Age

New Materialities and Maker Paradigms in Schools

PETER LANG
New York • Bern • Frankfurt • Berlin
Brussels • Vienna • Oxford • Warsaw

Library of Congress Cataloging-in-Publication Data

Names: Justice, Sean, author.
Title: Learning to teach in the digital age:
new materialities and maker paradigms in schools / Sean Justice.
Description: New York: Peter Lang, 2016.
Series: New literacies and digital epistemologies; vol. 78 | ISSN 1523-9543
Includes bibliographical references and index.
Identifiers: LCCN 2016015263 | ISBN 978-1-4331-3319-0 (hardcover: alk. paper)
ISBN 978-1-4331-3318-3 (paperback: alk. paper) | ISBN 978-1-4539-1887-6 (ebook pdf)
ISBN 978-1-4331-3720-4 (epub) | ISBN 978-1-4331-3721-1 (mobi)
Subjects: LCSH: Maker movement in education—United States. | Education—
Effect of technological innovations on—United States. | Actor-network theory.
Classification: LCC LB1029.M35 J87 2016 | DDC 371.102—dc23
LC record available at https://lccn.loc.gov/2016015263

Bibliographic information published by **Die Deutsche Nationalbibliothek**.
Die Deutsche Nationalbibliothek lists this publication in the "Deutsche
Nationalbibliografie"; detailed bibliographic data are available
on the Internet at http://dnb.d-nb.de/.

The paper in this book meets the guidelines for permanence and durability
of the Committee on Production Guidelines for Book Longevity
of the Council of Library Resources.

© 2016 Peter Lang Publishing, Inc., New York
29 Broadway, 18th floor, New York, NY 10006
www.peterlang.com

Printed in the United States of America

For my parents,

Ann Haight Justice and James W. Justice,

my most important teachers:

Your stories and adventures weave through my every act of learning.

ACKNOWLEDGMENTS

This book is a shared achievement; it would not exist without the concerted efforts and goodwill of many people. First and most obviously, thank you to the teachers and administrators at the school where the study was situated: Without your fearless generosity, this work could never have gotten off the ground. I'm especially thankful to Kieran and Amanda for the welcome you showed throughout the eighteen months of the study, including your willingness to engage so thoroughly with this project, in endless conversations, in emails, and by reading sections of the narrative: You helped me understand what I was hearing and observing.

Secondly, I am thankful to so many people from Teachers College, Columbia University, and elsewhere that it's impossible to name everyone— mentors, colleagues, confidants, and fellow lifelong learners; each of you, in different ways, were indispensable to the doing of this study and the writing of the book, even though I suspect some of you might not even be cognizant of that fact. Thank you, Angela Allmond, John Baldacchino, John Broughton, Judy Burton, Marta Cabral, Sarah Cunningham, Jaymes Dec, Carol Guasti, Erol Gündüz, Olga Hubard, Jesse Jagtiani, Richard Jochum, Michele Knobel, Colin Lankshear, Victoria Marsick, Joy Moser, Kylie Peppler, Rocky Schwartz, and Lyle Yorks. I'd like to especially thank Victoria and Lyle for your methodological wisdom and guidance; John, for your mentoring in the way of art; Marta, for your insight and collaboration in material inquiry; and Judy, for your dedication to art education and teacher education, two passions that will fuel the rest of my career.

And finally, to my family, without your support this work could not have been done; thank you for bearing with me during this long journey. Connor and Brendan, following you has catalyzed this work; thank you for teaching me so much about learning and knowing in the digital age. And Diana, your strength and generosity are fundamental to this achievement; there are no words I can use to adequately express my gratitude to you for making this work possible.

Sean Justice
New York, NY
March 2016

CONTENTS

LIST OF TABLES

INTRODUCTION

The mistake I see a lot of schools making is that they don't view technology as a tool for learning. That's why I never use the word "integration"—because you don't integrate reading into your English curriculum. Right? It's a core skill.

— Bradly, K–12 technology director

I have a commitment to deciphering objects and texts, and that's what I've done my whole career. I get the feeling that something else is about to happen where instead of deciphering objects, I'm going to be thinking about creating [them]. I mean, we're about to reconceptualize the object.

— Amanda, high school history and humanities teacher

This is a story about a study that explored how a handful of K–12 teaching practices began to connect to digital making and learning pedagogies. Since about the mid-2000s a new generation of digital tools and materials have been appearing in schools and after-school spaces, cropping up in newly built FabLabs and makerspaces, stoking enthusiasms for project-based or problem-based learning. These new tools, such as 3D printers, laser cutters, robotics and microelectronics kits, and the cascade of new teaching and learning opportunities that they supposedly initiate, excite educators, students and the general public about the potential for reforming schools. In fact, hopes that maker education will fuel a schooling revolution run so high in some circles that a kind of evangelism has begun to appear at normally staid educational technology conferences.

Recently, in an emotional appeal at the conclusion of a digital fabrication conference, a university researcher told an overflow audience that if we failed to reinvent schools this time around, we might as well give up on the democratic values at the foundation of our society. The message resonated strongly for many of us who, for one reason or another, have become disillusioned with the rising tide of instrumentalism in schooling—for example, the high-stakes testing and jobs training that push the "useless" arts to the periphery of school agendas. This time it'll be different, we tell ourselves; the maker movement, digital fabrication, the rise of STEM and STEAM, the Internet of Things— everything has changed, and we really do stand on the threshold of renewal. We're encouraged in these hopes by teachers who report the achievements of students who have been motivated by maker education to take charge of their own learning. Time and again, teachers, administrators, and even some parents have told me that the problem of schooling will be solved when every grade looks more like kindergarten, where play with materials and make-to-learn activities overflow like the cornucopia on our Thanksgiving tables.

And in fact, for many observers, the metaphor of the makerspace saturates the imagination—that workshop filled with a buzzing rush of students exploring and experimenting, collaborating with and encouraging their co-learners, sharing, questing, tinkering, doing what they need to do, not because some teacher told them to, but because they're driven by their own interests and curiosity, their own need to know. Often, no further proof of maker education's effectiveness is required beyond the contrast between a busy makerspace and our memories of those rows of desks from childhood classrooms, or from the classrooms in that other school down the road, the one that doesn't yet have a makerspace.

While this might sound like an exaggeration if you haven't hung out with teachers who are committed to maker education, it isn't. In fact, excitement about making in schools has spread beyond the classroom and taken root in the tool design and toy industry—a sign of the movement's expanding relevance. For example, today (in the last quarter of 2015), a Google search for makerspace furniture returns advertorials not only from companies that have traditionally produced school furniture, but also from newcomers to the field like IKEA and Steelcase, as well as paid messages from architecture firms vying for a slice of the expanding market in makerspace design. In fact, the commercialization of maker education might explain the skepticism of some teachers and administrators who wonder if the hoopla is just a fad, and if the 3D print-ers and laser cutters will disappear into backroom closets along with other new technologies that failed to change teaching and learning. Others consider the incessant marketing coming from the maker industry as a simplification that might diminish potential. For instance, in October 2015, a school technol-ogy administrator told me that he didn't like the words STEM and STEAM because they separated science and math from English and the humanities. For him, this trivialized the problem-based learning he wanted in the curricu-lum. Similarly, the head of a middle school discussed her makerspaces without once using the word *maker* or any derivative of it. When I called her attention to this, she said that the word itself—*maker*—had become associated with just one kind of tool: 3D printers. To resist the diminishment this represented, she refused to even use the word. When I asked what word(s) she preferred, she said, "*inquiry-based learning.*" For both of these administrators, clearly, the language itself has begun to obscure the reason they want teachers to engage with maker education (or whatever we might call it) in the first place.

These anecdotes get to the questions and conflicts that propelled me into a K–12 school in 2013 to study teachers' learning. By that time, the maker movement had been gaining traction in schools for a while, due in part to the popularity of *Make* magazine and its DIY extravaganza, Maker Faire (founded in 2005 and 2006, respectively), but most research into how or if project-based, making-infused teaching and learning worked for school-ing had focused only on student learning. Left unasked were questions about how teachers and administrators connected with making in education. This, it seemed to me, was an oversight—especially if a resurgence of hands-on learning were to help reform schooling.

A different trajectory is apparent in the digital media and learning move-ment (known as dml). Stemming from the new literacies movement that emerged in the early to mid-1990s with the advent of the internet and the Web, more than 10 years before the maker movement showed up, dml has attended to the way digital text and Web 2.0 practices like blogging, gaming, and social media participation have changed learning and knowing. For example, multiliteracy movements like the New London Group have been exploring changes in teaching and schooling since the emergence of digital text, especially in Australia and the United Kingdom (see Green and Bigum, 1993, for an early exploration of the challenges teachers would come to face in the digital age). Today, thanks in part to the support of the MacArthur Foundation, dml is a leader in research on 21st-century pedagogy, including teacher training and professional development (see their website for the breadth and variety of dml work in education: http://dmlhub.net). In fact, as I'll show in Chapter 2, dml is a key strand in maker education, even though its tools and materials (e.g., new literacies such as blogging and gaming) are sometimes thought to be tangential to the making and building that goes on in makerspaces. This is changing, however: As Smith, West-Puckett, Cantrill, and Zamora (2016) remind us, "writing [is] a form of making" (p. 3).

Nevertheless, in spite of that early work, and the rising enthusiasm about the affordances of digital media for students' learning, new literacies and digital media learning research does not appear to have provoked maker education to ask how *teachers* adopt, integrate, or otherwise come to terms with digital tools and materials, and whether doing so changes their practices. This, then, is where this book begins: Researchers agree that new tools are changing learning, but we haven't yet looked closely at how (or if) teaching is changing in schools.

How do new tools and materials affect teaching, or change how we learn to teach? The study began with two propositions: first, that tools and materials are important components of teaching and learning; and second, that studying tools and materials in actual learning ecologies, such as schools, can catalyze new ideas about how teachers learn to teach with those tools. As you might already suspect, in this book, *digital* tools and materials—for example, computers, smartphones, the internet; and peripherals such as laser cutters and 3D printers; and the microelectronics found in makerspaces, such as circuits with sensors and lights that blink or buzzers that buzz—are considered a subset of a vastly broader suite of technologies that weave through teaching and learning. In the words of a third-grade teacher who participated in the study, "That pair of scissors is a technology...and your pencil sharpener is a type of technology, [too]."

In this book I explore these questions by focusing on a particular school in a particular setting. To be clear, this is a local study. That's not to say that what I've learned won't be relevant to other schools, libraries, or makerspaces— I hope it will be!—but rather to suggest that the way it is relevant rests on holding practice as an emergent phenomenon rather than a generalizable set of rules. In saying this, I'm following qualitative, sociomaterial research traditions that come from ethnography, science and technology studies (STS), and emerging scholarship in new materialisms. In these traditions, data collection and analysis is a recursive and entangled enterprise. That is, instead of deploying numbers and statistics to measure or prove cause-and-effect correlations,

I gather stories and impressions and overlap them with metaphor to report what I've observed; in asking how a particular group of teachers began to understand the place of digital tools and materials in their teaching, I did not try to standardize what they told me according to benchmarks established ahead of time, but rather to describe what they did, and how and where they did it. In this, I am trusting that the value of the work will be in how what I've learned might inform teaching in classrooms, or in a teacher education curriculum.

Organization of the Book

This book is comprised of twelve chapters, a bibliography, and an index. Additionally, distributed between the chapters are narrative snapshots of some of the projects and activities I observed during the study. These "Field Notes," as I call them, are meant to immerse you in the kind of teaching and learning that I encountered.

This begs a question: Who is the "you" who is reading this? A teacher or administrator who wants to learn about project-based, making-infused teaching? A researcher or graduate student who wants to explore the methodology? A teacher educator who wants to bring making into a preservice or professional development program? In fact, whether you're one of these or someone else, I've tried to make the book accessible to a broad audience of educators and education researchers, even if some of the specifics (about maker education, digital technology, school reform) are unfamiliar in form, content, or language. To that effect, I invite you to dip into and out of these chapters based on your interests, and to use this map to plan your route through the stories and conversations I've collected.

In the first chapter I'll trace the story of the thinking that led to the questions that launched the study. To ground the book on both accounts—the thinking and the approach—I'll describe my background as a teacher, artist, and researcher. In the conclusion of Chapter 1 I'll talk about what I hope to achieve in writing this book.

Chapters 2, 3, and 4 discuss the shape and conduct of the study, both the theory that informed it and the dispositions that guided me in implementing it. Specifically, Chapter 2 looks at pedagogical traditions that undergird maker education, such as constructionism, artistic development, and interest-driven, or connected, learning. These traditions are compared and contrasted with each other in order to construct a maker-oriented teaching framework to help analyze observations and interviews. Chapter 3 introduces and describes digital materiality, a ubiquitous material affordance of contemporary learning ecologies. Chapter 4 describes the design of the study—the methods and practices I employed in conducting interviews, observations, and data analysis. Chapter 4 also traces the development of the inquiry questions by describing two dispositional frameworks that guided me: sociomaterialism and actor-network theory.

Chapters 5 through 10 report the major findings of the study, including empirical material collected from interviews and observations, as well as interpretative analyses. Chapter 5 introduces the school where the study was situated, and the individual teachers and administrators who shared their practices with me. Chapters 6 and 7 assemble and discuss interactions between traditional and project-based, or making-infused, teaching practices. These interactions, which I think of as *contact points*, are collected in the Ways and Challenges, a typology of practice-based interactions. Chapter 8 puts the typology to use by building and then interpreting several integrated narratives based on specific teachers. Chapters 9 and 10 extend this narrative analysis by looking in more detail at one teaching practice, that of a high school humanities and history teacher.

Chapters 11 and 12 conclude the study with a summary of what I think I have learned about learning to teach in the digital age. It begins with a summary of how participants enacted teaching practices that were informed by and entangled with digital making and learning. Then, by way of addressing the inquiry questions that guided the study, I discuss the Ways and Challenges as a heuristic for identifying and assessing pedagogical goals. Finally, I draw out some implications for teaching and teacher education by considering practice itself as an enactment of knowing and learning.

FIELD NOTES (RACECARS)

A 50-foot wooden track undulates across the cafeteria floor. Lunch tables have been pushed to the walls; chairs are scattered awkwardly here and there. Throughout the room, sixth-grade girls huddle around stations, building racecars. In teams of two they sort through bins of parts and tools, passing wheels and axles back and forth, and adding or removing weight from their chassis with washers and tape. One pair works with screwdrivers and pliers to remove the motor from a battery-powered toy. "There's no rules," one girl says, a bit defiantly. At one station, students streamline the aerodynamics of their cars by smoothing corners and creases, while conversely, at another station, other students are glue-gunning feathers and fuzzy pipe cleaners to theirs.

"Three, two, one—go!"

From across the cafeteria, at the highest point on the track, another run begins with a cheer and the flip of the starting lever. Two cars leap across the starting line and zip down the steepest part of the slope. One car immediately jumps out of the grooves in the track and falls to the floor, but the other one accelerates to the bottom of the first dip, rockets to the crest of the middle bump, catching air as it passes the high point, and zooms down the second incline, a sleek blur of fine engineering. As it crosses the finish line, a sixth grader taps her stopwatch, and from the starting line 50 feet away, her partner yells, "Was it faster?!" As they gather to compare and plot their new data on graphs posted along the walls of the cafeteria, analyzing the fractional changes in speed produced by the washers they've added, the other team picks up their fallen car to ponder what went wrong. "I think the axle broke," one girl says. "No, there's too many feathers," her partner replies.

This is the Nerdy Derby, an annual weeklong extravaganza that has the sixth graders build cars from cardboard, plastic, and assorted craft materials, and then race them against each other. Derived from the famous derbies of an earlier generation's Boy Scouts, each team designs and tests, and then iterates and reiterates their build in order to create the fastest car, the slowest car, and the car that can stop at a precise point on the track—as well as the sleekest car, the prettiest car, the most improbable car, and paradigm cars of other categories that spontaneously appear as the week progresses. Classes have been canceled for the duration of the tournament, but Kieran, the technology teacher and FabLab coordinator, and teams of science, art, and math faculty are fully engaged. At the start of the week teachers had scattered throughout the North Building to facilitate independent learning stations where the girls explored race-critical characteristics like mass, friction, and drag. Games and activities had included various ways of bundling objects of different densities together, and then timing and graphing their descent along ramps of varying steepness. The hands-down favorite of these had been the parachute drop, where fanciful double- and triple-decker concoctions of coffee filters, plastic bags, feathers, string, paper towel tubes, and various other fuzzy components had been set free from the third-floor mezzanine; and where each contraption's wafting descent—or plummeting fall—had been tracked, measured, and documented by smartphone videos and stopwatches amid the screams of laughter and roars of disappointment from the more than thirty sixth-grade teams.

Today, Thursday, before the final races, what the girls have learned about physics is being built into cars at the assembly stations scattered throughout the basement cafeteria. Materials on offer include washers, wooden dowels, bolts and nuts, bamboo skewers, toothpicks, tape, metal fasteners, pipe cleaners, feathers, clay, sticky tack, bottle caps, cat toys, wiffle balls, marbles, paper cups, coffee filters, string, and some laser-cut acrylic, wood, and cardboard wheels. Students can't use prefab or store-bought wheels, but pretty much anything else goes—including, it turns out, secret weapons like battery-powered motors, which haven't been expressly forbidden. In an aside, Kieran tells a concerned teacher to let the girls work out a dispute among themselves, because, anyway, they'll have to figure out how to attach the drive train to their cardboard wheels in order to get any advantage whatsoever—and if they can do that, they deserve to win.

Tomorrow morning there'll be a brief period of last-minute testing, where the girls can add or remove mass, tinker with axle design or wheel diameter, and reduce or increase drag. Then after lunch, faculty and visitors from the other campuses will begin to arrive, fifth graders from the lower middle school will take their trackside seats, and with a favorite teacher's enthusiastic baritone announcing the festivities, the races will begin.

Datasheet: Age group: sixth grade. Content domain: technology, science, art, math. Lead teacher: Kieran. Collaborating teachers: Vanessa, Aidan, Susan, others. Timing: one week in April.

· 1 ·

TRACING THE EMERGENCE
OF THE INQUIRY

I come to this research as an artist and art educator. In the 1980s, while doing an MFA in studio art, concentrating on photography and video, I started teaching high school photography and writing. A few years later I taught photography and the history of photography at a community college. During that time, I was also working as an arts organizer and grant writer, exhibiting photographs and video art in galleries, and beginning to make photographs and videos for magazines and marketing agencies. Later, as my freelance practice grew into a commercial studio business, I dropped the arts advocacy and cut back on the fine art. While I regretted setting those aspects of my career on hold, the studio thrived, and by the mid-2000s we had several employees, dozens of assistants, and clients worldwide. In fact, at about that time the commercial practice stabilized, so I returned to teaching and making art again.

Trajectories of Changing Tools

Along the way, the tools of photography and media changed radically. My journey into computers had begun in graduate school, when I took an administrative job in my university's psychology department. I remember beginning 1986 with a brand new IBM Selectric typewriter, thrilled to be working with such an excellent machine, and ending that year with a desktop PC attached to a dot-matrix printer. In some ways, office life didn't change—managing communication between students and professors still involved endless back-and-forth iterations and chaos—but in others ways the office became unrecognizable: Stacks of yellow legal pads and loose-leaf binders disappeared, replaced with boxes and boxes of floppy disks. What sticks with me, though, is a discombobulated sense of wonder about that PC. What was happening in there? I remember the silence: The gray box and dark screen, the glowing green characters, the buttons on the keyboard and the hieroglyphics of the DOS commands—compared to the electric typewriter, that computer was dead quiet.

Later, when I was a high school photography teacher, and then a moderator for the school yearbook and newspaper, we transitioned from paste-up mechanicals to computer typesetting on laser printers in less than 3 years; I remember feeling the act of writing shift from product-oriented commitment to a fluid, exploratory process. As a video producer with an art and commercial practice I remember when digital buttons replaced analog cameras that had to be calibrated with small screwdrivers and paper targets. I also remember when the thrill of the post-production studio became equivalent to field work, at least in terms of storytelling. And as a photographer, after years of practice with chemicals and mechanical equipment, building darkrooms and ventilation systems along the way, I remember beginning to develop the different kind of precision that computers and digital equipment required, and finding myself thinking about pictures as process rather than object. That is, as with writing and video, photography on the computer changed what I thought I knew about making pictures. I remember huddling around a screen with a friend in about 1992, exploring an early version of Photoshop, amazed by what it could do: Make the picture darker! Make it lighter! Make it greener! But I also remember wondering how we were going to *make* a picture—that is, how were we going to get the picture out of the computer and show it? At that time, before email, the Web, and today's ubiquitous photo printers, that question had no answer we could articulate. In fact, thinking about the problem itself was difficult—what did it mean for a photograph to be *inside* a computer? If there was no way to get *outside*, could the *inside* truly be a place?

I remember another friend's more sanguine response—"Don't worry about it," he said. "When or if computers matter to photography, we'll learn about it as we need to. In the meantime, who cares about making the picture lighter or darker in the computer?—that's what we do in the darkroom. What's the difference?"

His lack of astonishment shocked me, but perhaps he had a point: Maybe the tidal shift we'd been experiencing was something else entirely. Perhaps the evolution in the tools was not an evolution of the object *as* an object, but rather a change in our relationship with it. I remember wondering how to think about what was happening. In the late 1980s and early 1990s computers were changing language, graphics, and pictures, but my experience of those changes felt slippery and difficult to grasp, especially since so few of us had ever put our hands on a computer, much less used one in our studios.

The Hand Makes the Brain

This idea captivated me when I heard it for the first time, in the mid-1990s, from a jazz singer who followed anthropology and the emerging field of brain imaging. He said, "The brain makes the hand, but the hand makes the brain." This was before Frank Wilson (1999) and Antonio Damasio (1994, 1999) had popularized the entanglement of intelligence, imagination, and emotion, or the recursive enactment of body as it acted in the world; it was new to me at the time. But the singer had said it matter-of-factly, in a conversation about intuition and improvisation, when we had asked about singing in relation to a song's history, or to what he knew about it musically, either as a score or as he had performed it previously. This happened during an interview I was video-taping in Tucson, Arizona, for a series of short films about the art community there.

Later, in post-production, we fiddled with the singer's implication that creativity, intuition, and intellect were inseparable from the physical performance of any particular song. The idea resonated strongly, but its appearance in the interview surprised us, changing the film in an unexpected way, as if we weren't really in charge. Suddenly, that video reprised the singer's ideas about improvisation and connected to our unspoken reasons for telling the story in the first place. That is—articulating this from a distance of 20-plus years, with language I did not have at the time—my co-director and I held our practice as an entanglement of action and language with tools and materials, and we wanted that relationship to be visible in the video. We thought perhaps this artist—a singer of jazz standards and a former railroad worker—shared our feelings, but we had not confirmed those suspicions before beginning production. Rather, we had started the project on a whim, with no idea what we were doing, and it had become an improvisation in itself. In the editing room and then later at screenings, there it was: an emotionally resonant picture of innovation emerging from the entanglement of intuition and intellect with material (i.e., the song) and performance (i.e., the singing of the song).

The conversation started by that project influenced my teaching. Shooting and editing that video showed me a community of artists approaching the entanglement of intuition and intellect as a practice of making and doing; I remember feeling that my teaching had to be just as participatory. At the community college where I was teaching the history of photography, I prompted students to connect to picture making as a historical practice, and the course became an exchange of objects, with students making pictures and cameras, and sharing them. Together we enacted a learn-by-doing pedagogy, just as when, several years earlier, I'd converted my high school photography classroom into an open learning lab. In that transformation I'd been inspired by Nancie Atwell's *In the Middle: Writing, Reading, and Learning with Adolescents* (1987) and captivated by her enthusiasm for the kind of teaching espoused by the whole language movement, which was in its ascendancy. At that time, in my first real teaching job, the apparent chaos of the classroom discombobulated me, and some of my colleagues, but we all acknowledged that student achievement had soared. Results at the community college were similar; students learned history by making and sharing artifacts. Our success made me want to keep learning about good teaching. This happened, ironically, at about the same time I stopped teaching in order to focus on the commercial photography business.

Return to Teaching

In 2008 the financial markets collapsed, taking down several of my largest clients and obliterating most of my commercial income. Unfortunately, my wife and I discovered, our robust photography practice had a weak foundation. After thinking about rebranding, we decided to leave the commercial art world altogether. As wrenching as those changes were, we realized that the collapse had created an opening. Our small enterprise had become too big for us, too all-consuming and too stressful, and the work had shifted from making pictures to managing a business, which didn't align with our passions.

As I look back at it now, I see a delicious circularity in the story I'm tell-ing: In 2008, the digital networks that had helped inflate and then burst the financial bubble set up the conditions that turned me toward studying digital media making and learning. Of these conditions, perhaps the most instrumen-tal in terms of this book was my return to full-time teaching in art schools and university art programs. That return made me recognize the challenges that digital tools were bringing to education. For example, in 2001 computers were only a minor element in photography courses, but by the time I was teaching at the end of decade, *photography* had fully morphed into *digital photography*. In the early days, student frustration with the new tools was understandable but low key. In fact, when students became tearful or angry, their emotions were easily defused. The first time an outburst happened in the middle of class, how-ever—in perhaps 2005 or 2006—I was stunned. Later, around 2009, temper tantrums had become commonplace, and I had learned to predict when and where the frustration would break the surface. I remember being taken by surprise, though, when a student stood up, screamed at me, threw a pencil, and stormed out of the room. I also remember discovering that my faculty colleagues were experiencing similar incidents. What surprised all of us was how raw students' reactions were, and how out of place they seemed, coming from people who were college age and older. Why were they so upset? Clearly, something in the environment had changed. I remember paying closer atten-tion to *how* I was teaching, and to how students were responding.

I realized, gradually, that photography students felt fragmented. Photo-graphs made with traditional tools—film cameras and darkrooms—felt like a different kind of artifact from photographs made with digital tools. But why? The results were identical, or nearly so. And studio critiques posed the same questions, whether digital or traditional tools had been used. Why did they feel fractured in spite of day-to-day conversations that addressed picture making as an integrated practice?

The Appearance of Technology

That was when I noticed technology. That is, students used the word *technol-ogy* to talk about computers and digital cameras, but not about darkrooms and film cameras. This didn't make sense to me; why was one set of tools and not another called *technology*? Photographers had always used *technology* to make pictures. For example, calculating f-stops and shutter speeds is the same with digital or analog tools, and in countless other ways the tools are similar if not identical. But a student once told me: "I'm an analog photographer." Where was this distinction coming from?

I began to wonder how our behavior traced to the language. That is, students *described* themselves as fragmented, and they fell to pieces. I was fascinated by this overlap and wondered if, in turn, changing the language might change the learning. Looking back to my high school teaching, and specifically to that whole language photography classroom, I decided to change how I approached the studio and seminar room. The first thing I did was talk about technique in relation to what we were making. Instead of computer menus and digital procedures, studio sessions became stories about pictures. When I did talk about computers, I used metaphors that connected the tools to experience. For instance, I explained digital file characteristics with stories about Thanksgiving, European vacations, and backpacking trips, and compared pictures to road maps, city maps, and trail maps. And, following W. J. T. Mitchell's *What Do Pictures Want?* (2005), I talked about pictures as agential: What does this picture want to say? How can we help it tell that story? I found that narrating from the picture's point of view helped connect with a sense of purpose that did not begin and end with the tool. Suddenly, it didn't seem to matter as much whether the picture had been made with digital or analog tools.

After a few semesters, I noticed that students had stopped talking about their work in tool-based chunks, and the temper tantrums subsided, too. I don't know if the change came from the way I was talking about pictures, at least not as a simplistic causal effect, but students enjoyed themselves more. And yet, I was conflicted: Why would using metaphors in the digital art studio matter?

At this point in my story, two currents converged. The first came from a crisis at my son's high school, brought on by his teachers' rejection of digital media in the classroom. My son's imagination thrived with digital video games and social media, but the school discouraged their use, and nothing that we said or did seemed to have any effect at all. Further, in the school administration's diatribes and draconian restrictions I recognized some of the anxiety I'd experienced with my art students. While not surprising, given the general response that schools have had to digital media, especially in that time period, the anxiety felt very different once it was aimed at my son. The second current came from my decision to begin studying for a doctorate at a university college of education. Not long into my studies, also perhaps not unexpectedly, I found myself teaching digital methods classes for preservice teachers. What did surprise me, though, was that those graduate students— from history, English, math, science, international relations—displayed the same frustrations with computers that I'd noticed in my art students. These two entangled things—debates about digital media with my son's teachers and with my graduate preservice students—put tool-based learning anxieties front and center, but in a newly visceral way. I remember recognizing an overlap; my son's teachers, my education students, and my art students all saw digital tools as a disruption. It occurred to me that what was happening in my son's high school and at the universities was a multidimensional challenge to teaching and learning in digital ecologies.

Technology as a Way of Thinking

A breakthrough came when I began to read philosophy again, in my doctoral seminars, something I hadn't done since college and art school in the 1980s. I remember thinking—again, or for the first time?—that both ancient and modern traditions positioned logic, intuition, sensory knowing (for example, touch, taste, smell), and *techne*, or craft-knowing, as overlapping ways of learning, though each had its own characteristic voice. As Aristotle and Heidegger reminded us, *technology*—making things with tools and materials—is a way of thinking. For me, the notion that intellect, intuition, and imagination were inseparable from the sensuous material of the world felt true to my life as an artist and teacher. Its impact, however, stated so succinctly—*technology is a way of thinking*—felt new. I remember wondering how teachers (both my son's teachers and the preservice teachers who were now my students) would learn to teach with digital tools if their experience was filled with anxiety and fragmentation. Could the storytelling approach I had used in the art studio help? And, taking that line of thinking further, if teachers' biases created fragmented learning spaces (e.g., darkrooms versus computer labs), might the conversation itself be foreclosed? That is, how do we teach something that we can barely talk about?

This chicken-and-egg conundrum fascinated me, but was not being addressed by teacher educators (at least not directly, not in 2010). While the effect of digital media on children and youth learning had been robustly explored (see, for example, Seymour Papert's *MindStorms*, 1980, and *The Children's Machine*, 1993; and James Paul Gee's work on video game learning and situated literacies from 2004 and 2005), there had been little research into how teachers learned to use digital tools and materials. A correction to that deficit has recently appeared (for example: Honey & Kanter, 2013; Martinez & Stager, 2013; and Peppler, Santo, Gresalfi & Tekinbas, 2014), but at the time I was first exploring these questions, conversations with K–12 colleagues and preservice teachers suggested that not much of the enthusiasm from the digital media and learning literature was finding its way into classrooms.

This is where a gap appeared: A question was not being asked. Was fragmented teaching producing fragmented learning, and was it, in turn, leading to fragmented schooling? Conversely, I wondered if learning to use digital tools holistically, for example, in the context of metaphor making, would help teachers enact learner-centered, interest-driven learning.

In coming to this last question, I realized, I might be wrong: What if it didn't matter how teachers came to use digital tools, but only that they did, in fact, bring them into their classrooms? Anxiety and fragmentation might be intrinsic to living, after all. Or, what if digital tools had no effect whatsoever on learning, in spite of so many scholars' enthusiasms?

Finally, in asking this question (*How might I be wrong?*), the trajectory of this study snapped into place. In observations and interviews I would investigate how and in what ways a select group of teachers was coming to use digital tools and materials in their classrooms, and I would ask if doing so was changing their teaching. I remember my sense of confidence as I proposed the project to the administrators at the school that would eventually host this research. Eight months later, with interviews and observations underway, most of that confidence had evaporated, and the simple through-line of my questions had become a tangled mess of uncertainty. Such is often the case with research, I've learned. Before getting to that part of the story, however, I want to step back from the personal narrative to discuss the theoretical and pragmatic foundations of the book.

Motivations and Goals

The longer I reflect on education, the more curious it becomes to me. What is a proper education? How do we know when we know something? What is learning? Plato's questions in the *Republic* feel as urgent to me today as they must have felt to him 2,400 years ago. And judging from the passion with which so many of us engage with these questions, I would argue that writers down the centuries feel as I do, as well. And yet, despite our bulldog determination, we seem no closer to understanding those complexities in the 21st century than we were in the 18th century, when Rousseau tackled nature-nurture in *Emile*, or in the early 20th century when Dewey wrote *Democracy and Education*. Neither, for that matter, does it seem we've budged an inch toward more effective or engaged schooling, even after travelling for decades down the path blazed by Piaget's developmentalists, and more recently by the cognitive neuroscientists. After all this time, do we in fact know anything more about teaching and learning than Plato did? Judging by the similarity of the questions that nearly identical actors continue to bring to an unchanging stage, I would argue that we don't. In fact, to my mind, the conversation about education has gotten stuck in a loop, and educationalists and policy makers appear to believe that narrowing our parameters and refining our metrics can find a solution to the loop. But in what sense is education a problem to be solved, rather than an ongoing and constantly renewable exploration of values and ways of being? The dream of leaving no child behind, or of racing to the top, not to mention the repetitive national scripts about testing, accountability, and competition, look like fantasies of completion rather than a desire to understand knowing and learning. But can we ever close the book on education?

This is my first motivation in writing this book: to explore the conundrums that swirl through our conversation about education. I don't want to still those whirls and eddies, however, but to hold their energies in play. Yes, I want schools in the future to be better than they are today, whatever that means, but I don't think that locking in a definition of "better" moves us toward that goal. Rather, I hope this work holds the conversation open, and counters the diminishment of wonder that narrow definitions of learning appear to require. I also hope the book becomes useful to teacher education. To help you follow me toward these goals, I first need to clarify what I mean by learning.

Defining Learning

In the literature of education, learning has been theorized from across a wide variety of positions that include developmental, cognitive, behavioral, social, and psychological approaches, to name just a few. I want to hold this multiplicity open, but I am particularly intrigued by John Dewey's arguments that good learning happens when teaching connects to the present needs of the individual learner; by Jean Piaget's investigations of developmental characteristics that reliably complexify what learners are capable of; and by Seymour Papert's (1980a, 1980b, 1993; Papert & Harel, 1991) aggregation and extension of these ideas in his observation that learning is stronger when we make and share artifacts. I will explore these ideas in more detail in Chapter 2, but it's important to say at the beginning of the book that I hold learning as a constructivist activity of meaning making and meaning doing. This nice line from Dewey to Piaget to Papert is tangled up, however, with several other ideas about learning that make just as much sense to me; particularly the situated, participatory learning of Jean Lave and Etienne Wenger's (1991) communities of practice, and the co-emergent, ecological trajectories of sociomaterialism, as described by Tara Fenwick, Richard Edwards, and Peter Sawchuk (2011).

Further contradicting what I've just written is the resonance I feel with Kieran Egan's (1997, 2002) arguments that explicitly reject some of these ideas. I live with this complexity everyday, so it seems right that I lay it out in the open at the beginning. Basically, Egan suggests that our experience of knowing, as an action, doesn't fit very well with either constructed or situated theories of learning. In making this argument Egan reminds us that anyone who spends time with young learners will find that their mind-bending fascination with talking rabbits and dinosaurs challenges our assumptions that learning be useful, developmentally appropriate, or community centered. In showing how cognitive tools inform curriculum as ways of thinking, Egan points to Lev Vygotsky's early 20th-century experiments with physical materials and social interaction. Though it seems to me that Vygotsky aligns more closely with ecological theories of co-emergence like sociomaterialism, his work shows up in the background of many who enlist progressivism, constructivism, and situated learning theories to explain the need for contemporary school reform (for example, Gee, 2004; Ito et al., 2013; Martin, 2015; Martinez & Stager, 2013). This overlapping and interweaving mesh of ideas about how learning works, and about what knowledge is, will be explored throughout the book, so perhaps the takeaway at this point is simply this: Multiple, contrasting and sometimes contradictory ideas about learning and knowing have influenced my writing, and the complexity can't be easily simplified. Actually, *contradiction* is the wrong word. It's more accurate to hold these currents as evolving tides in a vast educational conversation. And perhaps the tensions don't need to be resolved, either. To my mind, the longevity of progressivism, constructivism, and situated learning; and the dynamics of newer ideas like sociomaterialism; and the internal consistency of Egan's cognitive tools approach, suggest that educational theory and research are more open than the public policy conversation sometimes lets on. I find this theoretical turbulence exciting and, in itself, a further reason for writing this book. In fact, pulling at these overlapping threads even further, I'd say the story of this book begins with the proposition that learning is a way of doing the world—a gesture, an action and an interaction *with* the world in the construction *of* the world. Putting it this way surfaces a second motivation for writing this book: to learn how to replace *construction* in that last sentence with the word *enactment*.

Derivatives of the word *enact* figure prominently throughout the book—as a verb, noun, adjective, compound modifier. To introduce my use of it, I would point to Tara Fenwick's (2000) *enactivism*, with which she describes ecologically co-emergent, practice-based knowing. In her view, enacted knowing and learning entangles the learner and the context of learning as an action in the world. An example: In "City Hall enacted the mayor's policy on economic relief," there's an implication of multiple actors coordinating multiple kinds of work for a negotiated goal—the mayor, advisors, industries, and the public, all banding together to make compassion and charity available to designated members of an urban community. There are other implications, too (rhetorical, metaphorical, political, etc.), but in this very common sentence, "enacted" suggests a distribution of agency throughout a relational system, rather than the consolidation of a singular will.

To illustrate with an example from daily life, consider a conversation, where participants contribute, reflect, and respond in patterns that are generated by their participation in the conversation itself. In other words, the content of the conversation does not exist outside of the speaking and listening. Content is emergent: Speaking generates listening, which generates further speaking, and so on. And in especially robust conversations, where we become completely absorbed in the stories we're sharing, losing track of ourselves and our sense of time, knowing is a thorough give and take, or flow, a relational process that seems to create itself. In such conversations, amplified as much by the exchange between us as by the information we're sharing, we sometimes hear ourselves say something that we didn't even know we knew. In other words, good conversations are about *doing* the conversation, as embodied and gestural as they are linguistic. But this is not extraordinary; rather, conversation threads organically through our day-to-day existence. It's just what we do.

In schools, however, knowing as emergence seems rare. For example, if I hold that *to enact* an object of some kind (say, a history curriculum) is to work cooperatively and purposefully to bring that object to presence, I'm acknowledging that any individual actor is unlikely to control the way that object becomes real. But schools obsess over control, and who is in control—usually the teacher—and how outcomes can be controlled and measured. So the view of action that I'm proposing with *enactment* pushes against the way schools work. That is, the teacher-knows-best disposition, or the rows of desks that make standardized testing more efficient, don't encourage questioning of curricular goals (e.g., as evolving or as predetermined), or the structure of classrooms (e.g., dialogically or hierarchically). This reasoning about and interest in emergent knowing has influenced my writing, leading in fact to descriptions of teaching practices without teachers at their center.

An example from another field might further clarify the sense of emergence that I want the word *enact* to make available here. In *The Body Multiple: Ontology in Medical Practice*, Annemarie Mol (2002) argues that describing the diagnosis and treatment of disease as enactment implies a similar disruption to established norms: "If an object is real this is because it is part of a practice. It is reality *enacted*" (p. 44, original emphasis). As such, Mol intends her book as a *praxiography*, "a story about practices" (p. 31), that opens a new space, that reconfigures the topology of space, in order to imagine new potentials for the doing of a practice—in her case, medical practice, or the doing of disease and the treatment of disease. My book is also about practice, teaching practice, and about how digital tools and materials might entangle with and change the enactment of that practice.

For now, let's leave it at this: The sense of learning that I'm after feels like a complex and sometimes acrimonious relationship with action in the world, like a push and pull, like an oscillating tension that foregrounds doing. This view contrasts with the well-ordered workshop metaphor implied by Piaget's constructivism, and with the compassionate consensus metaphor suggested by Lave and Wenger's situated learning. In the chapters that follow, I will use observations and analyses from the study site to test my evolving understanding of this dynamic in order to contribute, at least in some small way, I hope, to changing the language of learning. To further unpack the baggage I'm carrying on this journey, I'll lay out the following four matters of concern; each has occupied me while writing this book, challenging and shaping my desire for doing so.

Matters of Concern

New materialisms. Across multiple domains of inquiry, encompassing industries, political institutions, and schools, and both the natural and social sciences, cultural theorists are reconceptualizing materiality and the role of matter in how social systems work (for example, Barrett & Bolt, 2013; Bennett, 2010; Coole & Frost, 2010; Fenwick et al., 2011). This so-called material turn is shifting scholars' attention to flow over stasis, to process over object/subject, and to co-emergence over individual agency. These changes in interpretative strategy have fueled a critique of notions of accountability rooted in the Enlightenment-era human-centered concept of production, presencing instead an ecologically distributed model of action, where the will to do and make, the urge for becoming, and even ideas about growth and development are conceptualized as a mesh of oscillations weaving together human and nonhuman intentionalities. From art and art education, jan jagodzinski and Jason Wallin (2013) argue that "theorizing creativity and art as emerging from the gap or chiasm between nature and culture" requires theorists to integrate material agency into their analyses of phenomena (p. 31). Speaking more broadly, in *New Materialisms: Ontology, Agency, and Politics*, Diana Coole and Samantha Frost (2010) claim that "foregrounding material factors and reconfiguring our very understanding of matter are prerequisites for any plausible account of coexistence and its conditions in the twenty-first century" (p. 2). Following that line, philosopher Rosi Braidotti (2010) argues for an ethics of sustainability that puts collective altruism ahead of neoliberalism and global managerialism, particularly in the context of the genetic engineering that is changing what we eat and how we live. From a slightly different point of view, William Connolly (2010), a political theorist, deploys the language of neuroscience to describe the materiality of perception, arguing that "self-organization in a thing, species, system, or being" cannot be ignored in contemporary political discourse (p. 179). For these writers, the agency of materials contradicts our human-centric, Enlightenment-era understanding of the world, requiring a change in the language we use to understand action and intentionality. But posthumanism, as this change has been called (Braidotti, 2013; Hayles, 1999, 2012), sounds confusing, gloomy and even threatening. The challenge is significant. Conventionally, matter is passive and mute, compliant with human desires and intentions, whether for making rocket ships, roads, or theories, a relationship of *thinking* to *making* that forms the bedrock of our scientific method. Today, however, scholars argue that this old relationship no longer holds. Katherine Hayles (2012), in *How We Think: Digital Media and Contemporary Technogenesis*, argues "humanities and qualitative social sciences are... facing a paradigm shift [that] can no longer be ignored" (p. 2).

Following educational researcher Tara Fenwick and her colleagues (Fenwick & Edwards, 2011, 2012; Fenwick, Edwards, & Sawchuk, 2011), I would argue that schools cannot ignore this shift either. In fact, new materialism's agential matter and posthumanism's decentering of humanism challenge the definition of learning that I've sketched above to become even more complex and more indeterminate than it already is. Today, in the age of the internet, where learning and knowing is sometimes considered synonymous with digital literacy, an additional paradox surfaces: The virtual matters as much as, if not more than, the material. The conundrum of internet materiality is not new; it underlies objects as diverse as video games, blogs, Skype, and the database structures that support them, including the electrical grids and transportation networks of our days and nights—streetlights, parking meters, rail crossings, drawbridges, and more and more often, thanks to the Internet of Things, even the temperature of the milk in our refrigerators at home. This dependence of (physical) matter on immaterial (data) indicates a need to come to terms with what I will call *digital materiality*. Throughout the book I will ponder the costs and benefits that this material/immaterial paradox makes available to teachers, students, and other stakeholders in schools, especially as pedagogy becomes more thoroughly entangled with digital tools and materials.

Decentered embodiment. Among the cultural effects of new materialisms and digital materiality that interest me, one of the most widely talked about is the shift in agency and embodiment. As the writers mentioned above observe, contemporary social science de-emphasizes human-centered agency in favor of distributed, or decentered, agency. We see this in their analyses of manufacturing, governing, teaching, and other coordinated activities. In effect, researchers and policy makers recognize that complex practices cannot be adequately understood by holding action in isolation from the ecologies that comprise those practices. For Coole and Frost (2010), this co-emergent entanglement leads to a different kind of causality; new materialisms, they argue, "compel us to think of causation in far more complex terms" (p. 9). To contextualize the effect of this decentering, new media philosopher Mark B. N. Hansen (2004) identifies amplified embodiment as digital media's "reaffirmation of the body as the enframer of information" (p. 20). For Hansen, *enframing* identifies the body as the location of knowing, implying that new materialisms' argument for decentering is not an open-and-shut case. Annemarie Mol's (2002) descriptions and analyses of the diagnosis and treatment of arteriosclerosis model the complex empiricism that this paradox of decentered agency and amplified embodiment produce. By charting the presence and simultaneous absence of arteriosclerosis in a patient's legs, and the corresponding treatment of the condition across the hospital—in the clinic, the surgeon's office, the operating room, and the pathology lab—Mol shows that the intentions of doctors, clinicians, scientists, and even patients cannot entirely account for the way in which the disease is enacted in practice. Rather, she argues, an analysis of complex material presences—the multiple ontologies of her title—must include complex explanations if they are to be useful in real clinics and operating rooms. To get at that complexity, Mol describes agency as an entangled choreography undertaken simultaneously by multiple human *and* nonhuman actors. Importantly, Mol articulates the challenge that decentered agency presents to traditional research methodologies by arguing that the dance of ontology happens only in its specificity, in a particular location for a specific purpose, and cannot be generalized to nonlocal participants. While distant from my study in topic, discipline, purpose, and most every other detail, Mol's example has deeply influenced the writing of this book. Firstly, I've used it as a model for deploying complex empiricism in the analysis of day-to-day teaching practices; and secondly, for me it is a provocative and paradigm-bending intersection of empathy, exquisite attention to detail, and clear-eyed wonder about practice in the world.

Material learning. Following from these first two matters of concern, I am drawn to a way of knowing that I have come to call *material learning*. Pulling from my experience as an artist, art teacher, and teacher educator, I define material learning as what sometimes happens when a child loses herself in a painting, when a mathematician stumbles onto a proof, or when a composer plucks a melody from the air. In his moving tribute to woodcarving, David Esterly (2012) writes that he learned how to carve by following the wood; and in his anthropology of making, Tim Ingold (2013) admits that the book told him how to write it. Ingold argues that he finds this kind of recursive, co-emergent learning-action dynamic consistent with all kinds of making, which he describes as a "correspondence between maker and material" (p. xi). Another way to say this is that material learning happens when human and nonhuman agencies become entangled with noninstrumental materialities. But putting material learning into words can be counterproductive (as that last sentence proves); just as explaining a tune cannot reproduce the experience of music, talking about material learning cannot replace feeling yourself give over to the agency of a piece of clay or a line of poetry. Nevertheless, I can point to characteristics of material learning: surprise and sudden realizations (e.g., *aha* moments), a sense of shared agency (e.g., "the characters in my novel spoke to me"), a sense of time and space disruption (e.g., flow), and unexpected mistakes, errors, and screwups (e.g., serendipity, or the happy accident).

Material learning can also be illustrated by recalling the words of artists, musicians, writers, scientists, mathematicians, and winners of the Nobel and MacArthur prizes when they talk about their innovations and breakthroughs. In so many of these cases, when we read their stories (or hear them interviewed), we catch their sense of surprise, breakthrough, loss of control, and the importance of making mistakes. They tell us again and again that learning to innovate feels different from other kinds of learning, especially where intentional agency and quantifiable goals rely on narrowly instrumental, scalable pedagogies—as in schools. Instead, they say, innovation is unforeseeable, unknowable, and in fact, not thinkable. This means that school teachers are faced with a paradox: The outcomes they have been hired to bring to presence—for example, innovation and achievement—depend on a kind of serendipity that runs counter to the assessment requirements of their jobs. Simply, when poets and mathematicians describe their greatest innovations, they aren't talking about worksheets, book reports, or standardized tests.

This conundrum highlights one of the most intractable conflicts of our educational conversation. We can't elevate achievement by tightening the screws. And yet, how can we be sure that holding the object of the curriculum more loosely will enable pedagogies of innovation to be enacted in classrooms? This is the Holy Grail of the maker education movement and, it seems to me, the place where dreams of renewal begin to wither. My concern is that establishing maker education in schools might require acquiescence to methodologies, such as standardized assessments, that would kill it. Paradoxically, the success of making in the curriculum might be signaled by the arrival of heavily marketed educational products that tout developmentally appropriate maker activities—or, innovation in a box. To my mind, the arrival of such kits would be a sign that material learning in schools has been foreclosed.

New paradigms. If digital making and learning practices gain traction in schools, new teaching and teacher education paradigms might become available, too. But school leaders and other stakeholders (for example, principals, head teachers, parents, and teacher educators) might be challenged by the existing features of their institutions (structural, spatial, and otherwise) in trying to enact those paradigms, especially if new or expanded ways of knowing no longer fit within their outdated structures and frameworks. This challenge, famously described as a paradigm shift by Thomas Kuhn in 1962, interests me very much. How do we know what we know? How do we make room for what we don't know? And how do we even recognize what we haven't yet named? These are ancient questions, but teachers and scholars who engage with the maker movement and the digital learning movement write with enthusiasm about the potential for make-to-learn methodologies to reform schooling. In fact, maker education might be nudging school practices across a threshold of learning and knowing where everything changes; or we might find that predictions of the old paradigm's demise have been grossly exaggerated. Or, a third option—we might be asking the wrong question. How do paradigms actually work? Instead of imagining a tipping point, a cataclysm of change, we might ask how paradigms overlap and juxtapose to reveal practices that are neither singular nor fragmented but partially connected, or as the anthropologist Marilyn Strathern (2005) puts it, "more than one but less than many" (p. 35).

In thinking about this question I'm intrigued by the analyses of educators like Kieran Egan (2002), who talks about a paradigm shift as a change in the angle of view on a given phenomena, rather than as a wholesale rearrangement of knowing; and of social scientists like John Law (2004), who argues that paradigms are recursive, simultaneously helping us to discover new knowledge as well as to enact it. Following Strathern, Annemarie Mol (2002) proposes something more challenging: Paradigms, like cultures, describe processes that gather materialities within a singular framework, thus stifling differences. She therefore avoids methodologies that theorize new paradigms. She asks, instead, what if practice were like an assemblage that lived in more or less unstable configurations of potential? The sense in which she poses her question—*What is it to hang together?*—emphasizes a notion of *assemblage*, described by Deleuze and Guattari (1987) as connoting a decentered and indefinite, continually unfolding, processes-oriented rebuilding of knowledge. Jane Bennett (2010) understands assemblages as ad hoc groupings of diverse elements "that are able to function despite the persistent presence of energies that confound them from within" (pp. 23–24). The paradox of an effective practice that barely holds itself together is a recurrent theme of this book. What is required and what is detrimental to such an outcome? Based on her observations of medical practice in the Netherlands, Mol (2002) replies that, in *practice*, this question is probably not answerable, at least not in ways that traditional paradigms of knowing presume. In this book, my exploration of teaching in the age of digital making and learning has brought me to wonder about structural and spatial incompatibilities in schools. In what ways might a paradigm clash open a space for reconfiguring the assemblage of teaching and learning?

Digital Making and Learning in Teacher Education

Theorists and researchers from overlapping pedagogical traditions, for example, constructionist artistic development and socially centered learning, suggest that project-based, making-infused practices will revolutionize teaching and learning. These enthusiasms have spread widely but unevenly across schools, after-school programs, clubs, camps, community centers, and other learning ecologies. This unevenness shouldn't be surprising given the unequal access to computers and the internet, not to mention 3D printers, laser cutters, craft electronics, and the other tools and materials commonly found in FabLabs and makerspaces. How will digital making and learning take hold in a school that has no access to digital tools and materials? Just as important is the question of teacher education: How will teachers enact digital making and learning practices if their own education never addresses them? During the study and while writing this book I have turned that question around and around, drawing from a diverse body of literature to inform my observations and analysis. In the coming chapters I'll review some of that work in detail, but here I want to particularly acknowledge James Paul Gee's (2004, 2007) influence, especially his descriptions of the complex literacy practices of young children. For example, I found his analysis of card and video games, such as Yugioh and Age of Mythology, relevant not only for how I evaluated what I heard in classrooms, but also for my parenting of two young sons.

In tracing these personal and theoretical overlaps as I have—that is, with a detailed chronology of my personal journey—I have been modeling a proposition about the relationship of knowing and learning to practice. To be clear, this book argues for robustly embodied and passionately empathetic teaching. Knowing, as an action, and learning as an enactment of knowing, are emotional trajectories that entangle tools and materials with action and affect in and with the world; teachers are the guides, facilitators, mentors, coaches, tutors, and experts who nurture and sometimes initiate those relationships, but neither stance nor outcomes can be determined in advance of the day-to-day enactment of their practice. In a manner of speaking, I have written this book as an antidote to the accelerating conversations around STEM and STEAM—frequent substitute terms for maker education—that sometimes foreground curricular goals, assessment standards, and instructional approaches that depend on a simplistic or instrumental view of teaching and learning. To my mind, this is contrary to the ideas at the heart of maker education (see, for example, Seymour Papert's call for broadly expansive and richly open-ended learning in *Mindstorms: Children, Computers and Powerful Ideas*, from 1980). I would also argue that narrowly conceived curricular goals are contrary to our national interests because they frustrate the mandate that we educate for inclusion, participation, and innovation (Darling-Hammond, 2010)—goals that require a different way of holding education. That is, despite researching and theorizing 21st-century learning that stretches back a decade or more (Jenkins, 2006), and that heralds a transformation of schooling rooted in digital media learning (Gee, 2013), interest-driven arts learning (Peppler, 2013), and in-depth expertise (Egan, 2008, 2010), the conversation around contemporary education continues to narrow in on frameworks that look a lot like the banking model that Freire (1970/2000) excoriated more than a generation ago. As a result, in our age of accountability (as described, for example, by Biesta, 2010; Eisner, 1985; Schwartz & Arena, 2013; Sullivan, 2010), we pursue efficiency in the hope of growing jobs, but end up with an impoverished educational mission linked to the production of human capital—a connection that pervades our newspapers, political platforms, and casual conversations.

In their MacArthur Foundation report, *Measuring What Matters Most: Choice-Based Assessments for the Digital Age*, Schwartz and Arena (2013) argue that 21st-century tools offer a way out of the accountability quagmire our conversation has fallen into, but that it requires a change in how learning outcomes are defined and valued. But where will such change come from? Schwartz and Arena write that "with new developments in technology, it should be possible to advance goals that were beyond the reach of prior assessments" (p. 6), but recognize that results have not yet appeared. James Paul Gee (2013) shares their hopes and also laments the paradox that makes powerful digital tools "[separate] from, rather than blended with, face-to-face interactions, physical spaces, and deep educational uses that go beyond entertainment" (p. 198). And yet in spite of these hesitations, digital technologies are routinely discussed in relation to the emergence of new kinds of learning behaviors, called the *new ethos* (Lankshear & Knobel, 2011), or the *new culture of learning* (Thomas & Brown, 2011).

I remain optimistic about this conversation that shows no sign of concluding, but I would argue that remaking the language we deploy to enact these supposed new cultures is crucial to their eventual emergence. That is, the irony of so many scholars' good intentions is that the focus on outcomes sometimes mistakes the flow of the conversation for a completion-directed endeavor. But the tide comes in and the tide goes out, and marking the moment of its reversal requires slow and sustained attention, patience, and the generosity to suspend snap judgments. In other words, talking about outcomes can be counterproductive to figuring out what to do next.

Whether or not we are actually approaching a new ethos and new culture of schooling, my desire for engaging with teachers as they connect with digital tools and materials, and for asking whether doing so changes teaching practices, overlaps with my desire to hold making and doing as ecologically interwoven with speaking and being. Needing to know about this overlapping assemblage of action and desire stems from my life as an artist and art teacher, and from my life with two sons. In other words, everything I know points to the irreducibility of tool and material entanglement with learning and knowing: We make and do the world as the world makes and does us. That's simple enough to say because the tool I'm using, the grammar and syntax of the English language, encourages linear, active, causative propositions. But how might describing these challenges in this way affect schooling, or learning to teach?

My overall goal in doing this study, then, was to learn if the relationships of practice that I've noticed in my own work could be observed and described in the practice of other teachers. My goal in writing the story of the study is more practical: How might such descriptions inform teacher education, including preservice training, in-service professional development, and teachers' ongoing personal growth in the profession?

FIELD NOTES (ROBOTS)

For the third graders seated on the rug in their bright, fourth-floor science classroom, the challenge is to make a robot that can kick or pull or push a small bouncy ball a distance of four feet. Grace explains the only constraint: You can't add any extra parts to your Lego robotics kits, and you have to use the motor. One girl says "Easy," and another replies, "Of course," and then Grace tells them that they'll have today's class for planning and sketching, and tomorrow's for building and sharing.

"Let's talk about motors," Amber, her co-teacher, says. Seated at the whiteboard with large, colorful markers, she asks the girls what they already know about motors—how they spin, start, and stop. Hands go up immediately, and she calls on a student in the middle of the rug.

"Well, there's this thing that you attach to the motor...?"

"Yes," Amber says, "That's a gear. That's a good tool, and you might use a gear. Also, think about your leg when you kick a soccer ball. What does your leg do?"

"Oh, it goes forward!"

"Yes, but first it has to go backwards, right?" On the whiteboard, Amber sketches a stick figure with directional arrows animating its leg. From the rug come oohs of recognition and then excited whispers as the girls start sharing ideas about kicking, bouncy balls, and motors. One pair says they want to make a rabbit, and asks about putting ears on their machine.

"If you want to make a bunny rabbit with cute little ears, that's fine," Amber says. "But you might run out of time. Today, let's focus on making the ball move."

And with that, the girls are up and scattering towards their tables. Purposeful chatter fills the room, and paper, pencils, and rulers appear. One girl from each team is called to the shelves to retrieve a Lego kit, and immediately they're exploring parts and sketching. I see arms that swing and mechanical legs that look like punching rams, or pistons. I hear: "But we don't know how to make an arm," "What if we put the gear right here?" and, "What do you call this?"

Grace and Amber circulate, encouraging these explorations with questions. "What will that arm attach to?" "What can you use to elevate that leg so it's high enough to kick the ball?"

Some of the girls pull pieces from their kits to see what they look like, carefully labeling their drawings; others begin exploring how things attach. One team is back on the floor with a glue stick and a motor arm, trying to figure out if the swinging motion they've sketched will actually work. Pointing at their drawing, Grace asks, "How are you going to elevate that piece high enough to kick the ball?"

The girls are confused. The contraption in their sketch has a swinging arm that floats in midair, without any kind of platform to support or hold it in place. Grace points at the drawing and pulls the Lego kit closer, saying, "You only have the pieces in the kit." Together they look inside and take out the largest and flattest pieces they can find. As they turn them over in their hands, propping them on edge and leaning them against each other, they get it—the pieces don't connect to anything. They can't make a platform at the right height because the pieces in this kit aren't built that way. Suddenly they're quiet again, huddled over their drawing, revising their plan. As she walks away Grace reminds them, "Don't forget, you're using Scratch to program the robot, so try to figure out which motion comes first and which comes second."

Later, the whole group gathers again on the rug, this time in a circle spread out around the edges. Amber brings the classroom tortoise out of its enclosure and places it in the center. The girls giggle and whisper and watch with excitement as it ambles randomly around the rug. "Look! He knows it's your birthday!" one of them says a little too loudly as it comes near. "Shhh," comes the response from around the circle.

At the beginning of class Amber had told the girls that there was no booklet for what they were about to do, that they would have to invent what they're going to make. She'd said, "We're trying something new today and we're not sure how it's going to work out." Now, retrieving the tortoise, she asks, "How are you girls feeling about the challenge tomorrow?" To their half-hearted replies of "good" and "okay," she says, "Well, I can't wait to see how it turns out."

Datasheet: Age group: third grade. Content domain: science. Teachers: Grace and Amber. Timing: two days in May.

· 2 ·

TRADITIONS OF LEARNING
AND KNOWING

These next three chapters set up the study. Each takes a slightly different approach, however, and as I mentioned in the introduction, readers might want to read one chapter before the other, or *instead* of another, or, in fact, read none of them and skip directly to the study itself, which begins in Chapter 5.

My goal in this chapter is to draw a relationship between the literature of maker education and the study I'm writing about in this book. Frankly, weaving together the intellectual and cultural traditions that a study pulls from is fraught with difficulties. How do tradition and new knowledge connect to each other? As authority? As disruption? As critique? And how is that relationship enacted in the structure of the writing? Some writers reference their framework in footnotes with small type, like an archeology that constructs the new on top of layers of the old; others spiral off in lengthy tangents within the text itself, like an uncle showboating his wandering erudition. And others barely acknowledge their traditions at all, with, for example, endnotes that might not even be keyed to the body of the text, like secrets at the back of the book.

One of the most inventive and effective solutions to this problem that I've encountered is in Annemarie Mol's (2002) *The Body Multiple*. Here the text is set in two blocks on each page, with the empirical narrative at the top and the philosophical narrative (that is, the story about books and traditions) at the bottom. As Mol says, the reader is invited to decide individually how to encounter her text—to read the story of the study straight through, or in chunks that alternate with the literature review that informs it, or even by alternating pages or lines of each! And indeed, it's possible to read the subtext as a separate work altogether, skipping the empirical work entirely. What an engaging way to reprise one of the most interesting and challenging questions her work addresses: How do we, as active knowers, structure our relationship with knowing? To what extent are we simply thrown into the midst of a practice and required to trust that we'll figure it out as we carry on? On the other hand, how much guidance and hand-holding can we expect along the way? And, what is to be gained or lost by adhering to either trajectory, or to some other one? In fact, Mol argues, there are multiple answers, in a text as in life, and the practice of knowing, as an action, proceeds in complex choreographies of doing: forging ahead, backtracking, reflecting, spinning off on tangents, and otherwise alternating between holding loosely or clenching tightly to our relationships and desires.

In this book, the discussion of tradition is consolidated (for the most part) in the next three chapters, without further reliance on footnotes or endnotes. I want to minimize tangents and digressions in describing what captivated me—realizing that confusions of interpretation are impossible to predict or eradicate. You are invited to skip around as you wish, of course, and to chain through the citations, but you can also read straight through without concern that you're missing additional material.

Relationships Within the Literature

Two different but related theories of learning and knowing braid through maker education in schools. Each can be described as a separate strand in the weave of progressivism, that long tradition in Western education that includes Herbert Spencer, John Dewey, and Jean Piaget (Egan, 2002). In my telling, each strand is itself composed of multicolored threads. As educational researchers Erica Halverson and Kimberly Sheridan (2014) have suggested, educators who study *making* in education draw connections between objects as distant from each other as cave paintings and the "new industrial revolution" (p. 496). Within this wide swath, however, most research begins from a similar starting point, at least in terms of progressivism's learn-by-doing emphasis on learning *to be* over learning *about*. And yet, within this commonality we find diverse intellectual approaches: from linguistics (Gee, 2007, 2013) to anthropology (Ito et al., 2009, 2013) to literacy studies (Lankshear & Knobel, 2011) to computer science (Blikstein, 2013) to media and communication studies (Jenkins, 2006) to engineering (Gershenfeld, 2007) to art (Peppler, 2013) to education (Martinez & Stager, 2013).

The hubbub from these different voices and dispositions can be disconcerting, especially for those who imagine classrooms with the schoolteacher standing in front of polite rows of desks. This is not the relevant image, as these writers would certainly argue, because new tools, materials, and patterns of discourse have irretrievably altered learning (though not always teaching) since the end of the old industrial revolution. This in fact points toward more differences: These researchers write about and advocate for different tool sets. For example, those who align with Seymour Papert's *constructionism* (Papert, 1980a; Papert & Harel, 1991) tend to write about makerspaces, FabLabs, and electronics (for example, Blikstein, 2013; Martinez & Stager, 2013); while those who follow Jean Lave and Etienne Wenger's (1991) theories of situated, participatory *communities of practice* tend to focus more on Web 2.0 affinity spaces, such as social media, blogs, games, online zines, and immersive environments (for example, Gee, 2004, 2007). There is overlap, to be sure (for instance, both camps advocate for low-floor and high-ceiling pedagogies that deploy computer programming tools like Scratch), but to describe the flavor of making in education as a strawberry-vanilla swirl is not inaccurate. This is why the first task of a study that asks how teachers are coming to making-infused teaching is to decide what counts as such. This is why Halverson and Sheridan (2014) argue for having a "common frame of reference" (p. 496).

In my reading, the first component of such a framework is composed of constructionism (Papert, 1980a; Papert & Harel, 1991; Martinez & Stager, 2013). To this I'll add artistic development (Burton, 1980, 2009; Lowenfeld, 1947/1957), and refer to the assemblage as *constructionist artistic development*. In knitting these traditions together, I'll call on new materialisms, introduced as a matter of concern in Chapter 1, because both constructionism and artistic development foreground the role of materials and materiality in learning, though perhaps not in the same way. The second component of my framework is connected learning, or digital media learning, also known as situated or interest-driven learning (Gee, 2004, 2007; Ito et al., 2013; Lankshear &

Knobel, 2011; Lave & Wenger, 1991; Peppler, 2013; Peppler, Santo, Gresalfi, & Tekinbas, 2014), an orientation toward collaborative, systems-oriented learning and knowing that holds digital networks as crucial to new definitions of literacy. I will refer to this strand as *socially centered learning*.

In Halverson and Sheridan's (2014) definition, "the *maker movement* refers broadly to the growing number of people who are engaged in the creative production of artifacts in their daily lives" (p. 496, original emphasis). This understanding is broadly consistent across the field of maker education (Agency by Design, 2015; Blikstein, 2013; Martin, 2015; Martinez & Stager, 2013). Countering this broad agreement, however, is doubt about whether, or how, making actually belongs in schools. As Halverson and Sheridan note, "many educators and researchers have raised the question of whether learning through making is a fad" (p. 500). This question of stability (*Is maker education a temporary enthusiasm, or will it rebuild the foundations of teaching and learning?*) goes directly to one of the questions that launched this study: Does digital making and learning affect practice? Addressing this skepticism at the beginning of the book helps set up an important question: Are stakeholders—parents, teachers, administrators, and school boards—evaluating project-based, or making-infused, learning practices in comparable ways? For Halverson and Sheridan, "perhaps the greatest challenge to embracing the maker movement [in education]…is to standardize, to define 'what works' for learning through making" (p. 500).

I am skeptical of a move toward the kind of standardization that would diminish complexity in the name of assessment. However, I recognize that standards also help forge the common language that makes a conversation about teaching and learning possible in the first place (Darling-Hammond, 2010). Keeping this paradox available in the digital making and learning framework that I'm assembling here is paramount. Importantly, my purpose is to hold *what works* open to the multiple voices of the diverse teachers who are learning to bring digital making into their practices. In my approach to framework building I share Fenwick's (2000) skepticism about the role of frameworks more generally. After assembling her multifaceted typology of perspectives on experiential cognition (which I'll refer to throughout these discussions), Fenwick admits that frameworks "that pretend to totalize distinct currents of thought and pedagogical energies must themselves be disrupted, put off balance," and invites her colleagues to "challenge and debate or extend and modify" her categories (p. 266). I am emboldened by her grit and perseverance to make a similar invitation.

Constructionist Artistic Development

Constructionist artistic development combines three intellectual traditions that are relevant to maker education. The first, *constructionism*, derived from Jean Piaget's constructivism, is an approach that Seymour Papert, a mathematician and pioneer researcher in artificial intelligence, and co-founder of MIT's Media Lab, formalized in the 1980s and 1990s (Papert, 1980a, 1980b; Papert & Freire, 1980; Papert & Harel, 1991). The second, *artistic development*, focuses on art making as a constructive process of identity formation (Burton 1980, 1991, 2000, 2009; Lowenfeld, 1947/1957). Interweaving through both of these is a disposition toward materiality that reprises aspects of *new materialism* (Barrett & Bolt, 2013; Bolt, 2007, 2010, 2013; Carter, 2004, 2010).

Constructionism

"Constructionism—the N word as opposed to the V word—shares constructivism's connotation of learning as 'building knowledge structures' irrespective of the circumstances of the learning. It then adds the idea that this happens especially felicitously in a context where the learner is consciously engaged in constructing a public entity, whether it's a sand castle on the beach or a theory of the universe" (Papert & Harel, 1991, p. 1). As such, constructionism is "both a theory of learning and a strategy for education [because it argues] that knowledge is not simply transmitted from teacher to student, but actively constructed by the mind of the learner. Children don't *get* ideas; they *make* ideas" (Kafai & Resnick, 1996, p. 1, emphasis in original). In other words, when teachers enact constructionist practices, students solidify their learning by making objects. Importantly, these *objects* can be of different materials and take various forms—sand castles, theories—as long as they are held as "public entities" (Papert & Harel, 1991, p. 1) or "external artifacts" (Kafai & Resnick, 1996, p. 1) and shared.

Sharing is important to constructionism because, through sharing, Papert's *public entity* becomes a recursive, process-oriented object. Mitchel Resnick (2008) wrote about this iterative process as a "spiral of creativity" in which "people *imagine* what they want to do, *create* a project based on their ideas, *play* with their creations, *share* their ideas and creations with others, and *reflect* on their experiences—all of which leads them to *imagine* new ideas and new projects" (p. 18, emphasis in the original). This cycle of make/share/repeat is at the core of constructionism.

As a mathematician, Papert wrote and spoke passionately about constructionism's recursivity, but his ideas resonate strongly with arts learning as well. Papert argued that the goal of math education was "to find ways that children can use mathematics to *make* something—something interesting, so that the children's relationship to mathematics is more like the engineer's, or the scientist's, or the banker's, or all the important people who use mathematics *constructively* to construct something" (Papert, 1980b, n.p., emphasis in original). Papert focused on learning that connected to a way of being in the world; that is, not as merely learning *about* engineering or math, but learning *to be* an engineer or mathematician, an idea that resonates strongly with contemporary notions of learner-centered education (see for example, Atkinson, 2011; Hickman, 2010; jagodzinski, 2005; Peppler, 2013). Echoing this concern with authentic connections, art researcher and educator Judith Burton (1991) wrote: "Put directly, children's art in all its forms embodies profound sensibilities about the connections which bind self to world" (p. 36). In fact, in 1991—the same year Burton wrote these words—Papert explicitly linked art education to math education. It's worth quoting him at length on this point:

> More than 20 years ago, I was working on a project...to allow a seventh grade to "do Logo" [the programming language first developed for educational use in 1967] instead of math....But the story I really want to tell is...about the art room I used to pass on the way....I dropped in periodically to watch students working on soap sculptures and mused about ways in which this was not like a math class. In the math class students are generally given little problems which they solve or don't solve pretty well on the fly. In this particular art class they were all carving soap, but what each student carved came from wherever fancy is bred and the project was not done and dropped but continued for many weeks. It allowed time to think, to dream, to gaze, to get a new idea and try it and drop it or persist, time to talk, to see other people's work and their reaction to yours—not unlike mathematics as it is for the mathematician, but quite unlike math as it is in junior high school. I remember craving some of the students' work and learning that their art teacher and their families had first choice. I was struck by an incongruous image of the teacher in a regular math class pining to own the products of his students' work! An ambition was born: I want junior high school math class to be like that. I didn't know exactly what "that" meant but I knew I wanted it. I didn't even know what to call the idea. For a long time it existed in my head as "soap-sculpture math." (Papert & Harel, 1991, p. 4)

With his revelation in an art classroom, Papert reprises a contested idea about art education, perhaps unwittingly—namely, as described by the historian of art education, Arthur Efland (1990), teaching for content versus teaching for expression (p. 263). Indeed, outside of the art department, the relationship of content to noncontent—even to the point of identifying which is which—remains fraught across the K–12 curricular landscape, as we are reminded time and again (Darling-Hammond, 2010; Kirp, 2013). Long after this encounter with soap sculpture learning in the 1970s, Papert (2001) continued to argue that the most engaged learning occurs when teaching "meshes with interests that particular kids have…[enabling them to] work in communities of common interest on rich projects that connect with powerful ideas" (n.p.). This focus on the emotional connections that sharing makes available to learners reiterates constructionism's overlap with a much older proposition about school practices—namely, quoting John Dewey from 1916, "the criterion of the value of school education is the extent in which it creates a desire for continued growth and supplies means for making the desire effective in fact" (Dewey, 1997, p. 53). The emphasis on *desire*, and the tension between learning *about* versus learning *to be*, or between academic content and life content, is not exclusive to constructionist artistic development; indeed, as a theme, it will recur throughout the book.

Artistic Development

Viktor Lowenfeld (1947/1957) mapped children's psychological development onto the material artifacts they made, from scribbling at 2 years old to the pseudo-realistic art of adolescence. According to art education professor Judith Burton (2009), Lowenfeld's framework remains a primary influence on art education, even after 6 decades. For many teachers, Lowenfeld's insights about how artifacts change as the child ages provide a foil for understanding identity as an emergent relationship between self, world, and practice. Art teachers who attend to Lowenfeld can chart their students' learning journeys by holding changes in mark making as indications of an evolving ability to control and vary gesture, which in turn catalyzes iterative and recursive cycles of individual growth. Burton (1980) claims that for the child, these mark-making behaviors lead to a "momentous new discovery—they have made something where nothing was before" (p. 7). But, warning against reducing the complexity of human development, artistic or otherwise, to a simplistically linear set of chronological stages, Burton (2009) reminds art teachers that Lowenfeld "was consistent in the emphasis he placed on relational-knowing at the heart of art practice, aesthetic experience, and as a reflection of creative intelligence" (p. 324). To keep such relationality present in classrooms, Burton (2000) urges art teachers to deploy unscripted conversation as students engage with materials. "Teaching through dialogue not only opens children to new ways of thinking—it empowers their understanding… [and] inhibits the kind of uniformity of outcome in making and appraising that is the consequence of 'telling and demonstration'" (p. 344).

Conversation, whether as open-ended dialogue, studio critique, or otherwise, plays an important role in the teaching of art (Burton, 2000; Daichendt, 2010; Garoian, 2011; Hetland, Winner, Veenema, & Sheridan, 2013), but the primacy of materials in artistic development cannot be underestimated. Lowenfeld's (1947/1957) theory was literally drawn from material artifacts— for example, scribbly lines versus purposeful lines, open forms versus closed forms, and arbitrary placement of details versus top-bottom or left-right organization of details. Importantly, however, he does not hold materials to be static entities. Instead, as Burton (2000) argues, Lowenfeld's materiality was relational rather than ontological: "[Lowenfeld] wrote, we do not paint and draw objects in our world; we paint and draw our 'relationships' with them" (p. 333). This relational approach underpins Burton's scholarship and teaching, where we read repeatedly about "a world of materials…each with their own distinguishing physical characteristics such as weight, texture, plasticity, density and color" (Burton, 1980, p. 7); and about how "the range and depth of children's understanding of materials will not only empower the journey *into* the imagination but also the journey *out* towards the creation of visual forms which link inner and outer experiences" (Burton, 1991, p. 40, original emphasis); and that "materials bring responses into focus, they simultaneously act as vehicles of reflection provoking new shades of meaning and enriching the immediate significance of the originating thought, memory or event" (Burton, 2000, p. 334). Further, this relational materiality implicates the body in learning: "[T]hrough the body come powerful ideas, feelings and moods, seeking wordless forms of expression" (p. 334). As such, there is a performative aspect to Lowenfeld's theory. For Burton, it is the body in relationship with materials that launches the "momentous and mysterious" developmental advancements of young children as they "swoosh paint, or pummel clay and announce that the outcomes are 'something'" (p. 336). Indeed, this entanglement with materials as enacted learning and knowing pervades Burton's teaching, where courses "talk a lot about the 'voices of materials'" and where preservice art teachers are encouraged "to foster a playful yet analytical investigation of the distinguishing characteristics, possibilities and experiences that individual materials call forth" (personal communication, April 29, 2014). It's this *calling forth* that artistic development points to most often, where materials, identity development, and meaning are interwoven with conversation that gives teachers and students "insights into how knowledge is constructed and is expressed in and through visual images" (Burton, 2000, p. 344).

This emphasis on *construction* points to an overlap between artistic development and constructionism. Making objects has been important to art education for a long time (Hickman, 2010; Sweeny, 2013), as Papert acknowledged with his soap sculpture anecdote. However, Halverson and Sheridan (2014) point out that while "studio art classrooms have long embraced a learning-by-doing perspective, there has been little scholarship that meaningfully incorporates the history of artistic practices into the constructionist frame" (p. 498). Kylie Peppler (2010), a learning scientist with an interest in art and art education, agrees that the literature of art education has not been strongly influenced by constructionism. This might be held as a challenge to art education—to specifically theorize art making as a constructionist knowledge practice.

On the other hand, constructionism has not filtered its own theory of making through the literature of artistic development, such as Lowenfeld's insights about what kids make, or how the making process changes as learners age. That is, in spite of recognizing Piaget's constructivism, and his stage theories of human development, scholars of constructionism have rarely looked at maker practice in terms of identity development. This might be changing, however, with the release of Agency by Design's (2015) study on making in education, titled "Maker-Centered Learning and the Development of Self." Here, the authors argue that "the most salient benefits of maker-centered learning for young people have to do with developing a sense of self" (p. 7)—although they make only the faintest reference to psychological theories of development, or to the kinds of objects that students make, in coming to this conclusion. This, then, might be artistic development's challenge to the maker movement—to explicitly chart identity development through the material artifacts that a learner constructs.

New Materialisms

Another overlap between constructionism and artistic development is that both recognize the importance of materials in learning and knowing. Constructionism's public artifact presumes a material substrate if it's to become sharable—though Papert's "theory of the universe" (Papert & Harel, 1991, p. 1) begs a question about the role of the immaterial as well. Similarly, artistic development grounds itself in material characteristics such as weight, texture, and plasticity. New materialism both amplifies and challenges these traditions to be more explicit about these dynamics. To be clear, neither the literature of constructionism nor artistic development explicitly touches new materialisms, which is an emerging, loosely interwoven stream of thinking; in fact, in ways that I'll explore below, new materialism's claims of decentered agency and co-emergence go explicitly against the grain of the human-centered making that anchors both constructionism and artistic development. Nevertheless, I am arguing here that both traditions open space for new materialisms because they hold materiality's contribution to learning as an iterative, spiraling process (Resnick, 2008), and as a conversation with material voices (Burton, 2000). My thinking on these relationships is informed by multiple traditions, including art and art history, new media theory, and posthumanism. In this section, as a component of the braided tradition I'm calling constructionist artistic development, I'm exploring new materialisms via art and art education; in later chapters I'll fold other voices into the conversation as well.

In her introduction to *Carnal Knowledge: Towards a New Materialism in the Arts*, Barbara Bolt (2013), an artist and art historian, points to a material turn in philosophy and the natural sciences, a new sense of materialism that challenges the anthropocentrism at the foundation of our Enlightenment-era image of ourselves. Bolt is skeptical of the way that traditions of learning and knowing such as constructionism and artistic development regard making as an act of human-exclusive agency: "Put simply, the idea that the world is a passive resource for use by active humans is no longer sustainable" (p. 3). Instead, she argues, contemporary relationships with technology decenter the human subject and disrupt the privilege of human-centered agency, resulting in a primary tenet of new materialisms: "At the core of the material turn, is a concern with agential matter" (p. 3).

Coming to grips with agential matter requires a difficult turn of thought, perhaps especially for teachers and curriculum designers, because schools require that teachers remain in control of each and every activity in their classrooms. Also, conventional wisdom is highly skeptical of materials that talk or move around. Dancing rocks and singing trees are not the point, however. Rather, Bolt argues that paying attention to materiality opens practice to new configurations of knowing and learning. That is, as an artist, Bolt wants to retrieve art as making from a language-centered functionality. In her view,

20th-century formalism and medium specificity, and the emphasis on original-ity and genius, relegated art to a social object. That is, when modernism (and postmodernism) elevated the *ideology* of the painting (i.e., what it means) over the *practice* of painting (i.e., the handling of materials), it positioned art as a discourse anchored in language. Consequently, practice as a way of *doing* knowledge, or as an encounter with an extra-, or pre-, or nonlinguistic *material* world was lost. As such, Bolt opposes the cultural turn that represses embodied, material engagement. She argues that "central to the constructivist position was the assumption that discourse prescribes what can be thought and what can be represented—whether in writing, speaking, acting, dancing, music, filmic or visual representations" (p. 4). Countering this linguistic focus, and echoing Papert's soap sculpture math and Burton's material voices, Bolt (2010) points to material practices that hold knowing as a trajectory of action in the world.

Bolt illustrates her argument with two examples: one from her life as a painter, when linguistic rationality succumbed to material thinking; the other from David Hockney's (2006) explorations into 15th-century European painting technologies, and his insights that emerged from handling tools and materials. About her own experience, she writes that while working in the unrelentingly harsh climate of Western Australia, she confronted a way of knowing she hadn't expected. "In the fuzziness of practice, out in the desert, the principles foundational to my art education were no longer of much use to me....Light does not always shed light on the matter. Under the harsh glare of the Australian sun, light fractured form rather than revealed it...a move-ment from logical rational thought to material thinking" (Bolt, 2010, p. 32). With respect to Hockney's research, she writes that his visual arguments were specific to his art practice as a drawer, and that those experiences "fashioned the nature of the question, the methodology and the types of realizations that emerged from (his) investigation" (p. 27). Bolt argues that paying attention to how materials enact meaning in practice—such as how paint renders form either tangible or intangible in the desert sunlight, or how the characteristics of a line can be more or less confident than another line—is fundamental to a way of knowing that comes with handling, and that might make available the "shocking realizations that occur in practice" (p. 34).

Bolt's new materialism recalls constructionism's and artistic development's proposition that learning and knowing are anchored in material engagement. That is, Bolt rejects modernist and postmodernist configurations that collapse materiality into history, culture, or ideology, a move that renders matter as mute, dumb, irrational, and passive (Bolt, 2007, 2010, 2013). Burton (2000) does not disagree: Materials have "voices" (p. 335) that cannot be silenced. Papert (Papert & Harel, 1991) concurs as well: Those soap sculptures "came from wherever fancy is bred" (p. 3), not from intentional design. In fact, both constructionism and artistic development see material as agential, though not to the same degree as new materialisms. In this way, Bolt's notion of handling is a critique of anthropocentrism that challenges constructionism and artistic development to be more explicit about the implications of their commitment to materiality.

Assembling Constructionist Artistic Development

Drawing from these sketches of constructionism, artistic development, and new materialism, *constructionist artistic development* is a learn-by-doing, productive activity that emphasizes individual learning; asserts that making things strengthens learning; holds knowledge as primarily interior and directed toward the construction of self-identity; and, in terms of teaching, practices a dialogic and relational pedagogy. Further, constructionist artistic development's emphasis on sharing implies recursive make/share spirals of creativity that position learning in a space of progressive improvement. As noted, a tension emerges from the way materiality is theorized. For all three strands, materials participate in learning, with their own voice and agency, but for constructionism and artistic development that participation is only partial, since those traditions restrict knowledge to an interior and essentially private construct of individual humans.

Socially Centered Learning

The tradition that I call *socially centered learning* stems from Lave and Wenger's (1991) theories of situated learning, where initial or peripheral participation in communities of practice leads toward full participation in those communities. In contemporary research this learning dynamic informs multiple lines of inquiry, including *situated learning, connected learning, digital media learning, new literacies,* and *interest-driven learning,* among others (Gee, 2013; Gee & Hayes, 2011; Ito, 2010; Ito et al., 2009, 2013; Lankshear & Knobel, 2011; Peppler, 2013). Both socially centered learning and constructionist artistic development hold knowledge as constructed by the knower, rather than as a hard-coded feature of the world, but they differ in terms of the identity of the knower and the goal of the constructive activity. Whereas construction-ist artistic development holds the knower as an individual and knowledge as leading to self-identity, socially centered learning theorizes the knower as the community and knowledge as a cultural configuration of that community.

For example, in his analysis of video game communities, Gee (2007) claims that social discourse implies "there are no private minds" (p. 6). The importance of language as a communal activity can't be overlooked in Gee's work on learning and knowing (Gee, 2004, 2007, 2010a, 2013; Gee & Hayes, 2011). Early in his career as a linguist, Gee (1999) theorized Discourse ["with a big 'D'" (p. 17)] to describe literacy as *action* in the world. For Gee, and for socially centered learning theory more generally, literacy is more than just reading and writing. In this expanded view, situated learning scholars point to a cultural turn that holds linguistic practice as key to understanding com-munities of actors who are embedded within institutions, expectations, and norms. This notion of (big D) Discourse as the engine of learning informs the digital literacies work of Lankshear and Knobel (Lankshear, Gee, Knobel, & Searle, 1997; Lankshear & Knobel, 2011, 2013), and Ito's work on connected learning (Ito, 2010; Ito et al., 2009, 2013; Ito, Okabe, & Tsuji, 2012). In this tradition, a systems-oriented approach to learning supports the work of "for-ward-thinking educators" who believe that "focusing on skill and drill rather than innovation and exploration,…[and] teaching to the test rather than teaching to youths' interests, were doing a major disservice to young people" (Peppler et al., 2014, p. xvii).

The pedagogical implications (big D) Discourse have been theorized since the late 1980s under the heading "social learning" (Lankshear & Knobel, 2011, p. 210). Pulling from the participatory learning frameworks of John Seeley Brown and Richard Adler (2008)—"We participate, therefore we are" (p. 18)—Lankshear and Knobel (2011) argue that social learning configures all learners as co-learners, and that the resulting coordination of Discourse enables learners to "apply one's knowledge and even to transform that knowl-edge for innovation'" (p. 219). This collaboration, as "a way of being together in the world" (p. 44), gathers a "new ethos" of learning from "interactivity, participation, collaboration, and the distribution and dispersal of expertise and intelligence" (p. 76). This distribution of knowing, as a dynamic action, is key to coordinating "classrooms, sports, friendship networks, church gath-erings, clubs, gangs, academic disciplines, discussion lists, chatrooms, types of women, weddings, funerals, families" (pp. 44–45). For Lankshear and Knobel, literacy (and literac*ies*) is a recursive and ever-widening relationship of context and pretext to the Discourses that "constitute the 'shape' and 'order' of the world. We enact them and they enact us" (p. 45).

Art educator and new media researcher Brigid Barron (2004) uses "the metaphor of a learning ecology" (p. 5) to describe the relational dynamics that suffuse the classrooms and sports fields described by Lankshear and Knobel (2011). In Barron's (2004) analysis, new media literacies have configured the internet as a vastly complex space of collaborative knowing, where an increasingly entangled knower and known is transforming learning into "a much more rapid, self-directed, spontaneous and interconnected process" (p. 5). Similarly, in her classic study of youth learning in the digital age, *Hanging Out, Messing Around and Geeking Out*, Mimi Ito (2010) explains that situated learning theory holds knowing as co-emergent because learners are not "internalizing knowledge, culture, and expertise as isolated individuals, but because they are part of shared cultural systems" (p. 14). This is why Lankshear and Knobel (2011) argue that social learning immerses learners in "ways of becoming full practitioners...[by] getting hands-on practice with their mental and material tools within authentic contexts" (p. 220).

Maker educators draw on this relationship between hands-on practice and community in their writing and research. In fact, long before the maker movement, Lave and Wenger (1991) described learning as a communal process that pulled novices (e.g., midwives, quartermasters, tailors, butchers) into associations of practitioners. Ito (2010) describes a similar dynamic whereby youth are invited to simply *hang out* on the periphery of a new media center until they feel inclined to get involved by *messing around* with the tools on offer, which might then evolve into deeper engagement as they are pulled into new relationships of expertise and encouraged to *geek out*. In both Lave and Wenger's communities of practice and Ito's *HoMaGo* spaces, learning feels like a pull toward action in the world, a trajectory of *doing*. Drawing on Brown and Adler's (2008) social learning theory, Lankshear and Knobel (2011) explain that this "'pull' approach assumes 'passion-based learning' that is 'motivated by the student either wanting to become a member of a particular community of practice, or of just wanting to learn about, make, or perform something'" (p. 228). Halverson and Sheridan (2014) state the relationship explicitly: "Makerspaces are communities of practice..." (p. 502).

Gee (2005) pushes back on the term *communities of practice*, however, saying that the "belongingness and close-knit personal ties among people...does not always fit classrooms" (p. 214). Instead, he suggests the term *affinity space*. The difference is that affinity participants share a common, interest-driven Discourse. Gee's objection pertains to the way schools are organized: Classrooms have in common a requirement for attendance; affinity spaces, on the other hand, exert a gravitational pull—learners want to be there. As such, social learning scholars describe affinity spaces outside of classrooms, for example, in after-school clubs, community centers, or libraries, and especially online (Gee, 2004, 2007; Ito et al., 2013; Peppler, 2013). Examples of online affinity spaces include Flickr, YouTube, fan fiction sites, and impromptu Wiki-spaces. In these digital spaces members share their work—photos, videos, stories— with the expectation that peer feedback will increase both the value of their individual contribution and overall community expertise. From the perspective of arts and design practices, Kafai, Peppler, and Chapman (2009), and Resnick, Rusk, and Cooke (1998) describe similar dynamics in the Computer Clubhouse, a face-to-face after-school program founded in 1989 in Cambridge, Massachusetts. And, in the series Interconnections: Understanding Systems through Digital Design, a four-book collection of curriculum ideas, learning scientist Kylie Peppler and her colleagues (2014) specifically and concretely describe such dynamics in video game design, computer coding, and craft electronics with an emphasis on participation, learn-by-doing, sharing, and spirals of iteration. (As an aside, I should mention that the Interconnections series directly addresses teacher learning and engagement with maker education, and, indeed, appears to be one of the very first projects to do so.)

Gathering Socially Centered Learning

As described here, *socially centered learning* situates learning as connected to and emergent from authentic communities. Like constructionist artistic development, it is a learn-by-doing, productive activity that emphasizes learning *to be* instead of (or in addition to) learning *about*. Unlike constructionist artistic development, however, it emphasizes the community over the individual, and holds knowledge and expertise as embedded in and distributed through (big D) Discourse as a way of being in the world. One consequence of this situatedness in discourse (and Discourse) is that socially centered learning theorists do not attend to materiality.

Overlaps and Contradictions

Teasing out the connections between constructionist artistic development and socially centered learning is an important first step in assembling a framework of digital making and learning. Table 1 identifies several points of contact between these traditions. At the risk of oversimplifying, we first should recall that maker education is an evolving pedagogy that traces to progressivism, a multistranded, centuries-long conversation about how education works and what its goals should be (Egan, 1997, 2002). Maker educators hold that this conversation is evolving, however, due in part to the way constructionism and situated theories of digital media learning handle the pedagogical challenges emerging from the new tools and materials that are washing over schools. In this chapter I've introduced artistic development and new materialisms to the maker conversation because I think they can strengthen the argument for why and how project-based, making-infused learning and knowing matters to schooling. To illustrate that claim, and to point to what's missing from current maker conversations, consider these several overlaps and contradictions between constructionist artistic development and socially centered learning:

First, both hold knowledge as constructed, rather than as a finite property of the world.

Second, both depend on learn-by-doing participation and dialog to fuel learning and knowing, and both emphasize learning to be over learning about.

These similarities highlight a contrast: Each tradition locates the place of learning and knowing differently. Constructionist artistic development positions learning as an individual act (as interior and essentially private); but socially centered learning holds learning as relational, distributed throughout and embedded within community (as exterior and shared).

Third, each tradition critiques conventions of subjectivity, though to different degrees. In constructionist artistic development, material agency nudges individual agency off center stage, at least slightly, and in socially centered learning the communal agency of the group subsumes the individual within it. This similarity highlights another contrast: For constructionism, decentering comes from the push of "physical characteristics such as weight [and] texture" (Burton, 1980, p. 7); but for situated learning, the gravitational pull of community decenters the individual. Certainly, the decentering effect is much stronger in socially centered learning. Compare Gee's "There are no private minds" (2007, p. 6) and Ito's "People learn in contexts, not because they are internalizing knowledge as isolated individuals" (2010, p. 14), with Bolt's "The idea that the world is a passive resource for use by active humans is no longer sustainable" (2013, p. 3).

Fourth, following from their learn-by-doing pragmatism, both traditions hold meaning as co-emergent with practice. As Fenwick (2000) observes, both constructivist and situated learning traditions recognize co-emergence, because *participation* leads to meaning making in each. In other words, there's a nascent sense of ecological enactment available to both constructionist artistic development and socially centered learning: Papert and Burton describe learners who share agency with tools and materials, where action in and with the world constructs meaning; and Gee and Ito write about the robust contextual dynamics of (big D) Discourse that distributes meaning and agency via communal literacies.

This shared commitment to enactment (which I would term *weak* enactment, since the overwhelming focus in each tradition remains on a purposeful calling forth and putting together of meaning and knowing, whether the actor doing the calling is an individual or the community), reveals another contrast: Despite having learn-by-doing strategies in common, each tradition holds tools and materials differently. There are two components to this. First, the tools differ; and second, their effect (why and how those differences matter to learning) is different.

Tools and Materials

For example, in constructionist makerspaces, learners build robots and wearable electronics with 3D printers, CNC routers, laser and vinyl cutters, programmable microcontrollers, conductive thread, buzzers, lights, and a wide variety of craft materials like wood, metal, cardboard, and fabric (Blikstein, 2013; Buechley, Qiu, & Boer, 2013; Gershenfeld, 2007; Martin, 2015; Martinez & Stager, 2013; Sheridan et al., 2014). In online affinity spaces or face-to-face media labs, on the other hand, physicality is downplayed in favor of video game design, blogging, coding, and movie making, among other digital literacy and Web 2.0 activities (Gee, 2013; Gee & Hayes, 2011; Ito, 2010; Kafai et al., 2009; Lankshear & Knobel, 2011; Peppler, 2013). For a visitor who is unfamiliar with what maker education looks like in schools, this difference might be the most visible contrast between constructionist and situated learning pedagogies. That is, from the doorway of a makerspace or media lab, it's easy to see whether kids are playing with machines and materials, or, conversely, if they're sitting at computers designing games or writing code.

As always, this image is too simplistic. In fact, in Philadelphia I recently visited a makerspace full of sixth graders working with paint, cardboard, glue guns, soldering irons, and a laser cutter. These students were building linguistic derivatives for their language class, however, not robots or Rube Goldberg machines as part of a STEM or STEAM class. One student told me that her word was *amicable*, from the Latin word for *friend*, so she was gluing laser-cut figures of people holding hands onto a painted collage of the Earth. "They're holding hands because they're friendly," she explained. My point is that as maker education evolves, easy distinctions between engineering, art, and literacy activities might begin to blur, and the view from the doorway will no longer seem as instructive. That is, according to education researcher Lee Martin (2015), although differences in tools and materials are readily apparent, they "should not be taken as absolute…[because] when the focus moves away from the tools employed to the mindset at work, these distinctions become less important" (p. 32).

This word *mindset*, which I take as *mind in the world*, is the second way these traditions differentiate tools and materials. That is, beyond the apparatus, constructionist and situated traditions diverge in the way materials matter to learning and knowing. From an engineering perspective, Martin (2015, p. 35) points to values and dispositions such as playfulness, a growth-oriented trajectory, an acceptance of failure, and collaboration. And from a new literacies point of view, Peppler and her National Writing Project colleagues (2014, pp. 10–12) emphasize participation, iteration, the need to know, publication, and change-agency. There are overlaps, to be sure, but a close reading suggests that STEM/STEAM pedagogies emphasize making objects to explore engineering and science standards, while new literacy teachers concentrate on telling stories to reform community. These are not the same goals, and they imply different pedagogical approaches, different ways of putting the mind to work, although I agree with Martin (2015) that locking in a definition of maker education based on specific tools and materials is too restrictive. Broadly speaking, however, it's accurate to say that constructionist artistic development focuses on building things, while socially centered learning focuses on building (and changing) community.

Articulating this contrast so simplistically will lead to further inaccuracies and omissions, as I've cautioned before, but the parallel grammar of that sentence is useful because it points to an important component of the digital making and learning framework I'm assembling. That is, based on the (presumed) orientation of any particular makerspace—STEM or STEAM versus new literacies—teachers might feel predisposed toward different kinds of activities. In her book on makerspace best practices, Laura Fleming (2015), a K–12 librarian, explains that she comes to making and building via "the unusual route of literacy" (p. 8); and from the other direction, Brian Gravel and colleagues (Gravel, Tucker-Raymond, Kohberger, & Browne, 2015) argue that their investigation of STEM literacy finds that "there is almost no literature that focuses on how people use literacies as they design and build" (p. 1). One writer (Fleming) addresses the perception that librarians don't build, and the other (Gravel) that engineers don't read or write. In effect, both researchers feel a need to explain why their work goes against the grain, suggesting that normative expectations in maker education might foreclose options for engagement, diminishing opportunities for learning. That's not to claim such foreclosure is preordained, only to highlight a relationship that might affect teaching practice.

Absent Materialities

The problem this brings up for maker education is that if art or English or engineering teachers presume particular kinds of makerspace or media lab projects are off limits, their students will encounter a diminished or depleted learning ecology. How might we recognize that depletion? As anyone who's ever tried to prove a negative understands, absence is notoriously difficult to point to. Addressing this blind spot calls attention to materiality: What is material to learning?

Contrast the sequential activities (imagine-create-play-share) that march progressively up and around Resnick's (2008) spiral of creativity, with the more ambiguous crossing-of-thresholds that happens when participants hang out or mess around in Gee's (2005) and Ito's (2010) affinity or *HoMaGo* spaces. What kinds of teaching practices are invited to appear in each? A response to that question depends on how teachers hold knowledge—as constructed or situated, as individual or communal—but it also relies on how they articulate the logic and use of tools and materials. And yet holding tools and materials as a way of thinking barely registers in the mainstream literature of maker education. In fact, with very few exceptions, this question is not adequately addressed in the literature of either of the maker education traditions profiled here.

For instance, in their constructionist study of three different makerspaces, Kimberly Sheridan and her colleagues (Sheridan et al., 2014) suggest that maker education is cross-disciplinary and hybrid, and that learning thrives in such spaces without restrictions imposed by normative expectations—but none of the three spaces they analyze exhibit any affinity with literacy-oriented constructivism. Why the one-sidedness? And why don't they comment on it? And from the tradition of socially centered learning, Ito (2010) reports that the most successful youth media programs are configured as open computer labs that "have plenty of unstructured time for kids to tinker and explore without being dominated by direct instruction" (p. 349). Rather than by domination, she argues, learning happens via peer-based coaching, facilitation, and mentorship—a "pedagogy of collegiality" (p. 349). Curiously, though, when it comes to describing the tool- and material-based expertise that kids need in order to coach, facilitate, or mentor their peers, trajectories that might lead to that expertise are not described. Why not? (For an example of where we might locate these missing aspects of the conversation, see Christa Flores's descriptions of the Reggio Emilia approach to materials in *Making Science*, in her forthcoming book exploring K–12 STEM teaching.)

My suspicion is that maker education's myopia traces to a thinly conceived sense of materiality. How do tools and materials matter to learning, and how do makerspaces and media labs nurture that relationship? Burton's material voices (from artistic development), and Bolt's material agency (from new materialism), point to the kind of materiality that's missing from mainstream maker education. In fact, I've included Burton and Bolt in this chapter specifically for this reason: to call attention to materiality's absence in the broader currents of mainstream maker education. That is, while I'm pretty certain Sheridan and Ito would agree with Martin's suggestion that *mindset* determines how a makerspace or media lab aligns with any particular teaching practice, or set of practices, or indeed with the ecology of any specific school, I'm not so sure that the interweaving of mind and materiality has been theorized robustly enough by either set of researchers to recognize diminished opportunities for making-infused learning, much less remedy that diminishment.

Pulling from the working definition of learning elaborated in Chapter 1—*a complex relationship with action in the world*, and particularly, as *an enacted push and pull*—I want to hold *mindset* as an ecological enactment of mind/world entanglement, a world-makes-world recursivity. That is to say, maybe mind doesn't precede space and materials, nor vice versa. Instead, perhaps space, materials, and mind are co-emergent in a given learning ecology. It could be that recognizing all three—mind, material, and space—as entangled effects of practice is the better way to go; or, to say it another way, that practice configures knowing. How would this affect schooling? What kinds of teaching would emerge in a space that explicitly held learning in these terms?

Exploring and eventually describing this interwoven mesh of mind and material entanglement, and enacting it in makerspaces and media labs, will require a more robust theory of materiality than is hinted at in the literature of maker education. In fact, I'm skeptical that maker education's dream of engaged knowing and learning, the new ethos and new culture of learning, can be adequately described, facilitated, invited to appear, or coaxed to presence by the relationship between constructionism and situated learning as drawn so far. We need a thicker materiality if we're to get traction on how making (with materials) and learning (with materials) matter to teaching. In this, I'm again pointing to Mol's (2002) exploration of the relationship between knowing, as an action, and doing, in her praxiography of arteriosclerosis in a Dutch hospital. The emerging discourse around new materialisms is here as well (Bennett, 2010; Bolt, 2013; Coole & Frost, 2010). And finally, I'm also alluding to Fenwick, Edwards, and Sawchuk's (2011) use of the word *sociomaterialism* to describe research that is refiguring the goals and purposes of schooling based on interweaving the social and the material.

The approach I'll sketch in the next chapter argues for holding materiality as a relational assemblage, and suggests that doing so makes the (sometimes counterintuitive) affordances of digital materiality available to project-based, making-infused teaching. To recall Deleuze and Guattari (1987), the sense of assemblage that I want to deploy here, using Bennett's (2010) words, is the gathering together of the "living, throbbing confederations…uneven topographies… [and] emergent properties…of an open-ended collective" (pp. 23–24)—a collective that I'll gather from ideas encountered in and borrowed from new materialisms, posthumanism, and new media theory.

Table 1. Making-Infused Traditions of Learning and Knowing.

Constructionist Artistic Development	Socially Centered Learning
Derived from the maker movement, art education, and new materialism, anchored by Papert and Harel's (1991) construction- ism and Lowenfeld's (1947/1957) artistic development:	*Derived from the digital media learning movement, anchored by Lave and Wenger's (1991) situated learning:*
1. Knowledge is constructed individually.	1. Knowledge is constructed communally.
2. Learning-by-doing depends on making and sharing in dialogic cycles that amplify self-identity, or learning to be oneself.	2. Learning-by-doing depends on partici- pating in communities, where learning *to be* is privileged.
3. Shared agency with materials decen- ters the human actor, implying that materials have voice and even agency.	3. Full immersion in practice emphasizes community over individual activity.
4. Meaning accrues to experience via the handling of materials.	4. Meaning is enacted within Discourse, implying that it is immersive and distributed.
Pedagogical Shape: Spiral of creativity (Resnick, 2008)	*Pedagogical Shape:* Affinity space (Gee, 2005)
Representative scholars and educators: Agency by Design, 2015; Blikstein, 2013; Bolt, 2010, 2013; Buechley, Peppler, Eisenberg, & Kafai, 2013; Buechley, Qiu, & Boer, 2013; Burton, 2000, 2009; Gershenfeld, 2007; Halverson & Sheridan, 2014; Hetland et al., 2013; Martinez & Stager, 2013; Resnick, 2002, 2008; Sheridan et al., 2014; Walter- Herrmann & Büching, 2013.	*Representative scholars and educators:* Brown & Adler, 2008; Gee, 2004, 2007, 2010a, 2013; Gee & Hayes, 2011; Ito, 2010; Ito et al., 2009, 2013; Kafai et al., 2009; Lankshear & Knobel, 2011, 2013; Peppler, 2013; Thomas & Brown, 2011.

FIELD NOTES (PARACHUTE DROP)

The project begins with friction and flow in water, air, and space. Aidan tells the girls to put away their computers and take out paper and pencils; they're going to draw pictures. He asks, "What hits the ground faster, a bullet fired from a gun, or a bullet dropped from my hand?" Hands shoot up, but one student stands and walks to the whiteboard to sketch her answer. There's chatter and sass as she does so, and the room fills with drama and loud voices. Aidan grabs a sheet of paper and enthusiastically crushes it into a ball, then raises his arms. In one hand he's got the crumpled scrunch, in the other a flat sheet. He releases them. "What's happening?" he asks, uncharacteristically raising his voice. The room replies together, "Friction!" and Aidan says, "Good! Now talk to your partner about friction."

Later, he spells out the parameters: Design a parachute that's as light as possible, as stable as possible, and that falls to the floor as slowly as possible. There will be a competition. They'll work in groups, but everyone will build her own parachute. First they'll explore coffee filters—how they fall or float— and describe what they find. Aidan holds up handfuls of coffee filters. The girls yell back, "What are our groups?"

After class, Aidan tells me that competition gets the girls to focus, because data collection is a social activity, but devising effective groups is a tricky business. He wants them to learn to observe what they do, and to pay attention to how the changes they make create differences in the parachute's performance. "But I want them to see it as connected to all the other stuff in life, too, not just to science class or parachutes," he says.

On that first day, the students play with coffee filters, dropping them from about head height and describing the way they float to the ground, and then folding, tearing, and taping them together to explore what happens next. After one iteration, a student says, "It drops like a dead bird."

In the following weeks, design and build phases will alternate with more testing and discussions. Materials include paper napkins, plastic bags, coffee filters, feathers, string, soda straws, tape, glue, staples; material interactions include folding, cutting, sewing, adding holes, layers and extensions, short strings, long strings, and rigid supports, and different ways of clipping their assemblages to the release mechanism that will be fixed to the ceiling.

On the last day, the girls push the furniture to the edge of the room, and Aidan rigs a drop line from floor to ceiling, made of kite string and a quick release clip. They take turns drawing their parachutes up, where a snap triggers the release. During test drops they tweak their designs, laughing and complaining and being melodramatic, and then the competition begins. Over a run of three trials, they drop and measure, drop and measure. One student puts tape on the floor to mark each parachute's drift, determining stability: the closer to center of the room, the less drift, and thus the more stable. Another student keeps the float time of each drop. Everyone measures her own mass. At the conclusion of the trials, Aidan announces a showdown: The top three parachutes will go head to head to determine the winner.

After the class has cleared out, Aidan explains that there'll be a critique of the project two days from now, after the girls have turned in their final reports, which will include measurements, calculations, and design drawings. He says, "I have to give them time to write and think about their performance before asking them to discuss it. They start to sulk otherwise. This is what I've learned from doing projects."

Datasheet: Age group: eighth grade. Content domain: science. Teacher: Aidan. Timing: three weeks in April.

· 3 ·

DIGITAL MATERIALITY

The previous chapter compared and contrasted two learning traditions that inform maker education: One described individuals making and sharing artifacts via reflective conversation (constructionist artistic development); the other drew learning as a communal process that situates, distributes, and connects knowledge through interest-driven affinity spaces (socially centered learning). As noted, a robust description of materiality is missing from that comparison. For me, this absence indicates, as education researcher Estrid Sørensen (2009) suggests, a "blindness toward the question of how educational practice is affected by materials" (p. 2). That is, though maker education emphasizes tools and materials such as laser cutters, cardboard, and programming languages like Scratch, among many others, the way these things contribute to learning is rarely analyzed or evaluated. For instance, when Martin (2015) distinguishes between additive and subtractive assembly tools, or when Halverson and Sheridan (2014) describe maker culture in three different makerspaces, questions of *how* and *why* are not asked: How might learning change if students explore cardboard instead of Plexiglas, or Python instead of Scratch, or the laser cutter instead of scissors and tape? These kinds of questions aren't available in the maker education conversation. In this, I'm in agreement with Sørensen (2009): "We should place a stronger emphasis on materiality in educational theory in general" (p. 8). In this chapter I'm gathering together ideas about tools and materials, and how they matter to learning. My goal is to arrive at a way of holding materiality that expands our collective sense of how and why learning in schools is shaped the way it is, and in doing so to suggest strategies for changing that shape.

Toward Materialities

Affordance and Connotation

The first way to figure materiality's place in a making and learning framework is to specify the obvious: *Materiality*, as a noun, names how a thing is or becomes present. From this beginning, four connotations are important. First, we use the word *materiality* to name matter, or physical substance: the clay of clay, the fiber of paper. Second, materiality connotes a quality of exteriority, or endurance, of being in or of the world. For instance, a bridge has a different materiality than a handshake or an itch on the back of my neck; and this difference can be named in addition to or alongside of the substance of these things, by specifying temporality, location, or scale, among other characteristics. Third, materiality refers to relevance. We hear this in legal jargon (in legal dramas on television when some attorney declares that a fact in a lawsuit is not material to the issue at hand), but the usage bears on curricular standards and pedagogy as well; for example, in how we might debate the ordering of algebra and geometry courses in a math curriculum. And fourth, materiality is affect. I mean this in the way you'd answer a question about how silk feels to the sense of touch or appears to sight—its *silkiness*: softness, smoothness, shimmering fluidity.

This fourth connotation entangles with the first three to reveal that things become present based on specific relationships, or affordances, with other things. For instance, a dress made of silk exists differently than one of cotton, wool, or cardboard, not simply because of its substance, but because of the combination of affordances that become available in the specific combination of its matter, exteriority, relevance, and affect. Importantly, I'm not talking about how an object is *represented*, but rather how a thing is encountered amongst the flow of life, in relationship with other things, that is, as presence with and through the world. In the hands of a designer, artist, or engineer, in fact, the relational assemblage of a specific materiality is crucial to the enactment of any given thing's presence—its usefulness, its desirability, its value. This is because the *feel* of a dress (or a bridge, or a sculpture) guides its unfolding trajectory in the world to such an extent that ignoring the complex interconnections of its affordances is not thinkable, or more specifically, not doable. (Note that, in order to keep the relationship of these four connotations available to the discussion about how materiality matters in a learning ecology, I will use *relational assemblage* as an occasional replacement for the term *materiality*, because we tend to read that word as "merely" substance or material.)

Each of these four connotations of materiality can be heard in everyday use, and found in common English-language dictionaries, even if their cumulative effect—as relational assemblage—is not articulated or even, at times, resisted. In his biography of Steve Jobs, Walter Isaacson (2011) offers several examples of such resistance. One of the most resonant is the story of the handle on the first iMac in 1998. Of the many debates Jobs had with his engineering and design teams—about color, translucency, the all-in-one design, the elimination of the floppy disk drive—the one that seems to have gotten the most pushback within Apple was about the handle on the top of the new machine. The Apple engineers "came up with thirty-eight reasons it couldn't be done" (p. 351), but Jobs pulled rank and insisted that they find a way to make it happen. Isaacson quotes Jony Ive, Apple's legendary designer, the one responsible for the look and feel of so many of the Apple products (and their derivatives) that clutter today's technology landscape, on why the handle was important: "If there's a handle on it, it makes a relationship possible. It's approachable. It's intuitive. It gives you permission to touch" (p. 350).

For some readers, Ive's analysis might hit with the force of a revelation, especially if you're able to remember your reaction to that first iMac: its whimsy, its friendliness. Where did that visceral goofiness come from? The handle: Yes, that simple, taken-for-granted feature of so many day-to-day objects had shifted dull functionality toward lighthearted serendipity. In other words, in the language I've introduced here, the handle figured as a relational assemblage that, in this specific instance, afforded an unexpected and surprising "permission to touch", thus making a new relationship with computers available. Up to that instant, remember, computers had not been fun, or friendly, or particularly approachable, at least not for most of us. In fact, Isaacson (2011) writes that, even in this case, desktop computers were not easy to carry around, so the handle "was more playful and semiotic than it was functional" (p. 350). Jobs nevertheless recognized its value, and the iMac subsequently helped launch computational appliances into everyday life. Whether you love or hate popular computing culture, an analysis of how computers became the things we know them as today goes through the materiality of that iMac handle.

While this is a rather unusual example of the kind of relationship that I want maker education to attend to, if only because the object itself (the first iMac), is so iconic, I would argue that holding materiality as a conversation, or relational assemblage is not extraordinary. For instance, the playful semiotics of the iMac handle (separate from or in addition to its dubious functionality) animates questions we ask ourselves everyday. Which shoes should I wear to work, or to dinner with friends? What color should we paint the living room, and how do we arrange the furniture once we've chosen that color? Or even, how do I end this email—Best, Sincerely, Warm regards?

These conundrums engage our curiosity, and open us to conversations with friends or colleagues. So when I say materiality is missing from the literature of maker education, I'm not talking about an esoteric aspect of learning theory; not at all. Rather, materiality matters in ordinary relationships because it's thoroughly entangled with our lives, as inescapable as gravity. And yet, maker education seems to attend to materiality only rarely, except to establish the brute fact that stuff (tools and materials) exists. For example, in their book *Invent to Learn*, Sylvia Martinez and Gary Stager (2013) suggest that "crayons and paint can and should co-exist with digital tools" (location no. 1975), but they don't explore *why* that co-existence is important to the way meaning becomes available in specific activities or their outcomes; and they argue, "Artists…draw, write, paint, film, compose, play, build, knit, sew, act, or direct to create personally meaningful objects, sights, sounds, or memories" (location no. 1563), but they don't elaborate on *how* any of these particular ways of making matter. Similarly, in her discussion of makerspace best practices, librarian Laura Fleming (2015) discusses tools and materials that might be found in a makerspace, but does so almost in passing (there isn't a chapter on materials, for example), and doesn't analyze how or why any particular toolset or type of material would be more or less appropriate to any specific activity.

Now, to be sure, I've learned a lot from each of these writers, so my critique is not simply pointed at their work. Rather, my claim here is that you can read far and wide in the literature of maker education without encountering the concern with materiality that occupied Jobs and Ives. This matters because, consequently, questions about how or why tools and materials contribute to learning, or how a made thing orders knowing in the world, become extremely difficult to ask when the relational assemblage of materiality is concealed.

Material Learning

In Chapter 1, I introduced *material learning* as a way of learning that addresses innovation. To be clear, material learning is the term I use to characterize what inventors and creative luminaries say when they talk about what innovation feels like, not a learning theory from the literature (e.g., Cabral & Justice, 2013). For instance, in biographies and interviews, and in speeches at conferences, or while accepting awards, we hear artists, writers, scientists, and mathematicians say that innovation feels like a surprise or a sudden breakthrough, that it's accompanied by a sense of shared agency or time disruption, that it's preceded by unexpected mistakes, errors, and screwups. From the field of psychology, Mihaly Csikszentmihalyi (1975, 2008) observed these characteristics in his research on enjoyment, optimal experience, what he called *flow*. And philosopher William Irvine (2014) chronicled a similar dynamic in the *aha* moments of Albert Einstein and Gustave Mahler, among other geniuses. And with a particular interest in the serendipity aspect of material learning, the science journalist Pagan Kennedy (2016) has called for more research into how we might enhance our ability to make the most of the happy accidents that appear to so often underlie innovation.

For my purposes, though, as an ingredient of the digital making and learning assemblage, I want to point to material learning's more pedestrian implications. That is, in addition to the mind-blowing insights from creative giants like Einstein and Mahler, or from the guy who invented the sippy cup (Kennedy, 2016), my claim is that materiality, as an assemblage of affordances, plays a critical role in even the most down-to-earth innovation, like discovering a faster route to school, or a better way to organize the furniture in your room. But schools too often ignore this kind of innovation. That is, *being* an innovator, or *doing* innovation, comes from a particular kind of relationship with the world that depends in part on surprises and mistakes. But we rarely if ever hear of a let's-see-what-happens curriculum, or of a serendipity test. Rather, we focus on knowing what we're doing, purposeful planning, being in control, and thinking by design.

Innovators tell us that it doesn't work that way. At a conference I attended in September 2013 at the Haystack Mountain School of Crafts in Maine, poet laureate Wesley McNair told a workshop audience that the poem guides itself into form, and then tells you when it's done. In his memoir about carving, David Esterly (2013) writes that the wood taught him to carve, explaining,

"[S]kill stimulates creativity. In the usual way of thinking, you have ideas, and then you learn technical skill so you can express them. In reality it's often the reverse: skill gives you ideas" (p. 84). The artist William Kentridge says exactly the same thing about drawing: Problems are solved in the process of working them out, in the materials—"the new emerges in and through the process of drawing" (Bolt, 2011, p. 87). And in October 2015, at a meeting of computer science teachers that I attended in New York City, Cynthia Solomon, partner in artificial intelligence research with Seymour Papert and Marvin Minsky at MIT in 1960s, said that she knows when a piece of computer code is getting good because it starts to take on a life of its own, and she begins to lose control of it.

In other words, for these inventors, innovating in poetry, wood, drawing, or computer code is a conversation *with* materials, not a working *on* materials to manifest a plan or an explicit purpose declared ahead of time. Innovation is a way of giving oneself over to flow, of holding making as entanglement, as a way of paying attention, as practice: not simply using tools to control docile matter. The salient aspects here—shared agency, surprise, time distortion, mistakes—figure materiality as a relational process. That is, the assemblage is not stable, not stationary, but constantly emerging. As a description of this dynamic, material learning points to the way learning to innovate unfolds for the learner, how it feels: innovation as affect.

The ideas behind material learning are not new, as the work cited above indicates. Here though, as suggested earlier, I'm explicitly folding in new materialisms' exploration of material agency, in order to articulate a resistance to "the idea of matter as passive stuff, as raw, brute, or inert" (Bennett, 2010, p. vii). This is where art and art education folds into the mix, too: with Burton's (2000) material voices, for example, and, on a slightly different trajectory, with Paul Carter's (2004) chronicle of place and space as a poetics of knowing in Material Thinking: The Theory and Practice of Creative Research. With respect to maker education, however, the notion that matter pushes back, like what happens between conversational partners, is absent; but it doesn't have to be. That is, material learning points to the boundary between things that maker educators know quite well (the everyday dialog that fuels the spiral of creativity, or the inward pull of social learning), and the tools and materials that suffuse their spaces and imaginations (cardboard, glue guns, LEDs, and code, for example), and other things that are missing or hidden in practice (materiality as a relational assemblage of affordances, as an agential partner in making).

Again, I don't mean this as an esoteric point of rarified theory; this is simply what innovators—scientists, engineers, artists—tell us about learning to innovate. In fact, perhaps because I'm so attuned to it these days, I hear this kind of talk all the time. As I was writing this chapter, in fact, the *New York Times* published an article titled "An Error Leads to a New Way to Draw, and Erase, Computing Circuits" (Markoff, 2015). The story is about researchers who lost control of an experiment and then noticed something new about the process they were exploring, a discovery that might hold the key to functional quantum computing. In the article, Evelyn Hu, professor of applied physics at Harvard, said: "I think the serendipity happens more often than not if you go into the history of science....The extraordinary thing behind every important discovery is not that it happened accidentally. The extraordinary thing is that the researchers noticed."

Following Professor Hu, the challenge to educators, especially maker educators, is to design learning ecologies that invite accidents while at the same time teaching students to notice them. How do teachers encounter and respond to the paradox of organized serendipity in a makerspace or media lab curriculum? Other than Seymour Papert's (Papert & Harel, 1991) musings on soap sculptures and his delight with the idea of soap-sculpture math, as discussed in Chapter 2, the notion that individual learning can lead to shared agency and productive purposelessness appears nowhere else in the maker movement, at least not that I've found. But this paradox, that skills counteract intentionality, that practice catalyzes loss of awareness, carries connotations of innovation that should animate maker education to its core.

Coming to Grips with Digital Materialities

When we bend the conversation toward the materiality of digital artifacts, the trajectory I've sketched so far changes. How does materiality matter to immaterial things? As Paul Leonardi (2010), a scholar of organization and management, suggests in "Digital Materiality? How Artifacts Without Matter, Matter," the question seems odd if we constrain materiality to physical substance. Following my discussion of materiality as a relational assemblage, however, I want to hold the conversation more open than that. The goal is to describe *digital* materiality as an assemblage that accounts for the affordances of digital tools. Leonardi's practice-based approach follows a trajectory that's similar to what I've sketched thus far: "Materiality is not a property of artifacts but a property of relationships between artifacts and the people who produce and consume them" (n.p.). Intriguingly, the literature of organizational man-agement has discussed digital technology in this way for years (for example: Orlikowski, 1992; Orlikowski & Scott, 2008). Most recently, information sys-tems scholar Kalle Lyytinen (Lyytinen, Yoo, & Boland, 2016) has asserted that digital networks require better theories about the affordances of digital materiality in order to improve the management of innovation. He warns, "This is a journey that is likely to challenge familiar ideas and beliefs about products, structures, relationships, and identity" (p. 71).

Closer to the theme of this book, educational researchers and cultural scholars have posed similar warnings about the challenges that digital net-works bring to schooling (Davidson, 2011; Gee & Hayes, 2011; Hayles, 2012; Thomas & Brown, 2011). For example, T. Mills Kelly (2013), in *Teaching History in the Digital Age*, argues that affordances of digital networks, such as the speed at which new sources become accessible, require new skills: "Where just a decade ago we had to teach students how to find enough primary sources to do interesting and original work, today we need to teach them how to pare down the results of their searches of such sources to something manageable in the context of a semester" (p. 127). Other scholars argue that internet-inflected changes to daily life are shifting what we mean by the word *culture*, from literature (Goldsmith, 2011) and the creative marketplace (Doctorow, 2014) to oral traditions (Foley, 2012), and from consumer capitalism (Shirky, 2011) to intellectual capitalism (Gee, 2013).

To unfold just one of these examples, consider the prompts that Kenneth Goldsmith (2011) gives his students, as described in *Uncreative Writing: Man-aging Language in the Digital Age*. In his university-level courses he calls on the copy/paste mechanics that internet searches invite to get students to play with a kind of writing that seems, on the surface, the complete antithesis of modern expectations. That is, he requires them to write papers entirely with downloaded text. Astonishingly, his students report that "writing" in this way brings about a relationship with creativity and self-identity that feels, to them, deeply authentic and original. The contradiction, or irony, is palpable. What might "original" mean in a copy/paste practice? And yet, in the digital age, at least for Goldsmith and his students, copy/paste (an affordance of digital text) reveals a way of doing writing that opens toward innovation.

In the language I've been using thus far, and keeping that iMac handle available as a reference, the teaching that Goldsmith brings to presence in his writing seminar enacts (some of) the affordances of digital materiality in order to change learning and knowing in his university seminar. Pointing to

Goldsmith's practice (and to Kelly's) begs the question of maker education: What digital affordances matter in makerspaces and media labs? And how might the *way* they matter be folded into the practice of teaching? In fact, these questions are similar to the one posed earlier about the way dresses made of silk or wool become present in the world. Drawing from the Interconnections book series mentioned above (Peppler et al., 2014), we might ask how a gaming practice is enacted as a board game, a game of tag, or a video game. What relational affordances become available in any particular instance of these enactments, and how does practice, or participation, change as an effect of those affordances? To explore that question in a classroom makerspace, we might analyze turn taking, the use of text, the rules, scoring, how one wins or loses, team building, the space of the game, how players experience embodiment in the game, and other characteristics. James Gee (2010a) proposes the methodology of the *worked example*, borrowed from mathematics and engineering pedagogies, as a way of describing these kinds of assemblages. In fact, in later chapters I'll adapt his methodology to my interpretation of interviews and observations from the study, but first, I want to puzzle through an affordance of digital materiality that has a direct and immediate consequence for making-infused teaching practice—a shift in the relational assemblage of knowing and learning that decenters agency but amplifies embodiment.

Decentered Embodiment

Introduced in Chapter 1, *decentered embodiment* is my neologism for an amalgamated cultural effect described by new materialisms as *decentered* or distributed agency (Barrett & Bolt, 2013; Bennett, 2010; Coole & Frost, 2010; Fenwick et al., 2011), and by new media theory and posthumanism as amplified *embodiment* (Braidotti, 2010, 2013; Hansen, 2004, 2005, 2015; Hayles, 1999, 2012). From the overlaps and entanglements these writers explore, I've simply adopted the two key terms: *decentered* + *embodiment*. Precisely how I want to use the terms, however, requires a brief digression into the new media theory of Mark Hansen and the posthumanism of Katherine Hayles.

Hansen: technogenesis. In *New Philosophy for New Media*, Hansen (2004) positions digital technologies at the center of the human. As such, the word *new* becomes problematic: "What is it about new media that makes them new?" (p. 20). Decrying the confusion generated by this question, Hansen writes that the conversation is polarized between "those who feel that new media have changed everything and those who remain skeptical that there is anything at all about new media that is, in the end, truly new" (p. 20). Hansen's solution is to hold knowledge as a phenomenological effect of (both old and new) media on the body of the media user. The root of his argument is that materiality produces a radical physicality—a feeling of knowing—that emerges from the body's affective presence in the world. *Digital* materials do so as well, and just as radically. He argues that this physical response is often not intuitive because *digital* is taken to signal *nonphysical*. For Hansen, this locates the source of new: Simply, digital media reveals the centrality of embodiment in a new way, a way that points to the arbitrariness of material relationships. That is, the more that digital media becomes *immaterial*—screen-based, code-based, and virtual—the more sensible the body's *physical* response becomes. For Hansen, digital materiality amplifies embodiment.

Hansen's word for this is *technogenesis*, which he describes as the body's capacity to reveal meaning, no matter what assemblage encodes it. He argues that this relationship of body *with* knowing "correlates with the fundamental shift in the materiality of media: the body's centrality increases proportionally with the de-differentiation of media" (Hansen, 2004, p. 20). This paradoxically figures the body, as a knowing site or space, as *more* important whenever materials become less physical: "The viewer must participate in the process through which the mediated digital image is transformed into a perceivable image" (p. 21). As such, Hansen argues that to insist on a divide between physical and nonphysical, at least in terms of embodiment, is incoherent and, in fact, counter to anything that we can sensibly name *as* experience. Rather, he argues, "with the flexibility brought by digitization, *there occurs a displacement of the framing function of medial interfaces back onto the body from which they themselves originally sprung*" (p. 21, original emphasis). For Hansen, the revealing of meaning, or how the body *feels* itself coming into a relationship of knowing, is characterized as a generative, emergent, active unfolding of action in the world.

Hayles: posthumanism. In *How We Became Posthuman: Virtual Bodies in Cybernetics, Literature, and Informatics* (1999), Katherine Hayles, a literature professor, admits that the term *posthuman* can evoke "deeply pessimistic" fears that "the age of the human is drawing to a close" (p. 290). Countering that fear, she explains that posthumanism stems from an observation of post-structuralist critiques of agency, resulting in the decentering of subjectivity and intentionality. This move, Hayles argues, invites us to reimagine ourselves in opposition to the "vision of the human in which conscious agency is the essence of human identity" (p. 288). As such, posthumanism suggests that "mastery through the exercise of autonomous will is merely the story consciousness tells itself to explain results that actually come about through chaotic dynamics and emergent structures" (p. 288). Here, in effect, Hayles describes a kind of emergent self-awareness that ironically depletes the agency of the will that brought that awareness to presence, a recursive loop of push and pull that changes the will's position in relation to its own affective acts of knowing.

For Hayles (1999), recognition of these changes comes, in part, from interactions with the internet, an ocean of connectivity that favors distributed expertise and participation over isolated autonomy. As such, posthuman refers *not* to the end of humanity but to "the end of a certain conception of the human, a conception that may have applied, at best, to that fraction of humanity who had the wealth, power and leisure to conceptualize themselves as autonomous beings exercising their will through individual agency and choice" (p. 286). By Hayles's analysis, an important characteristic of digital networks, an affordance of their particular materiality, is the social equity–based forms of knowing they bring to presence, such as collaborative and participatory problem solving, or shared expertise. She argues, however, that posthumanism doesn't make such utopian images inevitable, because unequal power distributions are not automatically eradicated by connectivity.

Overlaps and interweavings. Hayles's decentered agency and Hansen's amplified embodiment overlap in several ways. In terms of the materiality of objects, Hayles adapts Hansen's notion of technogenesis in *How We Think: Digital Media and Contemporary Technogenesis* (Hayles, 2012). From her reading of the history of the telegraph, a technology that precipitated the massive changes we now associate with *digital* technology, Hayles concludes that "objects...are more like technical individuals enmeshed in networks of social, economic, and technological relations, some of which are human, some nonhuman" (p. 13). This implies that human agency "codetermines what we call materiality....[M]ateriality, like the object itself, is not a pre-given entity but rather a dynamic process that changes as the focus of attention shifts" (p. 14). The notion that *paying attention* co-creates materiality amplifies the decentering she described previously (Hayles, 1999)—a logic of reciprocal, recursive depletion that counterintuitively enhances the *affect* of agency. In fact, here we see agency not only as decentered, but as diffused over a wide field of potential materialities. In terms of changing paradigms in classrooms, this diffusion blurs boundaries that often separate learning objects—for example, Papert's sand castle from his theory of the universe (Papert & Harel,

1991, p. 1), referred to in Chapter 2, a dynamic that I will argue has important implications for how teachers learn to teach in the digital age.

In another overlap, Hansen's (2015) recent work on 21st-century digital networks, what he terms *atmospheric media*, mirrors Hayles's posthuman dispersal of agency, amplifying the need to reconfigure subjectivity as a relational assemblage, and resisting the urge to regard human and nonhuman agencies as separable. With a nod to Alfred North Whitehead's early 20th-century reframing of subjectivity as process-based, Hansen agrees with network theorists Alexander Galloway and Eugene Thacker that "agency must be reconceptualized in a fundamental way. Specifically, we must rethink agency as the effect of global patterns of activity across scales in networks, where absolutely no privilege is given to any particular individual or node" (p. 2). Hansen then points to the way that digital networks rely on sensory perception constructed from algorithms, such as search protocols, that humans are not capable of perceiving. This paradox—perception without sensory awareness—indicates, "in our interactions with twenty-first century atmospheric media, we can no longer conceive of ourselves as separate and quasi-autonomous subjects" (p. 3) This interwoven entanglement, this thorough knitting-through of technology with perception and awareness, clarifies Hansen's idea that "subjectivity must be conceptualized *as intrinsic to the sensory affordances that inhere in today's networks and media environments*" (p. 3, original emphasis). In other words, Hansen argues, today, our awareness of individuality relies on a paradox: We are ourselves in spite of/because of the undifferentiated network tools we use to identify ourselves.

The Feeling of Decentered Embodiment

A thorough exploration of these interweavings between Hayles (1999, 2012) and Hansen (2004, 2005, 2015) would have to dig much deeper into the traditions that underpin their work, such as their critiques of Enlightenment rationality and humanist subjectivity, as well as the broader, contemporary currents of new materialisms and posthumanism, which I've only pointed to briefly (for example, in references to Bennett, 2010; Bolt, 2013; Braidotti, 2010;, and Coole & Frost, 2010). But this book is not the place to do that kind of thing (their books do it better than I could hope to!). And more to the point, my concern here is to question the *way* that digital materiality affects teaching, and a more thorough examination of Hayles's and Hansen's scholarship won't help us get a better grasp on that task. In fact, the words

I've used to map these ideas thus far (materiality as relational assemblage, and the effects of materiality as affordance, as a trajectory or presence in the world), and the examples I've provided of my own life trajectory as an artist and teacher (in Chapter 1), perhaps don't yet achieve the traction that I need. How can I know that you know what I mean? I suppose I can't. After all, it's plausible that even I don't know what I mean. And yet, affect remains. (And even that proposition can be contested.) Ah, what a tangle we make with so many words. In fact, let's leave the words behind (in a book?!), and gesture instead toward the *feeling* of decentered embodiment.

This is the how we start in the clay studio—by touching the clay: rolling it, kneading it, smelling it, tasting it—and how we'll start here, as well. But in fact, decentered embodiment, while paradoxical, is not unknown to you. You're already familiar with it if you've played computer games or explored virtual reality environments. Decentered embodiment is the emotional residue that accrues in your body while trying to survive your first night in Minecraft, or inside a multiplayer first-person shooter game, or while wandering through a nightclub or art gallery in Second Life. It's the physical contradiction you feel by the simultaneous presence and absence generated as you move through networked space. If you're like me, or my sons, or my friends and colleagues who like to get lost in digital topologies, you've experienced that wonder and curiosity when the clash of *he sees me!* connected to *I'm alone!* That unexpected encounter, that upwelling of excitement, fear, and wonder brought on by the paradoxical urgency of safety/danger or action/inaction oozing from your screen, through your headphones, and from sweat on your palms—that's decentered embodiment. If you're a habitual gamer, the exuberant anxiety I'm describing might be hard to remember because, just like a swoosh on a swing set squeezes your stomach, or a first kiss ignites sparkles down the back of your neck, the urgency of this presence/absence paradox is hard to hold onto against the background noise of simply attending to matters at hand. In this slide toward conventionality, the ephemeral rush of decentered embodiment resembles ordinary physiological mechanisms that compel thrill seekers to continually seek new extremes. If you fit this description, then you might not yet know what I'm talking about; if so, drop into a game you haven't played, or better, into a whole new genre of digital topology, and chart your awareness of the game's response to your avatar's presence. I don't know if this will work, but the shock of the new mechanics might open your sensory topology just enough to admit a renewed encounter with decentered embodiment, at least briefly.

Now, on the other hand, if you've never wandered around Minecraft, or spawned into a multiplayer tournament, or explored a world as an avatar (and perhaps don't even want to), you have nevertheless experienced decentered embodiment if you've ever used Skype, FaceTime, or Google Hangout. The emotional charge was probably less visceral than the fear and wonders that gamers experience, but the underlying dynamics were similar. I'm talking about the tingle of curiosity that meanders through your brain as you come to grips with the fact that someone sees you, and you them, even though neither of you is physically present to each other, at least not in a way that your bodies understand. This nonpresence that generates presence-like effects in your gesture, posture, and mood—that's what I'm calling decentered embodiment.

I hope that sketching decentered embodiment in this way makes clear the role of affect (and empathy) in its emergence. That is, decentered embodiment is a feeling of being in and of the world, but this particular feeling—a paradoxical presence/nonpresence—is an affordance of digital materiality, like a feeling of silkiness is an affordance of silk. In other words, digital materiality, a relational assemblage of tools and materials, matters to human sense-making because of the way it colors knowing. To reiterate, digital materiality is not a teaching tradition like constructionist artistic development or socially centered learning. Rather, it's a substance or mesh that interweaves individuals and communities in relationships of knowing and learning that are more complex than either of those pedagogies might be capable of describing. But this is not simply a "new media" thing. In fact, positioning learning as an enacted process, an entanglement of knower and known, or learner and context, is not new at all, as descriptions of exemplary teaching and teacher education imply (for example, connected, relational teaching is described by Darling-Hammond, 2006, 2013; Goldstein, 2014; and Rodriguez & Fitzpatrick, 2014, among others).

To be clear, my claim is that digital materiality is a characteristic of digital network ecologies, and decentered embodiment is an affordance of that materiality; a texture, force, or quality of the assemblage, like wetness in the Hawaiian rain forest, or the hardness of the floor of the Sonoran desert in midsummer, or like gravity anywhere on planet Earth. When you encounter the network, you encounter decentered embodiment. By analogy, when you walk in the rain forest, you get wet. Or, in a body/performance analogy: As you get dizzy by spinning yourself in circles, so the conundrum of presence/nonpresence accrues from logging into a multiplayer game, or from blowing kisses with your cousin's new baby on FaceTime. Or, to say it another way,

much like passengers on mid-19th-century trains thrilled to mechanized loco-
motion, or early 20th-century moviegoers panicked at the sight of those trains
barreling towards them, decentered embodiment is an empathic response to
contemporary tools. There are more complex and perhaps more accurate ways
to describe this entanglement, but my point here is that just as trains weren't
invented for the emotional rush of riding on them, nor movies for their illu-
sion of danger, the kick we get from decentered embodiment is an emergent
effect of the materiality of the network, an enacted encounter that was not
purposely designed into the assemblage. Further, this is not to claim a value,
either positive or negative; decentered embodiment is not good or bad in any
simplistic sense, just as watercolor or acrylic or tempera paints are not good
or bad. Neither is decentered embodiment a singular or isolated affordance
of digital materiality; the relational assemblage of the network is also associated with heightened collaboration, identity fluidity, creative remix culture,
the long tail of productivity, copyright redefinition, and shifts in qualities of
awareness, or the ability to pay attention. In each case, my question remains
nearly identical: How does the materiality of the digital ecology affect learning and knowing? How might we notice and call on this materiality in makerspaces and media labs in order to amplify and empower learning?

Implications of Digital Materialities

Knitting. This sense of expanded materiality that I'm after begins with tool
use as an encounter, in which we make and remake the world as extensions
of ourselves, while at the same time the world makes and remakes us. I've
discussed this world-makes-world recursivity as enacted knowing and learning
in Chapter 1, referred to it in my own work and life, illustrated it with the
image of a robust conversation, and pointed to it in the research literature
by recalling Fenwick's (2000) typology of cognition. Now, keeping before us
the exploration of materiality as a relational assemblage that makes certain
affordances available to practice, I'd like to extend those analogies with three
additional references.

First: Andy Clark's (1997, 2011) work in cognitive science and embodiment. His (2011) descriptions of "boundary disputes" between "brainbound"
cognition and extended, or ecological, cognition reprise the sense of enacted
encounter that I want to make available here, especially with his metaphor
of "mind as mashup" (p. 218), and his empirical interpretations that lead to
descriptions of cognition as "the complex interplay between morphology and

control" and as "active sensing routines that retrieve information from worldly sources just in time for problem solving" (p. 81).

Second, Bennett (2010) reminds us that Bernard Stiegler's (1998) study of early humanity's stone tools suggests that external action in the world becomes available to human beings as recursive spirals of internal reflection and external, or shared, response. Which leads Bennett (2010) to propose, "There never was a time when human agency was anything other than an interfolding network of humanity and nonhumanity" (p. 31).

And, third, I am especially moved by Lev Vygotsky's (1978) early 20th-century observations of very young children. "The child attempts to grasp an object placed beyond his reach; his hands, stretched toward that object, remain poised in the air. His fingers make grasping movements" (p. 56). It begins with gesture: An outstretched hand activates a parent's response, which in turn activates perception, which in turn catalyzes relation, and the recognition of relation, which in turn motivates an ordering of and with the world. This pre-linguistic dawning of sign-making evolves into sense, speech, and desire; an extralinguistic world-makes-world recursivity that co-emerges with play and things in the world; a way of thinking that will come to be called *technology*. Here, Vygotsky draws out the slow knitting together of mind and matter that interweaves bodies and materials as a relational assemblage. Later, the child will understand pointing and the affordances of pointing as an enacted dance of meaning, as a stutter-and-flow choreography of embodiment, of materiality, and as a gesture that leaves its own mark—a spark from which a topology of learning and knowing will cascade across the interconnected horizons of that child's life-world for as long as he or she remains on the planet.

Stepladder. To bring the analogy back to earth, let's consider a more pedestrian example, an everyday object: a stepladder. In the kitchen a stepladder extends our reach, but when the dishes are in the highest cabinets, it *requires* our reach. An apparently willing extension that feels like empowerment, like freedom, comes to be felt as dependence. At first, the ladder expands our world, but later it locks us in; we must use the ladder in the same way we first used it if we want to reach those dishes again. This is a recursively enacted, ecological relationship. With the ladder, we change our relationship to the environment, which changes our relationship to the ladder. As we enact one reality in response to the tool, we are no longer free to explore reality or the tool as we once did. Rather, we are now bound to a configuration of tool and world that stabilizes and becomes conventional, predictable, or black-boxed. Something similar happens with other tools, too.

This is not a new analysis. As an explanation for how tools and materials contribute to the construction of meaning, this shift from freedom to dependence was discussed in the 1930s by Lewis Mumford (2010), and has been explored by scholars, philosophers and cultural theorists who write about technology (Bolt, 2011; Eisner, 1985; Galloway & Thacker, 2007; Heidegger, 1977; Kittler, 1999; Maynard, 1997). But I want to unfold the analogy further by suggesting that these stepladder dynamics of expansion and dependence accrue to relationships with digital networks, as well. In my interpretations and analysis of interviews and observations in this book, and in my use of the framework of digital making and learning, I will call upon the materiality of digital networks to access this analogy of tool-world recursivity. And in doing so, I'll be interested in an additional shift, too: from tool to material.

That is to say, once the remade world has stabilized, become normative, or conventional, the tool-world recursivity that brought that stabilization to presence no longer appears as an interaction between tool and material but as a relational assemblage, as materiality. That is, as the tool becomes integrated within a construct, its affordances become inseparable from that construct. Imagine the naïve shopper at IKEA craning his neck at the high cabinets in the model kitchens. He asks, how was this made? Imagine a similar question from a surveyor of new homes. What gives this house its affordances? The answer: bricks and mortar; these are among the materials that enact this thing called "house." Back in the kitchen, we get a similar answer: the stepladder. That is, without the stepladder, those cabinets would be inconceivable; they could not have become present in this particular way. The stepladder, like the wood, hinges, glue, screws, and nails, is material to the construct.

Affect and agency. This interweaving of tools and materials with affect and agency suffuse this study. My claim is that we are knit through with digital network tools, like the internet, which extend and constrain the trajectories we trace in the world—implying relationships of learning and knowing just as stepladders imply relationships of countertops and shelving. As the stepladder becomes material, so too do digital tools. This is why holding digital materiality as a relational assemblage of internet, computers, smartphones, video games, blogs, social media, and digital protocol, among many other tools and types of tools, helps us articulate questions about how the maker movement and digital media learning become enacted in schools. In the stepladder analogy, we extend and become dependent on the vertical dimension—those high cabinets that were once beyond reach—and kitchens everywhere become enacted as similar topologies with similar affordances. Likewise, attending to digital materiality raises questions about the shape of learning and knowing in schools. Hinting toward a response, Hayles argues that materiality "is not a pre-given entity but rather a dynamic process that changes as the focus of attention shifts" (1999, p. 14), and Hansen that "we can no longer conceive of ourselves as separate and quasi-autonomous subjects" (2015, p. 3). How might paying attention to teaching as an interwoven relational assemblage affect the enactment of learning in classrooms?

A Digital Making and Learning Framework-Assemblage

The role of the framework-assemblage presented in Table 2 was to enhance my listening ability. I constructed it by weaving together characteristics of traditional and 21st-century teaching practices, and speculating about how the affordances of digital materiality might change those traditions. Characteristics in the first two columns have been culled from the numerous scholars and educators referenced previously (e.g., Burton, 2000, 2009; Hetland, Winner, Veenema, & Sheridan, 2013; Hickman, 2011; Jenkins, 2006; Martinez & Stager, 2013; Resnick, 2008). The contrast with traditional teaching, popularized as students in rows of desks (Blikstein, 2013; Martinez & Stager, 2013), has been extrapolated from the maker education research of Gary Stager (2014). It's important to keep in mind as you read the stories and analyses in this book that this framework-assemblage and its underlying logic continued to evolve throughout the study and in the writing of this book; in other words, as a heuristic tool, Table 2 does not represent a fixed set of standards or a catalog of benchmarks. Rather, its evolving matrix is like a weather vane that continuously swivels in order to indicate which way the wind is blowing, or like a netted shopping bag that stretches to accommodate the gathering assemblage of digital making and learning.

In terms of function, the framework-assemblage helped make comparisons available: between the making-infused pedagogies surveyed in Chapter 2 (center column), the affordances of digital materiality surveyed in this chapter (column 3), and traditional practices (column 1). Rather than try to bring each element into alignment with the others, however, or to launch a new paradigm, the goal was to draw out tensions and oscillations between practices. As discussed earlier, in this I was following Mol's (2002) work on arteriosclerosis, where she asked how multiple ontologies overlap and interweave in order to hold practices together. John Law (2002) asked a similar question, proposing the term *fractional coherence* to describe complex objects that function only when their constituent parts are not subsumed into a singularity, such as a British fighter jet (Law, 2002), or a French transportation system (Latour, 1996). For each of these theorists, the point in holding relational structures open is to coax to presence new ways of doing and acting in the world. Mol (2002) writes that doubt and confidence always alternate, and that ignoring one in favor of the other forecloses possibilities and shuts down practice. She argues: "In stressing ontological multiplicity my book lays bare the permanent possibility of alternative configurations; reality is never so solid that it is singular. There is [sic] always alternatives" (p. 164).

Similarly, in my study, the framework-assemblage became useful by helping me imagine new relationships between practices. For example, reading the top row of Table 2 from left to right suggests that remixing teacher-centered pedagogy with learner-centeredness, and suffusing both with digital materiality, particularly its affordance of decentered embodiment, might make teachers and students available to each other as co-learners. Or, in row 2, interweaving the teacher-knows-best disposition from traditional classrooms, which Papert (1980a) called instructionism, with the constructionist teaching that animates maker educators everywhere (Martinez & Stager, 2013; Peppler et al., 2014), might surface a new notion of content, or what teachers teach, as multiply sourced and perhaps even indeterminate. Overall, as I gathered observations and interviews, I used this evolving matrix to interpret what I was seeing and hearing. So, for example, if a teacher used a worksheet to prompt interest-driven learning, I referred to the framework to speculate about the kind of practice I was observing.

Methodology will be discussed in more detail in the next chapter, but I'll mention here that this process of compare and contrast suggested a conversational approach. For example, as Table 1 indicates, both traditions of making-infused pedagogy hold knowing as strongly constructivist (or constructionist); filtering that assumption through digital materiality's decentered embodiment (Table 2, row 2) suggests, paradoxically, that knowledge is neither individual nor relational but somehow both, and neither. Does this imply that digital making and learning practice is drifting toward decentered teaching? What would that look like? Or, how might Hansen's (2004, 2005) reconceptualization of embodiment challenge the material engagement that maker educators rely on? Perhaps more disruptively, what would either move—toward decenteredness or toward amplified embodiment—imply for schooling? Perhaps the question becomes whether or how digital materiality, as an assemblage of learning and knowing, rewrites the assumptions of constructivism.

Here, a question of topology emerges. If the shape of constructionist artistic development is a spiral, and socially centered learning an affinity space (see Table 1), what shape results from their combination? What happens when the twisting recursivity of Resnick's (2008) imagine-make-share cycle merges with Gee's (2005) and Ito's (2010) interest-driven, passion-fueled inward drift? In this, I imagine a dynamic morphology that both supports and challenges making-infused pedagogy, retaining its fractional coherence even as it expands into new territory. A Möbius strip comes to mind (Table 2, row 10). With a simple twist of a paper strip, topology blurs and dimensionality collapses—but not entirely. At any local point along the twisted paper strip, my fingers touch different sides of the structure, and differentiation remains. But tracing the topology reveals an irony: a one-sided multiplicity. What might this figure imply for practice? How might it chart new trajectories of learning and knowing? Perhaps pedagogy could be enacted with a light touch; with participants working collaboratively *and* individually, where expertise accrues from both shared and distributed expertise, *and* from disciplined, independent study. That is, the merging surfaces of the Möbius strip call attention to the potential for enacting new relations: Individual and community achieve relational symmetry, as do interiority and exteriority, and the knower and the known. Locally, while in stasis, these constructs differentiate, like two sides of a coin. But while circumscribing the loop—say, while enacting practice as an ebb and flow, as a relational assemblage, over the course of a term of study— we succumb to the curious gravity of the new topology, and new relations are generated from old objects. The role of the teacher in such a space might be to manage a circulatory system of enacted effects, at times coaxing stability from raucous fluctuations, at other times enjoining diverse voices to harmonize in a chorus of surprise and unpredictability.

These speculations gather attention to the potential effect of digital making practices in classrooms and other learning environments. But to repeat, the framework is not a predictor. Rather, like a weather vane, it helped me recognize learning ecologies suffused with digital materiality as I encountered them, leading me to ask whether I was observing new ways of teaching, or conversely, if teachers were doing the same old thing, but with fancy new tools.

As well, the framework-assemblage is a prototype—an early attempt to gather overlapping and contrasting traditions connected to the maker movement and digital media learning, traditions that are themselves still very much in flux. In fact, combining constructionist artistic development, socially centered learning, and digital materiality is a messy, speculative process. In that sense, the framework-assemblage reprises Law's (2004) observation that mess is unavoidable when research tries to clean up too much: "Simple clear descriptions don't work if what they are describing is not itself very coherent. The very attempt to be clear simply increases the mess" (p. 2). In this, I would reiterate Fenwick's (2000) cautions about the misrepresentations inherent to any framework: "Typologies that pretend to totalize distinct currents of thought and pedagogical energies must themselves be disrupted, put off balance" (p. 266). In fact, this aligns with the purpose of the framework-assemblage, which is to serve as a pin board matrix, or collage; that is, both conceptually and pragmatically, this framework should be messy enough to be useful, but not so haphazard as to fall apart when first applied to the task of describing and interpreting the findings from this study.

Table 2. Framework-Assemblage of Digital Making and Learning.

Traditional Classrooms	Maker Ecologies	Digital Making and Learning Ecologies
Teacher centered	Learner centered	Teachers and students as co-learners
Instructionism	Constructionism	Content is recursively and multiply sourced
Learning is Cognitive: Individual	Learning is Affect: Communal Engagement	Learning is Cognitive-Affect: The feeling of knowing
Cognitive: Learning in the head	Affect: Learning as engaged	Cognitive-Affect: The feeling of knowing
Locked to standards	Individualized pathways	Entanglement of world and materials
Goal-bound: Curriculum progresses toward pre-set objectives	Interest-driven: Curriculum progresses toward student-set objectives	Fractionally coherent: Curriculum enacts emergent encounters
Time controlled by teacher/institution	Time controlled by learning need	Time as intersection of iterative enactments
Focus: Reproduction	Focus: The new	Focus: Presence; recursive spirals of old and new
Achievement	Empowerment	Emancipation: A new ethos and new culture of leaning
Shape: Desks in Rows	Shape(s): Spiral of Creativity and Affinity Space	Shape: Möbius Strip
Trajectory: Control and deliver content	Trajectory: Liberate and amplify imagination	Trajectory: Enacted encounters with materiality

Representative Sources: Agency by Design, 2015; Barrett & Bolt, 2013; Blikstein, 2013; Bolt 2007, 2013; Brown & Adler, 2008; Burton, 2000, 2009; Coole & Frost, 2010; Gee, 2004, 2007, 2010a, 2013; Gee & Hayes, 2011; Halverson & Sheridan, 2014; Hetland et al., 2013; Ito, 2010; Ito et al., 2009, 2013; Jenkins, 2006; Jenkins et al., 2009; Kafai et al., 2009; Lankshear & Knobel, 2011, 2013; Lave & Wenger, 1991; Martinez & Stager, 2013; Papert, 1980a, 1980b, 1993, 2001; Papert & Harel, 1991; Peppler, 2013; Resnick, 2002, 2008; Sheridan et al., 2014; Thomas & Brown, 2011.

Table adapted from Stager, G. (2014). Making vs. school "reform." *Invent to Learn*. Available from http://www.inventtolearn.com/table/

FIELD NOTES (INVENTION CONVENTION)

Upstairs in the science room, Amber and Grace talk about inventions with the second graders. "How do we help people solve problems?" Grace asks.

Amber asks the girls where they think inventors get their ideas. After noisy speculation, they propose that inventors notice something not being done and then figure out a way to do it. In the brainstorm that follows, the girls consider dog alarms, light-up purses, and sunscreen applicators for the beach.

Grace tells me that earlier, they had given the girls a battery, two paper clips, and a lightbulb, and without giving explicit instructions, had told them to make the bulb light up. "That eventually leads to designing and planning an invention that can solve some sort of real-world problem," she says.

Four weeks later, tables line the perimeter of the drawing room on the parlor floor of one of the townhouses, and the girls dash about, finalizing their displays. Grace tells the assembled visitors—mostly parents and teachers, but some other students, too—that an important feature of this year's convention is the electronics and other high-tech tools the girls have used, such as Little Bits electronics and PicoCricket kits, and the 3D printers. Soon, the crowd ebbs and flows around the displays, and the girls launch into their explanations: automatic dog feeders, prototypes of door lockers, braille dice, and robots that clean under the couch. Next to each display is a poster the girls have made illustrating how their invention works and naming its price. A parent next to me asks if the items are in stock or if they're only available on demand.

Kieran comes up, and I'm surprised to see him, though he tells me that he's been back and forth between the North Building and the townhouses a couple of times already, troubleshooting the electronics. On the other side of the room there's a fifth grader, he says, who just told him that at her convention three years ago, they'd used mostly cardboard and tinfoil. But the extra running around doesn't bother him, because he knows it's worthwhile. In fact, on his way back to the townhouses a few moments ago, he'd crossed paths with a senior from Thomas's engineering class who'd said, "Every day is maker day around here!"

In the crowd, I bump into a student teacher I've gotten to know. He's doing his master's internship in educational technology at the school, and we chat about his impressions of the projects and about maker education more generally. He's excited by the energy and engagement of the students, he says, but wonders if the school is worried about protecting intellectual property, and whether the teachers have discussed copyright with the second graders.

Across the room I notice Beatrice greeting parents and testing some of the inventions. When she comes near, she asks how the research is going, saying she's happy I'm able to see this event. At that point, we notice the first graders coming single-file down the grand staircase above us. "Look how excited they are," Beatrice says. And when I say that they'll make teachers of their second-grade friends, she replies, "That's what learning is all about."

Datasheet: Age group: second grade. Content domain: science. Teachers: Grace and Amber. Timing: Spring, approximately six weeks.

· 4 ·

METHODS AND PRACTICE

This chapter describes the design of the study—both the methods and practices I used to collect data, and my process of interpretation and analysis. It also traces an iteration of the inquiry questions that were introduced in Chapter 1, and describes two dispositional sensibilities that guided the research.

General Research Design

Approach

This qualitative field study took place at a K–12 private girls school in a major metropolitan area of the northeastern United States; primary participants were the teachers and administrators who shared their work with me. Following Ito (2010), my approach was ethnographic and exploratory; I wanted to describe relationships by "grasping the contours of a new set of cultural categories and practices" (p. 5). That is, rather than analyze behavior at a granular level, my approach targeted digital making technologies across the curriculum.

Timeframe

In-depth interviews, observations, and conversations occurred from August 2013 through June 2014. Additional conversations and email contact took place until August 2015. Interpretation and writing occurred throughout the study period.

Participants

Teachers from various curricular areas (the sciences, humanities, language arts, and visual art), with varying lengths of service at the study site (from 2 to 15 years), were invited to participate in the study; five administrators (the headmistress, the director of curriculum, the directors of the middle and high schools, and the director of technology) were also invited. Altogether, 22 teachers and administrators were selected to join the study. Teachers shared their learning with me through in-depth interviews and multiple, casual interactions, and by permitting me to observe them in their classrooms as they taught. School administrators added descriptions of school culture, including demographics and historical overviews, and descriptions of the school's expectations of its teachers, including attitudes toward learning theories and instructional approaches.

Selection criteria for these primary participants included maximum variability across age, experience, and gender, and openness to talking about making activities in education, regardless of whether they expected to use digital fabrication tools during the school year. Each of these participants signed consent forms giving permission for audio recordings of interviews and publication of the study in this and other scholarly settings. I assured participants that their anonymity would be protected by the use of pseudonyms. As such, even the name and location of the study site have been kept confidential. Further, I took care that to the best of my knowledge, no participant felt pressured to join the study.

Additional participants included faculty who were not interviewed or directly observed in their classrooms, but who nevertheless welcomed me into the community; their spontaneous and serendipitous conversations helped me understand the interwoven fabric of the school. As well, the school itself—including the entry halls, cafeterias, stairwells, gymnasiums; the media events and art shows; as well as the myriad custodians and staff—should be considered a participant. That is, my presence during the 2013–2014 school year resulted in so many spontaneous interactions that the study site became a rich web of relations, and acquired its own, distinctive voice. Another category of participant includes the students. As discussed, I focused on teachers' learning, so students were not interviewed directly, but they were constantly present, and their learning was indeed the explicit focus of every other participant's work.

Site

The study site was a K–12 girls preparatory school in a large metropolitan area of the northeastern United States. The school was first established in a small rural community in the early years of the 20th century, but then later moved into the central urban area of a nearby city. Today the school occupies several 19th-century townhouses in a busy district of that city; three of the townhouses have been connected by extensive renovations, and a fourth remains separate. The school also occupies a large brick building about ten blocks north of the cluster of townhouses.

This school was an appropriate site for this study because it was committed to project-based, making-infused teaching across the curriculum, and because a general awareness of the maker movement was pervasive. In fact, in the year prior to my arrival, the school had constructed two FabLabs, a media lab, and several makerspaces. As well, the school espoused inquiry-based teaching and learning, and considered technology an important ingredient in progressive, constructivist education. Faculty from every discipline and grade level were encouraged though not required to explore the purpose and use of technology in their teaching.

A distinctive characteristic of the school that should be acknowledged is its affiliation with a major religious tradition, and its concern with social justice issues as espoused and practiced by that tradition. It was not unusual to encounter teachers talking about shared responsibilities for the underprivileged or socioeconomically deprived, for example. And yet, aside from this kind of discussion, religion did not overtly influence the curriculum; for example, religion was not visible in the science, history, or art classrooms that I observed. Neither did it appear to influence the daily routine, except that students were required to enroll in religion classes and to attend services at select times during the year. Further, the school was not managed or directed by religious officials, and membership in the religion was not a prerequisite of either admission to or employment by the school—indeed, more than two dozen different religious traditions were represented in the school population (Director of Admissions, personal communication, August 14, 2014). As such, though its religious character was indisputably woven through the fabric of the school, I would argue that it did not affect my methods or practice any more so than any other characteristic of the school.

Interviews

In-depth interviews with primary participants followed from Rubin and Rubin's (2005) responsive model, where the goal was conversational and expansive, like a conversation between partners. The process resembled Riessman's (2008) narrative interview approach that "gives way to conversation where interviewees can develop narrative accounts" (location no. 598). That is, I relied on open-ended prompts and encouraged participants to tell the story of their practice, often asking for clarifications and probing for details if they were not forthcoming. I also varied the way I asked questions, for example, by including fill-in-the-blank questions such as "Complete this sentence: In order for students to have a good learning experience with me, the most important thing I need to do, as the teacher, is _____." These prompts inevitably expanded into additional stories that sometimes meandered into examples or themes that I would not have known to ask about, leading to further follow-ups.

Interviews were conducted in classrooms, offices, waiting areas, and the cafeterias, or in other quiet areas where disturbances were expected to be minimal. That was not always an obtainable goal, however, and occasionally interviews were interrupted by the arrival of noisy students, unexpected faculty consultations, and, once, by a school-wide fire alarm that required the evacuation of the building (in that case, we continued our conversation onto the sidewalk). Audio recording was conducted with an Apple iPhone that was placed in plain sight between the participant and myself; in all cases, I asked the participant if it was okay to do so. During interviews, I also made notes on a yellow pad of ruled paper, primarily to keep my focus and concentration on the specific flow of the conversation, but also to mark moments of expressive emotion or gestural meaning that would not have been captured on the recording. All interviews were professionally transcribed by an online service that specialized in academic transcriptions and guaranteed secure data transmittal.

Observations

Two kinds of observations were conducted: scheduled observations of classroom sessions, and unscheduled semiparticipatory observations of the school environment at large, for example, in the lunch rooms, hallways, and stairwells. During both types of observation I took field notes using a notepad app on my iPhone. Frequently, especially at the beginning of the study period, I called participants' attention to my note taking to be sure that (a) they recognized me as a researcher who was recording my impressions of our interactions, and (b) they did not think I was rudely distracted by text messages during our conversation.

Classroom observations were scheduled ahead of time with each of the primary participants; at least two such visits were conducted with most teachers, but due to schedule complications, a few teachers were observed only once. Some teachers were observed as many as four times. During these observations I usually sat in the back of the classroom, or to the side, and took notes on the teacher's practice, paying particular attention to their sense of presence, flow, timing, and dialog with respect to materials, tools, and technologies. Classroom configurations varied greatly, however, as did lesson plans, so at times I walked around the room throughout the lesson. In some of the lab classes, or art classes, I spoke with the teacher during the session about how an activity related to what had happened in previous classes. Although in those cases I was a more visible and active presence in the room, I did not overtly participate in instruction. In some cases, though, especially at the start of the school year, teachers introduced me to their students as a researcher, and once in a while, particularly with older students, invited me to say a word or two about what I was doing. Once in a great while—perhaps five or six times in the entire school year—students wanted to talk with me about my work. For example, in an engineering class for high school seniors, after learning that I was an educational researcher, two students asked about careers in education. At the conclusion of a classroom observation, either immediately afterward or in some cases a day or two later, I followed up with the teacher, asking for their impressions of the session, for example, about what went well or not so well, or about aspects of the session that I had not fully understood.

Unscheduled observations occurred every day I was at the school. In these spontaneous conversations I was a participant, sharing stories about my own teaching or engaging in tangential conversations about popular culture or other common interests. In keeping with Latour's (2005) admonition that researchers follow their participants' lead, I wandered about the school, picking up snippets of conversation in the cafeteria, in the entry hallways, on the bus, on field trips, and at special events like the whole school art show, the second graders' Invention Convention, and the school's open community Maker Day. In this way I found myself engaged in the everyday hubbub as students, staff, administrators, faculty, and even parents passed through my zone of hearing. Often, participants would casually introduce me to other members of the community who might already know me from afar without exactly understanding my purpose. But sometimes I found myself with faculty or staff who had no idea why I was at the school; in those cases, I took it upon myself to introduce the study, which invariably led to further thoughts and opinions about project-based learning and making-infused teaching. In these spur-of-the-moment situations, I put away my phone because, even though they had just been briefed on my status and were openly willing to chat with me, they had not formally agreed to participate, nor had they signed consent releases.

Other Sources of Information

Documents. I collected syllabi and lesson plans from primary participants, as well as promotional and informational books and pamphlets produced by the school. About half of these documents were on paper, and half were in electronic format. These documents were used primarily as background information about teaching practices, or to help me understand the culture of the school at large. In some cases, participants emailed documents about observational issues or school-wide cultural issues. For example, when I asked how teacher education was perceived at the school, an administrator shared an aggregated list of email feedback she had collected from faculty who had participated in a professional development session. And, to address a question about the evaluation of maker projects, a science teacher emailed her notes from an assessment meeting she had conducted with faculty team members.

　　Photographs and videos. I collected photographs and videos of tools, materials, projects, and classrooms throughout the study period. These were sometimes given to me by faculty and administrators to illustrate specific student projects, but most were taken by me on my camera phone. Following Rubin and Rubin (2005), I thought of these images as physical artifacts that would help jog my memory of events, flesh out my notes, and even spur the development of interpretative concepts and themes. Following Yin's (2009) recognition that case study photographs "help convey important case characteristics to outside observers" (p. 110)—an idea that resonated strongly because of my background as an artist and commercial photographer—I took pictures of student projects and architectural features of the FabLabs and makerspaces to be used in reports, but because of confidentiality requirements, made sure that neither teachers nor students were recognizable in those images.

Field notes and memos. From the very beginning of the study period, even before on-site data collection had begun, I was making notes of conversations and observations, and converting those notes into narrative memos. Following Maxwell (2004), I considered these notes and memos as information sources. In practice, they were generated on an iPhone while waiting in the entryway at the school between interviews, or after lunch in the cafeteria, or on the bus on leaving the school after a full day of observations. For example, during a week-long event known as the Nerdy Derby, in which student teams designed, built, and then raced small vehicles down an undulating wooden track, I tapped on my phone continuously as I went from one conversation to the next, from one design and build station to another, and then from the starting blocks where the races began to the finish line where teams erupted in screams and cheers. At the end of each day, I had dozens if not hundreds of fragmented observations. These notes, and the memos drafted from them, informed future interviews and observations, helping to focus the research.

The Method Assemblage

In *After Method: Mess in Social Science Research*, John Law (2004) critiques the way that assumptions informing social science research are gathered into methodologies that are black-boxed or held beyond scrutiny, and calls attention to researchers who, by doing so, enact a version of the truth without calling that enactment itself to awareness. Citing Bruno Latour's (Latour, 1987, 1996; Latour & Woolgar, 1979) groundbreaking studies of neuroendocrinology labs and transportation systems, among other things, that described science as a social and cultural practice, Law argues that this entanglement of process and result underpins all research, even in the so-called "hard" sciences. However, in his view, equating an asymmetric coherence of method and result with "good" research, where results are clearly illuminated but the process that produced them is barely visible, is like a self-fulfilling prophecy. That kind of research, he insists, challenges the scientific process itself, casting doubt on what can be studied or known.

From a different sensibility, Law (2002) recommends an ontological generosity that doesn't rely on absolute coherence or simplistic correspondence, a trajectory that might feel strange to researchers steeped in modernist notions of purity, or in humanist notions of agency and control. He calls the idea *fractional coherence*, and uses it to describe the way that complex technological objects hold together, as discussed in the last chapter and in relation to Mol's (2002) work on medical practice. Building on fractional coherence as a methodology, as a corrective to Enlightenment-era methodologies anchored in rationalism, Law (2002, p. 41) coins "a (partial) neologism" by adopting "the term 'assemblage'…from the English translation of Deleuze and Guattari's *Mille Plateaux*": *method assemblage*. Here, research begins by "crafting… realities [as]…interactive, remade, indefinite and multiple" (p. 122). That is to say, by enlisting connotations of a decentered and indefinite, continually unfolding, processes-oriented reformulation and rebuilding of knowledge, Law proposes a counter-logic to coherence—one of overlap and juxtaposition, like a pinboard or collage, where relationships remain open, nonlinear, and up for grabs. This frames method as "a combination of reality detector and reality amplifier" (p. 14), rather than as a reducer of uncertainty, perhaps empowering a more accurate response to the flux of life.

In my study, following Law's (2002) description of the method assemblage as a research trajectory "that is at most, only very partially under any form of deliberate control" (p. 42), I looked for contrasts but held expectations loosely. So for example, rather than try to erase contradictions in the digital making and learning assemblage, or in what I was hearing and observing at the school, my goal was to hold dissonance in play so that new metaphors might appear. Collaborative and recursively enacted materiality is basic to my work in several modalities—artist, video producer, commercial photographer, teacher—as I've described at length, so it's perhaps not surprising to hear it again in this context too, that is, as a researcher. This point goes to my dispositional approach to the study, which I'll describe in more detail at the end of this chapter; here, though, it's important to call attention to the way Law's methodology informed my conduct.

Strategies and Tactics

Law (2004) implies that describing practice in language—or in any symbol system—silences it. In answer to this challenge, he argues, "There are no right answers" (p. 117). Rather, there is only a choice of metaphor: "craft, bundle,

hinterland, condensate, mediation, pattern, repetition, similarity and difference, object, gathering, allegory and representation" (p. 117). But the inevitable, ironic paradox is that every choice quiets relational dynamics because it
tries to establish fixity. "Perhaps, then, it is helpful to think of method assemblage as a radio receiver, a gong, an organ pipe...a set of relations for resonating with and amplifying chosen patterns" (p. 117). This analogy helped
me decide how to *do* the study, what methods I would use, because it made
me focus on relations and the ordering of relations, between participants and
practice, but also between artifacts of research, such as interviews and memos,
and the interpretation of those things, such as narratives and reports, which
were also artifacts.

Interpretation. Following Creswell's (2007) metaphor of the "data analysis spiral" (p. 150), interpretation was ongoing and continuous with data
collection throughout the study period, and involved several different methods. In addition to Maxwell's (2004) reflective memoing, described above,
I adopted Yin's (2009) recommendation to "play with your data" (p. 129),
assembling it into arrays, flow charts, or graphics, and arranging it chronolog-
ically to clarify the story of the study. As well, I adapted Rubin and Rubin's
(2005) dual-stage approach, which involved first sorting, bundling, and trimming concepts and themes noticed in the interviews, and then coding transcripts and other sources so that statements about those concepts and themes
could be retrieved; and in the second stage, comparing themes across sources
and assembling them into narratives. As such, interpretation and analysis
took from Creswell's (2007) spiral, Maxwell's (2004) reflective memoing, Yin's
(2009) playful listening, and Rubin and Rubin's (2005) dual-stage approach.
It's worth reiterating that because this was an ethnographic and exploratory
study, I held these methods as dispositional rather than strictly analytical;
that is, in sorting, trimming, and coding interviews, observations, and other
sources of information, my goal was to bring relationships of practice to presence, not to produce an all-encompassing explanation of the structural or
spatial contingencies of those practices.

Transcripts. In preparation for this kind of *thematic narrative analysis*
(Riessman, 2008), interview transcripts focused on *what* participants said
rather than *how* they said it. Other approaches were explored, including
interactional approaches and conversation analysis (Dijk, 1997; Goodwin &
Heritage, 1990; Malone, 1997), and performative action-oriented discourse
analysis (Gee, 1999, 2006, 2010b), but thematic narrative analysis seemed
more appropriate, if only because I was interested in "primarily what content a

narrative communicates, rather than in precisely how a narrative is structured" (Riessman, 2008, p. 80). As such, transcriptions contain normative spelling and standardized grammar, and elisions and slurred pronunciations have been cleaned up. For example, "I wanna ask you a couple questions" became "I want to ask you a couple of questions," and so on. In this book, ellipses have been used to clarify narrative cohesiveness, but only when doing so did not substantially alter the content of the participant's statement. For example, Amanda's story about Jimmy Heath and Emmett Cohen (in this chapter) begins: "And so they'd never met, I think they'd...maybe done some rehearsing that afternoon." The unedited transcript reads: "*And so they'd never met, I think they'd probably exchanged some MP3 but—and maybe done some rehearsing that afternoon.*" As this example demonstrates, transcripts were honed with an ear for the story participants were telling, in keeping with Riessman's (2008) call for narrative researchers to keep the story "intact" (p. 58).

Emergence. My approach to interpretation preserved and clarified the stories that participants shared with me. This book is filled with stories, from Grace's very short story about playing with paperclips, and Kieran's much longer story about learning to iterate, both in Chapter 6, to Amanda's multiple stories that take up the entirety of Chapters 9 and 10. In each case, the goal was to evolve a narrative amplification of participants' questions, challenges, and successes. These constructs, crafted to tell a particular story about learning and knowing in a particular environment at a particular time, figure as interpretations of my experience as a type of participant. That is, though I did not overtly try to influence what was happening around me—I didn't do any lectures, write any lesson plans, offer any tutorials—I nevertheless participated in the enactment of practice. In this, I'm in alignment with Riessman's (2008) argument that researchers and participants collaborate in the creation of narratives that speak to their common identities. Following Andrews, Squire, and Tamboukou (2013), my goal in this book is to hold in play the friction generated by stories as they brush up against experience, in order "to see different and sometimes contradictory layers of meaning...[because] as problematic as they are, narratives carry traces of human lives that we want to understand" (location 198–201).

Writing. In addition to coding, bundling, and trimming to weave a fractional coherence from what I was learning, the writing itself was crucial to my interpretative process. Richardson (2000) points out, "Although we usually think about writing as a mode of 'telling' about the social world, writing is not just a mopping-up activity at the end of a research project. Writing is also a way of 'knowing'—a method of discovery and analysis" (p. 924). Over the course of the research, memos and on-the-fly expositions, as well as long emails to participants asking about their experiences and offering my own ideas about what I was observing, were important to my gradual understanding. In reports of the study, including this book, this *writing as research* tactic is at the root of my analyses. That is, whether explicit or not, my work is informed by Richardson's notion of a "creative analytic practice ethnography...[that] displays the *writing process* and the *writing product* as deeply intertwined" (p. 930, original emphasis).

Recursivity. From early in the study through to my final conversations, and even in the writing of this book, I have found myself doubting the validity of collecting and retelling versions of my participants' stories, at least in terms of my inquiry questions. How might I, or anyone, know that my observations of and comments about learning and knowing practices in this school, with these teachers and administrators, have any bearing on the very large and very real questions about schooling that we collectively face? Even though, with Miller (2004), I am skeptical "that there are simple and transparent correspondences among 'identity,' 'voice,' 'experience,' 'memory'" (p. 52), and in spite of agreeing with Britzman (1995) that the "practice of narration is not about capturing the real already out there" (p. 237), I find myself longing for some sense of certainty, and wondering if the choices I've made, the path I've followed, have foreclosed the possibility that this work might have a practical effect, or that my conclusions can be trusted. In this crisis of confidence, another worry surfaced. Although I am comfortable with poststructuralist skepticisms about the practice of speaking and writing, while yet managing to continue to speak and write, I grew concerned about the ethics of collecting participants' stories. As Chase (2011) has cautioned, I understood that my research involved an "increase[d] risk that narrators will feel vulnerable or exposed" (p. 424) because of the conflicts their stories might reveal. That is, more than narrative snippets from their pedagogy, participants were sharing their passions, doubts, and struggles with me.

This recognition led to a tactical revision of my methods. Following Chase (2011), I decided to discuss validity and ethics with participants during interviews and casual conversations, in order to be as certain as possible that what I might write would not cause discomfort or, worse, compromise their work at the school. Additionally, I invited several participants (whose stories were pivotal to the overall conclusions I was drawing) to read and discuss the narratives I was constructing. This enhanced form of consent actually exceeded the standards of the formal consent they had already given, helping to relieve issues of ethics, but it also went toward enhancing the validity of the work. That is, by adding an explicitly recursive and collaborative dynamic to the study, by asking for confirmation that I hadn't misrepresented key participants' stories, or their frame of mind, at least not blatantly, I hoped that the overall trustworthiness of the work, to use Riessman's (2008) term, would increase. I realized, of course, that a shift in methodology didn't guarantee such an increase—which Riessman argues comes only with the pragmatic use of a scholar's work, over time, as "a functional measure of validity" (p. 195)—but it seemed to me at the time (and in fact, still seems) that acknowledging the indeterminacies pulling to and fro within the assemblage itself, tugging at the material of the overall research practice, gave the work a better chance of holding together, at least fractionally. The idea to iterate methodology, or strategy, by adding a new method, or tactic, at about the halfway point of the study, was in fact not unprecedented; that is, already, at the very beginning of my work at the study site, I had encountered an unpleasant surprise that required to me to reconceptualize the underpinnings of the inquiry itself.

Iterating the Research Design

In August 2013, as I began finding my way around the school, a flaw appeared in my study design. I noticed it in my first conversations with teachers and administrators, before I had even confirmed the principal participants of the study. It appeared as I came to understand that the school was in the midst of an enormous transition that only tangentially involved digital making and learning, when I realized that teachers' *digital* learning journeys were likely to be too entangled with on-the-job learning they were doing, such as absorbing the new divisional structure and calendar cycle (described more fully below), to be observed in the sense that I had originally intended, that is, as instances of tool and material learning. Instead, for these teachers, every interaction with digital making and learning would take place within diffused but densely interwoven—sometimes chaotically interwoven—changes to teaching and learning more generally.

Secondly, and more importantly, I began to suspect that my research questions were too narrow—in fact, my research participants told me so. That is, for these teachers and their administrators, digital tools and materials were important to the extent that they encouraged constructionist, interest-driven pedagogies, but no one was simply learning to use digital making technologies *as* tools in themselves. Rather, the tools and the teaching were entangled. My study design, however, asked first about teachers' learning as if it was distinct from their teaching, and only secondarily asked if the tools were affecting their teaching. In an early conversation with Bradly, the director of technology, this misalignment became clear. He told me that strong teaching was the goal, and "If it's strong with the FabLab, that's great, but if it's strong without the FabLab, that's great, too." In fact, when I asked about integrating digital making and learning into the curriculum, he said that *integration* was not the goal: "[Because] you don't integrate reading into your English curriculum, right? It's a core skill...and whether it's in a book or an e-book, that's a tool that you're going to use." He continued, "We spend a lot of time moving people away from...the device. And [toward]...the learning that's taking place with that device."

Kieran, the FabLab director, described it this way:

It's less about integrating the tools and more about integrating the project-based making mentality. The tools act as a bit of a hook. There's something that's cool, and people are like, "Ooh, it's 3D printing. Awesome." But really, they're like a Trojan horse to get *making* into the classroom.

Like Bradly's, Kieran's question was about mindset, a way of thinking—the "making mentality." He wanted to know if digital making would help bring that mindset about, but he was not interested in *how* teachers learned to use digital tools, at least not explicitly. In fact, Kieran and Bradly wanted to talk about changes in teaching first, and about FabLabs second—if at all. Simply, Bradly did not want to get distracted by the "device"; and Kieran saw digital making *as* a "hook," or a "Trojan horse."

Bradly expanded on the school's thinking about the purpose and place of technology in classrooms. He said,

It all comes down to learning objectives. What role does technology play? What role should technology play? And should technology play a role [at all]?...I remember doing a workshop, and the teacher was from [another school], and they'd just bought iPads. And the teacher said to me, "Yeah, we've been told that we have to use the iPads once a week." [That's] setting yourself up for failure...[because the first question should be] what learning objective are you trying to address by using this technology? So if you're not addressing a learning objective, you shouldn't be using it.

In collaboration with Cecelia, the director of curriculum, Bradly organized professional development sessions in order to discuss the opposition to the tool-first mindset. The goal was to explain the head of school's mandate to "rethink" education, he said.

> Beatrice [the head of the school] uses the phrase "transformation of teaching and learning." I don't think people understand what that means....I think what she's really trying to do is to move to a model where…it's not prescribed knowledge—it's student-constructed knowledge. And for some teachers to let go of prescribed knowledge, it's really tough.

In this, I recognized my own attempts to shift art students away from the tools and toward the meaning of their pictures. The congruence excited and challenged me. That is, focusing on digital tools as an agent of change was the same as focusing narrowly on any other tool; like my photography students, my questions had adopted a static focus on a device—in this case, ironically, the device of digital making and learning tools.

When I asked Julie, the head of the middle school, about the importance of digital tools and materials, she echoed Bradly and Kieran:

> I don't just see it as [exclusively] digital…digital fabrication pushed us towards embracing more of a making culture…to allow kids to expand their ideas and their inventions, and their imagination and create things, but I see it as more—…more of a studio model that includes things like video editing and video documentation and video creation and script writing and all of that stuff. I see that all happening in the same space.

Julie, too, wanted to talk about constructionist making, rather than about FabLabs, or how her faculty was learning (or not learning) to use 3D printers and laser cutters. Intriguingly, her comments reprised the mish-mash of the maker movement and digital media movement that I had identified in my study of maker-infused learning (as figured in Tables 1 and 2 in Chapters 2 and 3). Accordingly, we did not talk about digital tools and materials at all. Instead, I asked about the value of making-infused learning more generally. She said:

> The value of making is that it…allows you to get into a flow state. You're using multiple modalities to learn about something and you're discovering things about it as you go,…[it] solidifies things; it connects different areas of the brain;…it's going to stick with you a lot longer than going through fifteen math problems and writing down answers that you're going to forget.

This spontaneous shift in my interview protocol suggested a way forward. Up to that point I had been posing questions connected to my interests, but these three participants had explicitly pushed back. I had said, "Let's talk about x, because that's what I want to understand." But they had replied, "Actually, we'd rather talk about y, because we think you're not asking a very interesting question." This challenge messed up an implicit paradigm that I had not yet become explicitly aware of (i.e., researcher asks questions, interviewee provides answers). My participants and I were, if not exactly swapping roles, clearly muddying the separation between us. On the one hand, I recognized this relational confusion from the sociomaterial research literature (Fenwick et al., 2011; Fenwick & Edwards, 2012; Latour, 2005; Law, 2002, 2004). But on the other hand, I had not yet experienced it for myself. When I felt the contradictions internally, finally, the challenge to my design seemed potentially catastrophic.

On September 19, 2013, at the beginning of the data collection period, I wrote:

> This is a case of the school at large, and the culture of education and learning/teaching at the school, versus the individual teachers who are in the trenches with digital tools and materials. How do wider attitudes and personalities impact on the teachers' learning experiences? Need a rich description of the administration, the history of the school, the curriculum, the students, the facility itself, the community environs, and the resistances to change, in order to analyze the participants' learning in context. How important to their learning experiences are these variables? How accurately can I describe participants' learning without describing these variables? Does the methodology still work?

Clearly, the study had to open up, become more nuanced. The framework did not have to be reconceptualized from the ground up, but the inquiry questions had to evolve.

A fourth conversation from that early period suggested how this iteration might proceed. Amanda, a high school history and humanities teacher, told me she did not use the FabLab, and was skeptical about the place of digital making in her curriculum. She added, however, that she was excited about how the maker movement might change her teaching. She said, "I'm not sure what it means for education. Right now, in my life, right this minute, it has the ring of gadget about it." But then she said:

> I think there's probably something behind it. It's not there yet, and I'm not there yet, but this has the potential, given that as a story…I know what happened when mass

manufacturing moved in and displaced the individual craftsman, it was cataclysmic, both in a disastrous sense, right, it undid the status of the craftsman…and at the same time, it made enormous goods available to people, literally, like manufactured clothing and decent plates to eat off of, and people didn't get so sick. You ever try to get a wooden plate clean?

Amanda did not want 3D printing in her history classroom because she did not understand how it fit her learning objectives—"I made a plastic chair, I made a barrette. Oh bully, sweetie." But she was dissatisfied with her dismissiveness. In fact, she contradicted herself by inserting 3D printing into the narrative arc of the industrial age, thus connecting it to the core of her practice as a history teacher:

What I would want to know is…what are some of the processes? Not just about the making of the thing—to me, that's the filler at the end, that's not really the point. What about conceptualizing back to the object, because that's what I do now. I get them to look at objects and get to the idea…What is that chair? Who made it, what about manufacturing? They're going from the object to the idea. Makers are about the other thing; they're about—starting with the idea and building the object…. [But] the point of the process is not to make the object; the point of the process is to conceptualize and then to materialize what you made as evidence of the process.

The complexity of Amanda's response resonated because it paralleled the storytelling methods I had used in my digital photography courses and in my teaching methods courses that focused on creative coding and digital fabrication. I said, "This is fascinating on a couple of different levels. You are—you're reaching very deeply and struggling, I see, to articulate…." "Yeah, because I don't understand it," she replied.

But I asked her to pretend that she did understand, and to expand on the excitement she felt. Although she was skeptical of digital making, it seemed that the ethos of the digital making and learning had captured her imagination—even if she didn't articulate it that way. To explain, she told me about a jazz concert during the summer. It was more of a musical conversation, though, not simply a concert. On stage, Jimmy Heath played with Emmett Cohen, saxophone entangled with piano, and afterwards the musicians took questions from the audience. She described it carefully:

And so they'd never met, I think they'd…maybe done some rehearsing that afternoon. But it was all about jazz, and what was interesting is…there were a couple of guys [in the audience] who were playing troll, who said, "Well, we heard about electronic music last night, [but] what's so great about [live] jazz? *Why can't you just make an MP3?*" And Heath, who is a little old man, just bristled and said…"It's about the breath and the body. And of course we record jazz…but that's not what it is. [Jazz] is knowing the forms, and the variations on the forms. It's imagination…it's human… it's about the improv, it's about the moment. That's what jazz *is*. The recording is just evidence of it."

As we finished our conversation, Amanda clarified the role of "evidence" in her classroom by reflecting on the maker movement:

> Right now, where I sit, I have a commitment to deciphering objects and texts, and that's what I've done my whole career. I get the feeling that something else is about to happen.…

As I turned off the voice recorder and said good-bye to Amanda, I remember thinking that my inquiry questions had not foreseen the way a humanities teacher would speak about making. The study was off to a good start, and yet I was troubled: Her unfolding linkage between 3D printing and jazz, between concept, object, and process, and between the industrial age and an as yet unnamed, postmanufacturing age, did not fit my schema. My research questions rested on two assumptions: (a) teachers were learning to use digital making tools and materials, and then (b) teachers were changing the way they taught. But participants were telling me that both things happened simultaneously, and in a messier way than my questions could capture; in Amanda's case, (a) wasn't happening but (b) was.

In retrospect, I wonder why this surprised me. In a research memo, I reflected on what I was learning: Leadership wanted more student-constructed learning and less teacher-prescribed teaching. They wanted faculty to engage with digital technologies because they amplified student engagement. Leadership was concerned, however, that focusing on tools would obscure learner-centered teaching. That meant there would be no obligatory teacher training and that, in practice, if a teacher did not care to use the FabLab, she would not be forced to do so. The caveat was that faculty were expected to bring more project-based, experiential learning into the classroom, regardless. Clearly, this complex, contradictory dynamic was consistent with the motivations that had led me to the study in the first place, but it required a more subtle and flexible approach.

The way forward was to follow the participants, as Latour (2005) had suggested, by describing the conundrums and challenges they encountered on their "trail of *associations* between heterogeneous elements" (p. 5, original emphasis)—that is, from classroom to FabLab, from lecturing to making. Although the *way* teachers came to digital tools and materials would be difficult to isolate, at least in the sense originally envisioned, the invitation to observe the process had been sincerely given—by the head of school, her leadership team, and by the teachers themselves. As such, my study was feasible. The key was to hold the goal loosely—like studio art teaching and learning, by listening to the voice of the materials (Burton, 2000) and by letting go of assumptions of mastery and control (Bolt, 2013).

Dispositions

This study is grounded in a worldview that knits together poststructuralist empiricism, social constructivism, and pragmatism. To illustrate, consider this analogy from photography: When you make a photograph, the aperture and shutter speed must align with lighting conditions. If they do not, nothing can correct the imbalance. And if the calibration is too far out of balance, there is no picture: Simply, you must get the math right to make a photograph. But of course it's not that simple. Merely doing the math is not enough to guarantee a "good" photograph, no matter how you define that term. That is to say, after more than 25 years as a photographer, I'm comfortable with a world + tool relationship that isn't completely arbitrary. On the other hand, I'm also comfortable with a critique of that equation that recognizes contingent social structures in the ordering of our perceptions; that is, we can often talk ourselves into changing our minds about what looks good or bad. This paradox shapes my methods and practice.

My appreciation for multiplicity traces to my upbringing as the son of a public health physician who worked with indigenous populations. My earliest encounters with learning were informed by listening to my father negotiate the boundaries between Western and non-Western patterns of living. As he developed and implemented medical training programs for Native health professionals in remote locations around the United States, he had to transcode the certainties of Western epidemiology for practitioners who lived and worked in communities that responded to different rhythms and ways of knowing. My father's stories about these encounters permeated my youth and have permanently colored my relationship to the scientific process. Following his example, I'm not dogmatic about paradigms, choosing to adopt whatever approach can get the job done.

The story of this study unfolded through a multifaceted choreography of day-by-day conversations, but two research traditions specifically influenced my trajectory. The first is *sociomaterialism* (Fenwick & Edwards, 2011; Fenwick et al., 2011); the second is *actor-network theory*, or ANT (Fenwick & Edwards, 2012; Latour, 2005, 2013; Law, 2004). According to Fenwick et al. (2011), these traditions (a) consider whole systems as interwoven assemblages of human and nonhuman actors; (b) trace the emergence of objects to the effects of relational interactions within those systems; and (c) hold knowing and learning as embedded in material interactions (p. 6). Fenwick argues that this aggregate of dispositions "challenges the centering of human process in learning (often conceived as consciousness, intention, meaning, intersubjectivity and social relations)" (p. vi). This aligns closely with my own approach—for example, my methodology relied on an emergent, relational system of participants, on the decentered learning trajectories that I've called material learning, and on materiality as a assemblage of affordances.

ANT connects to this work because of its interest in materiality. Law (2004) explains that ANT holds materiality "as a continuously enacted relational effect,...[implying] that materials do not exist in and of themselves but are endlessly generated" (161). Sørensen (2009) concurs: "To understand materiality we need to move away from thinking of elements and more toward theorizing in terms of relations" (p. 70). Although ANT-inflected research on digital making and learning is rare, studies that explore materiality in education are central to my work. These include several that I've already discussed: Mol (2002), Law (2002, 2004), Latour (1996), Latour and Woolgar (1979), and Sørensen (2009). Many others remain at the periphery, including Koyama's (2009) study on the implementation of No Child Left Behind in New York City public schools; Nespor's (2002) study on school change as an interconnected network; and Mulcahy's (2011) study of teacher identity in relation to representational and performative standards. While the goals of my study did not require the kind of analysis that some of these others adopted, I nevertheless learned much from their grappling with language and process. In this sense, rather than holding to ANT strictly as an analytic strategy, I consider it a dispositional way of thinking about method.

And finally, in keeping with my pragmatic, by-any-means-necessary sensibilities, I've borrowed ideas from a variety of other studies, whether or not they live in the canon of ANT or sociomateriality. For instance (just two examples): Elizabeth Kasl and Lyle Yorks (2012) from adult education and transformative learning, and Jeanne Bamberger and Donald Schön (1983) from music education and urban studies. Both of these relate to the broadly ethnographic issues around learning and knowing that have informed my work, particularly in relation to the matters of concerns described in Chapter 1. For example, Kasl and Yorks (2012) conceptualize *presentational knowing* as a way of learning premised on gestural and experiential *knowing without thinking*. Particularly resonant is Kasl's story about an eyes-closed experience with clay—where she was asked to keep her eyes shut while manipulating clay, in order to explore an organizational challenge. For Kasl, the experience was bizarre, and even threatening, although it catalyzed "an epistemology vastly different from her usual way of knowing" (p. 512) that, in the end, pointed toward a resolution of the problem her group faced. Likewise, Bamberger and Schön's (1983) research on making—in this case, musical tunes and their symbolic annotation—explored learning and knowing that didn't depend on explicit intentions. Here, Bamberger and Schön hold knowing as a meandering flow, or as a way of paying attention, which leads to their conclusion that "unexpected insight *evolves* in the work of making" (p. 73, original emphasis). To my mind, both of these studies describe knowing rooted in materiality, a way of *doing* learning that I've described as familiar to artists and innovators from across multiple domains of inquiry—or *material learning*. As such, these studies exemplify the variety of interests and experiences that I will call on to interpret and analyze observations and interviews. In this sense, my methodological and dispositional sensibilities are like a collage, and I would point again to Law's (2004) pinboard logic of overlap that feels irrefutable to me.

FIELD NOTES (PROSTHETIC HAND)

"Bones and motion. Study your own hand," Isabella says as she distributes chicken wings. "How do muscles work?" she asks, as the girls begin dissecting them.

Later, she huddles with a team that's having trouble. Popsicle sticks, glue, tape, strings, and a yellow glove are scattered across their workbench. The girls are frustrated; one keeps walking away. "So if this is the hand," Isabella says, clenching her fingers to make a fist, and then opening them again, "How would this work?" She's pointing to the string and stick assemblage. After a moment she leaves the girls to puzzle it some more by themselves. As she passes me, she whispers, "I'd have thrown it across the floor. I would have hated a project like this at their age."

At a different bench, I hear her say, "This is the way real science works. You experiment, you iterate, you experiment again."

The assignment is to build a hand-like appendage that can grasp, lift, and release an empty soda can. Arrayed across the tables, students find cardboard, rubber bands, drinking straws, rubber gloves, plastic zip ties, and other household materials. They are to represent their learning by building a prosthetic hand that shares structural characteristics with real hands. For example, "bones" might be made of Popsicle sticks, and "tendons" of rubber bands.

But when a team suggests cotton balls for bones, Isabella understands that deep learning is not yet taking root.

On this particular day, the teams are fully engaged, though not each with the same aspect of the project; some work on their narrative reflections, others on the two-minute promotional video that is supposed to sell their prosthetic hand. And others are calculating their grades.

"How many points do we lose for a lasso-hand?" one team shouts from across the room.

"No lassos," Isabella repeats for about the fourth time. After class we chat about the prohibition on lassos, and she tells me that the rubric has evolved in order to force the girls to work a little harder. Lassos turned out to be too easy, it seems. "How do you put a grade on authentic learning?" she asks. "That's something I've been thinking about a lot."

Suddenly there's a scream, and the yellow glove team jumps to their feet, hugging and laughing, and crying. One student rushes over to share their success, yelling, "You're the best, Ms. W.!"

"Such perseverance," Isabella says. Shaking her head, she tells me that in seventh grade she was a total "type A" student who wanted facts and content. "This kind of learning wouldn't have had enough content for me," she says. "I don't yet know how I feel about it."

As the students scramble out to their next class, Cecelia appears at the door, asking how the project is going. Isabella shows off several hands at different stages of completion. One in particular catches Cecelia's attention: an inflated pink claw festooned with googly eyes and pipe cleaners. "I like this one a lot," she says.

On presentation day students queue up their PowerPoints and videos, and ready their prostheses. Some wear white lab coats to enhance the effect. "I feel so sciencey," one girl says as she stands up to present her work. During the final demonstrations of their hands, classmates cheer each other and jump up and down. Some of the spindly contraptions pick up and release the soda can, while others bump or knock it over, or crush it.

On the wall monitor, Isabella's screen saver floats an animated message: "Participate effectively. Doubt your limits. Enjoy the journey. Don't be afraid to fail."

Datasheet: Age group: seventh grade. Content domain: science. Teachers: Isabella and Jessica. Timing: April to May, approximately two weeks.

· 5 ·

PARTICIPANTS AND SITE

This chapter introduces the teachers and administrators who shared their work with me in interviews and casual conversations, in the classrooms, hallways, cafeterias, and offices at the school, on buses, and during field trips away from the school, and even, once or twice, on the city sidewalks in the neighborhood surrounding the school. These were the primary participants of the study. Secondary participants included faculty and staff who worked at the school but did not explicitly contribute to the study; although they were not interviewed or directly observed, they nevertheless knew who I was, and were openly candid with me as we passed each other in the hallways and sat together in the cafeterias. Another class of participants includes the students. As discussed, I was studying teacher learning, so students were not interviewed or explicitly observed, but they were present, and their learning was indeed the explicit focus of every other participant's work.

This chapter also introduces the space of the study, that is, the environment of the school, its situatedness as a learning ecology. The school cannot be considered merely a *container* of the study, a blank stage upon which various participants delivered their pedagogical lines, like a performance scripted by some director. Rather, following Latour (2005; Latour & Woolgar, 1979), and in alliance with ANT's propensity for casting object relations as interlinked network effects, I hold the school as a densely interwoven entanglement of individual and collective agencies, human and nonhuman, material and immaterial. As such, I will introduce the school as a participant in itself—a different class of participant perhaps, but a participant nonetheless. In this, my goal is to gather a sense of the school as an ecology, a living, breathing, unfolding space of learning, of knowing, of struggle, of success: a relational assemblage.

Teachers and Administrators

Primary study participants were the teachers and administrators who shared their work with me in interviews and by welcoming me into their classrooms. These 22 participants came from various curricular divisions and content areas. For example, teachers came from K–3 science, middle school art, and high school English, history, and humanities; and administrators included the head of school, the director of school-wide technology, and several divisional heads. An educational consultant who had once taught at the school, but had since gone into private practice as a consultant in school organization and curriculum design, also participated.

The length of participants' total teaching careers varied from about 1 to 40 years; the length of their teaching at the study site varied from 1 to 25 years. Eight participants were men and 14 were women; 16 were teachers, 5 were administrators, and 1 was a consultant. All 22 participants signed informed consent forms, agreed to in-depth interviews with me (though not every participant was in fact interviewed in depth), allowed me to observe them at work, and contributed additional information to the study in the form of notes, emails, lesson plans, and other curricular documents. Of the 22 participants, 11 were interviewed in depth twice, 6 were interviewed in depth once, and 5 were not interviewed at all. Of the 16 participants who were teachers, I observed 11 in their classrooms multiple times; 5 were not observed in their teaching. However, every participant engaged in conversation with me at multiple times during the study, in the hallways, at lunch, on buses, on field trips, and in the school's entry foyers. Importantly, all the participants were adults; no students were interviewed. The reason for this, as discussed elsewhere, is that the study investigated learning from the perspective of the teachers.

Below, each participant is introduced with a very brief narrative vignette or quote. Participants are sketched in this way to emphasize the variety of their career trajectories and dispositions, and so that they might be encountered as rounded characters, keeping intact the intersubjective relationships profiled in the coming chapters. Consistent with the guarantees of confidentiality extended to participants, all names are pseudonyms. For additional specifics about these participants, please see Table 3.

Participant Vignettes

Aidan, *middle school science, 2 yrs at this school (8 yrs teaching overall)*. Good learning looks "almost like moderated or controlled chaos, where kids are up out of their seats. They're engaged, sometimes even to the point of arguing with each other....Sometimes it looks a little funky to people who aren't used to that."

Amanda, *high school history and humanities, 16 yrs teaching, all at this school*. With her ninth-grade humanities students, glancing at the annotations they've made on their Roman history handouts, Amanda asks, "Did you write back to the document? When someone is talking to you, what do you do?... Respond." Looking closely at a student's notebook, she says, "Beautiful dialog with the document. It's talking to you."

Amber, *elementary school science, 5 yrs at this school (9 yrs teaching overall)*. "We're trying something new today," Amber tells the third graders sitting with her on the rug. Each time I'm in the classroom, it seems the girls are sailing into unknown waters. And each time, the children reply, "Easy," or, "Of course."

Barbara, *high school English, 3 yrs at this school (12 yrs teaching overall)*. Several boxes of brand-new books have arrived. Barbara tears open the flaps, enveloping us in the slightly tart odor of ink and binders glue. The literary magazine is here! Students surround us with oohs and aahs, and Barbara smiles. Via email, she explains, "I thought I would become a professor, but I discovered I liked teaching much more than research."

Beatrice, *head of school, 25 yrs at this school, (40 years in education overall)*. Beatrice has urged her administrative team and faculty to reimagine schooling. She told me, "If we are to really and truly contribute to the field of education, we cannot be afraid to disrupt what has been the same year after year."

Bradly, *director of school-wide technology, 16 yrs at this school (25 yrs teaching overall)*. Bradly is impatient with narrowly defined technology in education, especially when it comes to how computers can be integrated in schools. He said, "I never use the word *integration*—because...you don't integrate reading into your English curriculum, right?"

Cecelia, *director of curriculum, 17 yrs at this school (22 yrs teaching overall)*. When we talked about the changing school day, and about the opportunities that longer class periods might bring, Cecelia said, "I think the more powerful idea is getting students to tinker—not having it be teacher directed. How do you construct opportunities for students to tinker?"

Earl, *high school English, 3 yrs at this school (12 yrs teaching overall)*. In the cafeteria, Earl tells me that one of the challenges he faces is the vast diversity of learning styles and abilities. The ninth graders range from those with fairly significant developmental issues to those who are already capable of college-level work.

Emma, *high school art, 16 yrs at this school (20 yrs teaching overall)*. Sorting through a student's final project, I ask what Emma thinks the student has learned. "How to think; how to take risks. She learned how to have the courage to keep going, to get herself unblocked," she replies. "How do you Google that?"

Grace, *elementary school science, 9 yrs teaching, all at this school*. Grace thinks her interest in science education comes from watching her grandfather tinker in his workshop. She says, "Things really start working when I give the children the bare bones of what they need...and then let them...become the teacher in the classroom."

Isabella, *middle school science, 2 yrs teaching overall, both at this school*. Isabella is excited and perhaps even a little nervous about the challenges she faces. But, she says, "There is an atmosphere [here] that champions innovation and lets you experiment in the classroom."

Jerry, *educational consultant (independent), 18 yrs overall as a teacher and consultant*. Jerry talks about a "shift in education from the more abstract to the more physical." He says his role is to be "the bridge between what faculty and students say a school of the future should look like, and how it would help them be better learners and teachers."

Jessica, *middle school science and elementary school librarian, 11 yrs at this school (15 yrs teaching overall)*. During the time period of the study, Jessica taught middle school science, though normally she was in the library working with children with reading difficulties. Her primary career trajectory had been with K–5, so middle school science was a departure.

Julie, *head of upper middle school, 4 yrs at this school (22 yrs teaching overall)*. Julie first joined Beatrice's team as director of communications, and then later assumed the newly created position of middle school divisional head. She told me she is committed to "Beatrice's vision around reshaping teaching and learning."

Kieran, *FabLab director and technology teacher, 3 yrs at this school (5 yrs teaching overall)*. Kieran said he was surprised to find himself working as a teacher, especially because he "always felt school was really boring." Now, though, after having designed and built the FabLab, he said, "I was just thinking about how lucky I feel."

Mark, *high school history and humanities, 4 yrs teaching, all at this school*. Dealing with content that must get taught and projects that might be made is challenging, Mark admitted. "Who is Robespierre? When was the French Revolution? Teens don't even know they don't know," he said. "They have no way to ask these questions because they can't even see them."

Mia, *high school art history, 5 yrs at this school (8 yrs teaching overall)*. For Mia, balancing pedagogical styles was critical, especially with a content-heavy subject like art history. "There are benefits to traditional tools of education, and traditional methods, and I don't think any one thing should totally replace another," she said.

Miriam, *head of high school, 9 yrs teaching, all of them at this school*. For Miriam, the school's exploration of making-infused learning "is not just about objects and the use of technology, but is also about asking, 'How do I tinker with my gifts and talents and time so that I can make a positive change in the world?'"

Susan, *middle school art, 2 yrs at this school (10 yrs teaching overall)*. Susan loves woodworking, puppetry, and printmaking, but she's never had so many computers in the art classroom, and digital fabrication is completely new to her. She said, "We can work it out together. The students are pretty into... helping their teachers along with the tech stuff."

Thomas, *high school science and engineering, 4 yrs at this school (18 yrs teaching overall)*. Thomas teaches AP physics and honors chemistry, but he doesn't know how to evaluate students' creative engineering projects—are they useful enough? Are they frivolous enough? And he's exhausted with the demands of project-based teaching. "I am struggling a little bit," he admits.

Tyler, *middle school media arts, 6 yrs at this school (7 yrs teaching overall)*. "The days that most excite me are when the students are...driving the discussion because of their motivation and interest." With a green screen, he transports students to Egypt in his course on public speaking for media. He says, "They see the classroom looking at the screen and smiling, and they immediately become more engaged in their presentation, and their confidence increases because of [it]."

Vanessa, *middle school art, 10 yrs at this school (15 yrs teaching overall)*. "This is not about being pretty," Vanessa says, describing the dress project, where each sixth grader creates an outfit and then celebrates it on the runway during the school-wide fashion show. "This is about being proud of doing something."

The School

The school where this study was situated, taken as a whole, that is, as a collective, a network, a mesh, a tangle—of people, spaces, and things; entry halls, cafeterias, stairwells, chapels, gymnasiums; publications, media events, art shows; custodians and staff, and other faculty and administrators—must be held as a participant in the study, just as the teachers and administrators profiled above are participants. That is, after a multitude of interviews and casual conversations, and more spontaneous interactions than I can count, as the community went about its daily business, the institution grew to acquire its own personality and voice. The purpose of the multidimensional narrative I'm drawing here is to feed your imagination in a way that might evoke the space of the study as a relational assemblage, with recursively enacted affordances that pushed and pulled against practice. My hope is that in spite of the anonymous way I'm referring to the school and the city in which it's situated (in order, again, to preserve some measure of confidentiality), this narrative enables you to place the conversations and activities that follow, and my interpretations of them, in a richly interwoven field of relational materiality.

Placing

The study site was a K–12 girls preparatory school in a large metropolitan area of the northeastern United States. The school was initially established in a small rural community in the first years of the 20th century, but then later moved into the central urban area of a nearby city. Today the school occupies several 19th-century townhouses in a busy district of that city, three of which have been joined together by extensive renovations, and a fourth that remains unconnected. The school also occupies a large brick building about 10 blocks north of the cluster of townhouses. From about mid-century until the mid-2000s, that building housed a different school, but it subsequently closed due to financial distress and then was leased by the school at the center of this study. According to the school's website, a 2011 renovation of the brick building "focused on design education" and included the construction of a "FabLab, a media lab, a dance studio, an instrumental music room, a data visualization lounge, an additional gymnasium and stage, and over 20 classrooms, as well as a dining facility and student center." In these several different locations, the school serves more than 700 students and employs about 150 faculty and administrative staff.

Entering

A typical day during the study period began with my arrival by about 9 a.m. In the carpeted foyer, either at the townhouses or the North Building, I signed the guest register and then checked in briefly with the staff on duty, chatting casually with the receptionist or the doorman, and saying hello to the bus driver or to other visitors or passersby.

Of immediate importance was to double-check that I had properly coordinated my calendar with the school's 8-day cycle. In the North Building, the receptionist posted hand-crafted reminders that she had made herself so everyone knew what day it was—witty cartoons or decorative spin-offs from Dr. Seuss books, television station logos, inspirational aphorisms, or special holiday announcements. For instance, on Earth Day, her reminder card featured an illustration of a leafy green tree.

After synchronizing myself, I would wait for my appointment to be notified of my arrival and either come to the foyer to meet me or signal the receptionist that it was okay for me to make my way up to our meeting place. Sometimes, especially after I was well known to the community, I would go to the cafeteria for a cup of coffee and pass the time chatting with other faculty or staff.

Throughout the year, these in-between moments allowed me to soak in the culture and get accustomed to the rhythms of the school—teachers leading kindergartners to and from recess at the park across the avenue, teenagers jumbling past each other and laughing between classes, a teacher running to catch the bus to the other campus, a mother picking up her daughter for an orthodontist appointment, the custodial crew chatting about building a stage in the gym, or taking it down, and on and on. There were so many of these micro-interactions that it's impossible to catalogue them all; much of what I learned about the school culture, community, and even its pedagogy emerged from these unscheduled in-between moments.

Teaching

The school espoused a learn-by-doing, inquiry-based approach to learning, broadly defined. That is, it did not specifically identify itself as a science or technology school, much less as a *digital* technology school, but emphasized engaged, exploratory teaching and learning in all content areas. Perhaps partly as an effect of this mindset, computers and other digital tools were highly visible, and teachers from every discipline and grade level were encouraged, though not required, to explore them in their teaching. In a 2011 publication addressed to students and families, the head of school wrote that the school "celebrates the legacy of innovation....[O]ur school has always been filled with innovators willing to test boundaries, explore new territories, and advocate for social justice."

Both of these characteristics—boundary testing and social advocacy— were robustly present throughout the year. In an interview, Miriam, the head of the high school, offered an example: "The honors physics class had to create a project that used principles of physics, also principles of social justice [to]... come up with and then print a prototype using the 3D printer. One [group of students] came up with a ball that could be kicked around and also filter water at the same time." For Miriam, the project expanded the students' "concept of empowerment...[because] they were able to create something concrete that really solved a real issue in the world." As she understood it, that concreteness led the girls to ask, "What more can I do?" The big payoff, she told me, was that "our girls go into college knowing that, 'Wow, I could actually be part of something that makes a change.'"

Connecting

This sense of connectedness to the world—that what was learned in school connected to what was happening outside school—appeared in multiple ways, both large and small: from administrators and teachers at the front doors every morning and afternoon, where each student was called by her first name, to school publications that honored students' community internships and other social projects. As well, the internal cohesion of the student and faculty community was visible in the dining halls, where students and faculty ate together, sharing serving dishes and clearing the tables together afterwards, and in meetings, professional development workshops, and brief conversations overheard in the hallways and stairwells. For some faculty, in fact, the sense of community was palpable. Mia, a high school humanities teacher, said, "It is such a community of incredible support and kindness,…and while this is my profession and my workplace, the school thinks of their faculty [as people], and the faculty really support each other."

A corollary to this sense of personal community was the cultural and intellectual community. An admissions officer explained that in keeping with the mission of social justice and real-world connectedness, the school followed a comprehensive strategy for recruiting many kinds of diversity, including learning abilities. In fact, in the ninth grade, a traditional entry point for new students, admissions counselors specifically sought out students who demonstrated a "great spark" and who, though perhaps "not 'A' students,… had grit." This was in keeping with a wish voiced regularly by parents that their daughters "not feel entitled." An admissions brochure describing the student population noted that 22% received financial aid (a "huge carrying cost," according to an administrator I spoke with), 28% were students of color, and 21% were international students. The admissions officer told me that last year's middle school population was 35% students of color, and that about 30 different religious traditions were represented at the school. While confirming or authenticating these demographics is not a direct concern of my study, my conversations with faculty and my observations of teaching and learning during the year corroborate this sense of diversity. For instance, Amanda, a high school history teacher, told me, "This school really does embrace educational diversity in a way that's quite wonderful, beyond race and class,…but [also] style of learning."

Another important characteristic of the school was its affiliation with a major religious tradition. This tradition formed the bedrock of the school's culture and was broadly embraced, though neither faculty nor students were required to be practitioners, as borne out not only by the admissions officer's demographics of how many different religious traditions were represented at the school, but also by my own observations. In fact, as far as I could determine, religion did not directly influence curriculum at all. To that point,

Amanda, the high school history teacher, told me: "There's no expectation that I'm going to teach anything like a [religious] line. No one has ever told me what I can or cannot teach." An exception to this was that all students were required to enroll in religion classes and attend religious services at select times during the year. Otherwise, however, the school was not managed or directed by religious officials, and I did not experience religion as an overt organizing principle of the environment.

Computing

One aspect of the school environment that did directly impact the study was, of course, the presence of digital technology, whether in the FabLabs (the old one from 2011 in the brick building uptown, or the new one built in 2013 in one of the townhouses), the second-grade science classrooms, or in a nearby museum where art history classes sometimes met. In fact, the school prided itself on the ubiquity of digital technology: Large flat-screen monitors were installed in every classroom and in some hallways, and Apple TV servers ensured that teachers could access those monitors for demonstrations and presentations; every student from middle school forward carried a brand-new MacBook Air laptop with her; and the lower school was awash in iPads.

One sunny spring afternoon, on the leafy sidewalk outside the school, I passed what looked like the entire elementary school walking toward a nearby museum on a field trip, each child confidently holding an iPad, snapping photos as she walked, and the older ones pausing occasionally to tap a note to themselves about what they were observing. Bradly, the director of technology, told me with pride that they had a good relationship with Apple. A few years previously, in fact, Apple had formally recognized the school as a national leader in the use of digital technology in education. When I asked how and why the relationship had begun, however, he could not recall the details. He knew it must have been prior to his tenure, though, because he had seen a photo of an Apple IIe (the second computer model ever released by Apple) in a yearbook from the 1980s. He guessed that the relationship had grown organically from parallel interests and similar mindsets, and that this commonality continued to nurture it.

Later, I heard a story that corroborated this idea. When the second-generation iPad was due to be released, but before it had hit the shelves, the school's Apple sales and marketing representative came to Bradly with a few of the new devices, and asked him what the school would make of its new camera. In an interview, Tyler, the media teacher, told me that the Apple rep had asked the technology director "to experiment with this [new iPad]—and knowing my background with film and also knowing that I was teaching a class in drama, [Bradly] said, 'Is there something you can do with it?'" Tyler, in turn, gave the iPads to his class, who happened to be reading *Lord of the Flies*. Tyler explained,

> So each of the groups [made] a short film of what would happen if they showed up and there were no teachers, and the students were left to run the school by themselves... [and] that fit very well, very nicely into the curriculum that we had been doing anyway. Then [Bradly] sent [the videos] to Apple as an example of what we could do.

Those videos were a big hit at Apple and further strengthened their commitment to the school. In the year I was at the school, for example, a group of administrators had been to Apple's headquarters in Cupertino, California, to lead a webinar on educational technology; and back at the school, Apple had hosted an invitation-only conference for educators on the East Coast.

Despite the coziness of the relationship, it seemed to me that student and faculty attitudes about Apple's presence at the school were rather sanguine. I did not hear any debate or discussion about the ubiquitous use of Apple products, for example. A history teacher's reaction seemed typical: "You know, we're in love with Apple, we're in bed with Apple. That's fine. I'm not a big fan of the other platforms anyway. Apple is fine with me."

Indeed, Bradly seemed nonplussed when I asked him about potential conflicts of interest; he suggested that he and the school do what they want and need to do without regard to what Apple is selling or promoting, and that, anyway, "the other tech companies don't seem to care"—implying, in effect, that he needed whatever benefits he could get when it came to buying and maintaining expensive digital tools for the school. On this point—his nondenominational opportunism when it came to high-tech tools—he was insistent. "We spend a lot of time moving people away from the device," he told me. In his opinion, the important question was "about the learning that's taking place."

When Bradly and I crossed paths in the hallways or at the front doors, he occasionally reiterated his beliefs about the mistakes other schools were making—those that were fortunate enough to have access to new or emerging digital tools, that is. In our first interview he told me, "Another teacher at another school said to me, 'Well, I'm not going to use the iPad to do sentence structure because I can do it on pieces of paper.' So [I said], 'Then that's what you should do.' People are always surprised if you're at workshop or a conference, and you say that." For Bradly, the core of the relationship between teaching and learning, on the one hand, and technology of any variety, on the other hand, rested on a teacher's goals. He said, "It all comes down to learning objectives, learning outcomes. What role does technology play? What role should technology play? And should technology play a role in it [at all]?"

This iconoclastic attitude seemed just as much a point of pride for Bradly as his high-level recognition by Apple—perhaps he had come to it in part *because* of that recognition. In fact, as discussed above, Bradly's spirit of techno-recalcitrance—for example, his refusal to discuss the "integration of technology in teaching and learning [because] you don't integrate reading into your English curriculum"—was a catalyst for my iterations on the research questions. That is to say, talking with him alerted me to the complexity of the conversations already in progress at the school. Luckily for me and for the study, Bradly was one of the first people I met when I arrived at the school. In my notes after that first interview, I wrote: "Open and honest and generous; deeply reflective; articulate about learning dynamics."

Developing

A few months later, over morning coffee in the crowded basement dining room at one of the townhouses, Bradly and I talked about the school's professional development program. I asked how he would guide his faculty away from the trap of overreliance on devices, how he would point them toward learning objectives that accentuated the inquiry-based discovery models the school wanted to foster. He replied that everyone needed to recognize that "good stuff was already happening." He said, "If it's strong with the FabLab, that's great, but if it's strong without the FabLab, that's great, too."

To support the point, he told a story about respecting the specific affinities of particular tools, about how learning to graph by hand should precede learning to graph with software. He said that some skills needed to be learned the hard way, that is, without computers. On that point, I pushed back a little and reminded him of a story he had told me about shared expertise.

A few weeks previously, in his atmospheric science class, a lesson had become derailed by a faulty piece of equipment. Before he realized the extent of the failure, he noticed a group of students on the far side of the room becoming increasingly animated, laughing amongst themselves—though he could not make out what they were saying. As he came closer, he discovered that they were troubleshooting the equipment and getting excited about the challenges they were discovering. On reflection, he was filled with relief; thankfully, he had not lashed out when he saw them laughing. That would have been a mistake, he said. A new teacher might have seen those students chatting with each other as disruptive, but his years of experience in the classroom kept him from overreacting. And instead of a problem, he realized, just in time, their laughter had revealed a moment of interest-driven exploration, a sharing of expertise and knowledge that might lead to deep and authentic learning. He concluded that story by telling me, "That's the way it has to be all over the school."

In the dining hall that morning, after talking about learning to graph the hard way, I asked Bradly how the notion of shared expertise as experienced by his students in the weather science class squared with the idea that individually graphing data by hand was an essential step in learning to use a particular tool. To my mind, there was a conflict in the learning objectives. On the one hand, we were talking about classrooms where students learned by sharing and laughing; on the other, we seemed to be saying that the best way to learn was by individually suffering a difficult task. I asked him how differences in the affinities of different tools, iPads versus pencils and paper, for example, affected learners' experience of those tools, and how he might make those differences available to his faculty. Moreover, I wondered how those differences related to the school's focus on the "legacy of innovation."

This was a difficult question, we both agreed. I was asking, essentially, how Bradly was going to build a training program to help teachers create inquiry-based learning environments, while sidestepping the distractions of the fancy new tools that kept showing up. He admitted that he wasn't sure how to do that. He reiterated his point that everyone needed to acknowledge the good work that was already going on, and suggested that maybe "the Shangri-La is almost here." Perhaps, he said, the key is to have a "vigorous program, not a rigorous program."

Conversing

This kind of probing conversation that did not rush toward a finite conclusion was not unusual. While I was at the school, I noticed a willingness to ask difficult questions and wander around inside them, rather than insist on hasty, all-inclusive answers. In a sense, the quirky interiors of the townhouse assemblage reinforced this mindset, because there were a dozen different ways to travel between any two points: narrow halls and twisty stairways opening suddenly onto wide landings; a carved banister curving gracefully up toward a bright skylight; a wood-paneled reception room with marble fireplace mantels nestled beside a crowded administrative office the size of a closet. These architectural idiosyncrasies, born from 20th-century demands just barely accommodated by 19th-century buildings, were facts of life at the school, and everyone—administrators, faculty, students, visitors, and kitchen staff—turned themselves sideways to squeeze past each other on the narrow back staircases.

The intimacy of those fleeting encounters was casual, respectful, but also potentially transformative: What must it be like to literally rub shoulders with a teacher who has just given you a poor grade? Or with a colleague with whom you disagree? This warmly confrontational aspect of the school's personality wove through each conversation and relationship I observed.

Interviewing

For instance, in August 2013, when I arrived at the head of school's office to interview her, we sat together at an enormous old conference table that felt too big for the space, and I imagined the density of those interlocking townhouses pressing in on us. I wanted to understand how she—as a teacher of more than 40 years, and after 25 years at the school—viewed the potential and the challenge that digital tools and materials presented to teaching. Beatrice said,

> I would like to phrase it this way: In education, I think we have been stymied by road maps. We want to do things that have been tried and tested, that have very visible results, that has B following A…[but that] is antithetical really and truly, to pure learning.…[There has been too much] focus on the delivery, and therefore [on] assessment…and therefore [on] the standardization of learning, and therefore [on] the notion that if it's taught this way, then you are guaranteed this result. What is missing, particularly with adolescents, is a lack of meaning…because [school] is so disconnected from what is appealing to them, what makes them learn.…[And] the all-time equalizer, the democratizer of learning, which is technology, suddenly comes into the picture [but] is being met by resistance [from] the very people who are supposed to be inspiring and pushing [young people] to learn.…It is my sincere desire as an educator to make sure I do not relinquish my responsibility to make learners out of the teachers.

From the beginning of our conversation, Beatrice was resolute about her mission as an educator, and though she welcomed my presence as a researcher in her school, there wasn't a lot of space for me to question her direction.

She said, "I am so keen on how kids learn…in a very direct, very hands-on [way]." She had learned a lot in her career as an English teacher, from the Philippines to the Middle East, in boys schools and girls schools, across the entire range from kindergarten through college, and from working sometimes with children who did not speak a word of English. She knew what she knew about teaching and learning, of that I had no doubt, and reflecting on commonalities across so many cultures had catalyzed a path of action: "I talk about this dream of mine, this goal.…I keep talking about the power of engagement. I keep talking about the ownership of learning."

FabLabs, computers, the internet—if teachers would use these tools to enhance student agency, she said, "I know that learning can be much more dynamic." Almost as if reading my next question for me, she continued,

> So what is my responsibility as the head of school? To disrupt that thinking…if we are to really and truly contribute to the field of education…we cannot be afraid to break new ground. We cannot be afraid to disrupt what has been same old, same old, year after year. But the challenge is, how do you get your faculty to develop that same mindset?

I wanted to know where her ideas came from and how she had heard of FabLabs in the first place. "YouTube. *Wired* magazine…and then all this material from colleges, from MIT." But she had begun to formalize them, she said, during graduate school in 1980s, in her thesis research. "You will not believe what the name of the project was," she said, excited that I was interested.

"What was it?" I asked.

"Play."

"Really?"

"Yeah. So think about that. This was 25 years ago. Twenty-three years ago. I had these little three-year-olds and I was watching [them]…and I was saying, 'God, what have we missed?'"

There were several factors, she said, that led to constructing the FabLabs, to her focus on inquiry-based teaching and learning, but they all began with play. One component was the serendipitous introduction, a few years previously, to a young teacher who had recently finished an advanced degree in technology innovation at a major university. She said: "I don't even know how to discuss it, but he came up with all these ideas, and at one point he hosted a big treasure hunt all over the city. Now, I was so intrigued by that." So much so, in fact, that she hired him to help her imagine and build the technology curriculum at the middle school.

When I asked for her thoughts on her faculty's preparedness to teach with technology in a playful, exploratory way, she said:

> What has happened to the teaching profession is, we have been so focused on the fact that we have control that we dictate the pace and the direction and the volume of work that needs to be done. [But] technology just wiped it all away....How do you change your role from the center of the universe to the facilitator, the encourager, the inspirer, the affirmer? It's big. That's why you talk about mindset....It's good to have a combination of young and experienced teachers, because the young will lead the way in terms of that recklessness, but the old will also keep the young grounded. I think we always say, you invite, you make it less of a threat, and then you affirm, because it's very hard for someone to feel that they're [out of] control.

Challenging

Her administrators shared Beatrice's concern for the challenges faced by the teachers, and also her commitment to urging them to engage with the new tools and materials. Julie, the head of the middle school, empathized with the "ambiguity of not having everything mapped out." She explained, "Unfortunately, a lot of us who go into teaching were trained to make lesson plans and goals and objectives, and [to] time everything out and figure out how long things are going to take. So it's hard for us to transition to this place where we don't know where we're going exactly."

In offering her own interpretation of the professional development challenge, though, Julie said she remained "mindful of [Beatrice's] overarching message," and that "people have to be willing to deal with some ambiguity, because things aren't all mapped out." In that respect, Julie described the school as going through "a time of great change," with new expectations of the faculty, students, and even the parents. She said, "I think that parents are still sort of stuck in what education is supposed to be, [based on] what their education experience was—very much a linear process with right and wrong answers and test scores. So we're educating the parents [too]." In summing up the challenges ahead, she said, "We're trying to create a mind shift...driven by [Beatrice's] vision,...around reshaping teaching and learning, really reimagining teaching and learning, reimagining space and time."

Cecelia, the director of curriculum, recognized these challenges, too. She told me, "We've got these great teachers, and now we're telling them we want [them] to do a little bit more, and they're worried. 'Well, what is that *more* that you want us to do?'"

Letting Go and Tinkering

Bradly, director of technology, identified the "more" as letting go of teacher-directed learning. He said,

> [Beatrice's] vision is to really get people to rethink—…She uses the phrase 'transformation of teaching and learning.' I don't think people understand what that means at all. I think they think it's, "Oh, it just means we do something different." But I think what she's really trying to do is to move to a model where, again, it's not prescribed knowledge, it's student-constructed knowledge. And for some teachers, to let [go] of prescribed knowledge is really tough.

For Cecelia, the key component of the shift that Beatrice and the leadership team hoped for involved making in the classroom. Cecelia said,

> The more powerful idea for me is getting students to tinker. How do you construct opportunities for the students to tinker? Because if they're too busy, they're not going to [do it]. They're in the mindset, 'I have to do it because I have to do it, and then I go home.' These kids are highly overscheduled..... [We] have been talking about this for years, about the intrinsic motivation of students.

In their pursuit of these goals—minimizing teacher-directed instruction in favor of open tinkering and exploration—the school leadership had employed a variety of tools, including undertaking the science and technology renovation of the old big brick building, employing outside consultants, and holding administrative retreats (as Julie, the head of the middle school, told me, "Before we could ask the faculty to come with us on this journey, we had to do it, and [build] a common vocabulary and common experience among the administrative staff").

Restructuring

Another tool, with perhaps an even more powerful effect on the day-to-day life of the community, was the academic schedule. According to Cecelia, director of curriculum, "Another way of forcing the hand was rethinking even what the school day looks like." She explained,

> [Julie] and I were doing a lot of reading about what was going on..... Kids are more stressed out....They're focused on the test, they're focused on outcomes, they're not focused on learning....Wait a minute, what if we had longer class periods?...How does that work? Because there's only a finite time in the day. And the school day kept

getting longer, and there...[were] crazy ideas proposed, like just extend the school day. Or, have class on Saturday. How is that going to counter the stress that students are feeling? So we came up with a rotating schedule that wasn't date related.

The most immediately tangible result of this restructuring was the 8-day rotation, a schedule that effectively separated the school week from the calendar week. That meant, for example, the school no longer suffered Mondays. Instead, it put up with Day Ones or Twos or Threes, and so on, up to Day Eights—which might or might not fall on any particular day of the week. In practice, this required teachers and students to carefully synchronize school and real-world calendars so that assignments and holidays (not to mention after-school activities, field trips, and trips to the dentist) did not conflict. The great benefit of this change was the longer class periods it afforded: 75 minutes on average, but as long as 90 minutes, and even 2 hours on occasion. Cecelia said, "Having the longer class periods now forces everyone to say, 'How am I teaching my lessons?'...Shifting to a schedule in which 75 minutes is now the norm makes you think, 'Wait a minute, I have to do something differently.'" Bradly, the technology director, told me that when the changes were announced, "a lot of [faculty asked], 'Well, how am I going to cover my content?' But that's not the point. It's not, how are you going to cover your content? It's, what are you going to *do* with your content?"

The head of school and her administrators wanted the answer to that question to include learning-by-doing and project-based, and indeed, passion-based teaching. Julie told me she thought "digital fabrication pushed us towards embracing more of a making culture in our school,...allowing kids to expand their imagination and create things." To celebrate the school's success in moving toward this goal, the public affairs office produced a 90-second video titled "I Made This." In the video, students of all ages hold something up to the camera and say, "I made this." Examples range from a kindergartner's cardboard puppet, to a middle schooler's micro-controller audio squawk box, to a chlorine filter that a pair of high school students made for an NGO in Kenya; other objects on the video include a hotel for frogs, a portable phone charger, a prosthetic dolphin tail, teddy bears that report child abuse, picture frames, accordion books, Minecraft houses, clay sculptures of owls, robots, and the water-filtering soccer ball that Miriam described earlier.

As touching as the video is, however, Cecelia recognized challenges ahead: "What you can't do is have some teacher adopt something that is meaningless to her, that she doesn't understand." Bradly, in fact, expressed some frustration at the slow pace of change: "I walk around and I still see people lecturing for 75 minutes, and I'm like, 'Are you kidding me?'" I suspected that Beatrice might share at least a little of Bradly's impatience; in our interview at the start of the school year, she told me that when kids take off, teachers can "pull back"—but "it is a lot easier to do that with students than it is with faculty, because old habits are hard to change."

During the school year 2013–2014, I had a front-row seat from which to observe some of those changes. Beatrice was resolute in her belief that "if you build it, they will come," and sometimes the old townhouses themselves seemed to embrace her vision of a culture of making and imagination. In the basement, directly next to a classroom where ninth graders discussed Renaissance art history, custodians and a plumber puzzled over a detail of the infrastructure in the school's crowded machine shop, and in the hallway, the smell of oil and metal mingled with the odor of fabric softener as faculty and kitchen staff squeezed past each on their way to the lunch room. Meanwhile, in a sunlit FabLab three flights up, students used a computer-controlled vinyl cutter to make colorful decals of household objects, such as light bulbs and cutlery, and then added QR codes to link them to whimsical videos; later, a visitor who noticed one of the decals—say, of a light bulb attached to the banister of the grand, spiral staircase—and then scanned the QR code with his smartphone, might hear a young woman say, "Ideas are fired by inspiration and produced by your imagination."

When I asked Julie, the head of the middle school, how she was handling the demands of running a school while also rethinking education, she said, "We're kind of making it up as we go along." In meetings and interviews, watching teachers in their classrooms, chatting with the door attendants in the foyer or with administrators at lunch, my experience of this project has been like a rich conversation where almost anything could happen next; where FabLabs, art history displays, and violins made with a laser cutter entangled with 19th-century townhouses, leafy city streets, biodiversity dioramas, and marshmallow towers made with toothpicks.

In this chapter, I have described just a few of the many impressions that linger from my time at the school. My goal has been to weave these impressions into a richly varied fabric, in the hope that you will be able to situate the conversations in the chapters that follow within the interconnected and sometimes contradictory ecology of this study.

Table 3. Primary Participants.

Name	Role	Experience Total/Local	Interviews	Teaching Observations	Other Observations	Other Data Sources
Aidan	Teacher Middle School Science	8/2 yrs	2	2+	Parachute drop; Rube Goldberg machines	Lesson plans, rubrics, photos
Amanda	Teacher High School History Humanities	16/16 yrs	2	2+	Curator's Choice, Curator's Gallery	Document hand-outs, casual conversation, emails
Amber	Teacher Elementary Science	9/5 yrs	None	2	Marshmallow towers, robots	Casual conversations
Barbara	Teacher High School English Humanities	12/3 yrs	None	None	Literary magazine	Humanities team meeting
Beatrice	Administrator Head of School	40/25 yrs	1	N/A	At student showcase events; in the hallways; morning and afternoon greetings.	Published letters
Bradly	Administrator Dir. of Tech	25/16 yrs	2	N/A	Maker Day; Scratch Day; hallways.	None

Name	Role	Experience Total/Local	Interviews	Teaching Observations	Other Observations	Other Data Sources
Cecelia	Administrator Dir. of Curriculum	22/17 yrs	1	N/A	Classroom drop-ins; hallways; student showcases.	None
Earl	Teacher High School English Humanities	12/3 yrs	1	None	Curator's Choice, Curator's Gallery, iBook Box-folio	Lesson plan on Box-folio; team meeting notes
Emma	Teacher High School Art	20/16 yrs	1	1	Art show	Art show photos
Grace	Teacher Elementary Science	9/9 yrs	2	2	Marshmallow towers, kicking robot, Invention Convention	Lesson plans, photos
Isabella	Teacher Middle School Science	2/2 yrs	2	2+	Biodiversity; Prosthetic hand	Lesson plans, photos
Jerry	Consultant	18 yrs	2	N/A	PD workshops	Casual conversations

Name	Role	Experience Total/Local	Interviews	Teaching Observations	Other Observations	Other Data Sources
Jessica	Teacher Middle School Science	15/11 yrs	None	None	Biodiversity, Nerdy Derby, Prosthetic Hand	Group interview, casual conversations, email
Julie	Administrator Middle School Head	22/4 yrs	2	N/A	Nerdy Derby; hallways; morning and afternoon greetings.	Casual conversations, email
Kieran	Teacher FabLab Director	5/3 yrs	2	4+	Biodiversity Dioramas, Nerdy Derby, Maker Day, Scratch Day, lunch conversations, panel discussions	Casual conversations, photos, lesson plans, email
Mark	Teacher High School History Humanities	4/4 yrs	None	None	Curator's Choice, Curator's Gallery	Humanities team meeting; casual conversations
Mia	Teacher High School Art History Humanities	8/5 yrs	2	4+	Curator's Choice, Curator's Gallery	Casual conversations, emails, phone calls, Lesson plans, handouts, quizzes, photos

Name	Role	Experience Total/Local	Interviews	Teaching Observations	Other Observations	Other Data Sources
Miriam	Administrator High School Head	9/9 yrs	2	N/A	None, hallway conversations	Casual conversation, email
Susan	Teacher Middle School Art	10/2 yrs	2	2+	Nichos art project, Biodiversity science project, Wood cuts, FabLab	Casual conversations, emails, Lesson plans, photos, art examples
Thomas	Teacher High School Science	18/4 yrs	2	2+	Engineering class	photos
Tyler	Teacher Middle School Media	7/6 yrs	1	None	Video productions	Casual conversations
Vanessa	Teacher: Elementary & Middle School Art	15/10 yrs	1	1+	Logos; architecture; Biodiversity, Nerdy Derby	Casual conversations

FIELD NOTES (BIODIVERSITY)

Beneath the whale, Valerie is besieged with questions about stairs, steps, pyramids, boxes, and videos. "Should I use a still picture?" one student asks. "How about the laser cutter or the 3D printer?" another interjects.

Here at the American Museum of Natural History, on a rare and very special field trip, Valerie tells me that questions about how ideas become visual fascinate her, and that she's thrilled with her students' engagement, though she's having a tough time getting her head around the scope of the project she and her colleagues have unleashed on their seventh graders. At the museum, the goal is for students to immerse themselves in the interactive possibilities they might use in their dioramas. Valerie says she wants their research to lead their build, but the excitement is a little overwhelming. For a moment, we puzzle the relationship between what students are learning about biodiversity and the way they're conceptualizing the look of that learning—until we're interrupted again: "What if it's in the shape of a medicine cabinet?!"

Three weeks earlier, when they'd introduced the project, each teacher had made a short presentation. Kieran said that all the tools in the FabLab were available for their use; Susan explained that art classes would focus on the use of materials; and Valerie showed PowerPoint displays from her favorite museums—the Louvre, MOMA, the Franklin Institute. And then the science teachers, Isabella and Jessica, had introduced the topics students could pick from, including urbanization, deforestation, and climate change, among others. Students would work in pairs to research these threats to biodiversity and then present their findings in an interactive diorama.

On the day of the biodiversity convention, in the basement cafeteria in the North Building, students arrive before school starts to set up their projects. At 10:20 a.m. the choir is still practicing as Isabella snaps photographs of the installations. Students begin to appear, and then teachers, and then suddenly a lot more students. The hubbub increases exponentially as the choir wraps up and quickly exits. Isabella tries shouting to tell the seventh graders that one partner should stay with their diorama and give tours to the teachers, administrators, and visiting sixth and eighth graders—who have now also begun to arrive. But almost immediately, the cafeteria is crowded and warm with conversational chaos as everyone starts talking at once.

Letting myself be carried with the flow, I drift through cities that have been overbuilt, rain forests that have been cut down, and arctic ice floes that are melting. One team uses a game with little boats in an aquarium to explain that overfishing harms the oceans; another uses a roulette wheel to explain why ivory poaching accelerates the extinction of the elephants. And then I'm invited into a booth behind black-out curtains that immerses me in deforestation. Again and again, students tell me that making their research physical made it real for them.

I'm surrounded by projects constructed with cardboard, wood, Plexiglas, and electronics that turn on lights or motors, using Makey Makey, LittleBits, and serendipitous configurations of LEDs and batteries. Some dioramas are populated with animals made of modeling clay, or laser-cut figures, or 3D prints of houses, buildings, and street signs. Others are filled with store-bought components such as trees, fish, toy cars, and toy animals. And some projects include videos on iPads or laptop computers; one team has made an interactive video, hosted on YouTube, where I can click through the highlights of their research.

At the end of the morning, I help the teaching team clear the cafeteria. The students have rushed off to their next classes and the lunch crew is rolling tables and chairs back into place, putting out food even before the dioramas are tucked away. In the discombobulated rush, everyone is a little excited. Congrats and smiles fill the elevator, which is packed with gently disassembled fish tanks and curtain rods. On the way up, there's a spontaneous critique even as we try to make sense of the exuberance of it all.

"But why use a gun in the elephant display," Kieran asks. "Am I supposed to shoot the elephants?"

Susan says she loved the team who made the lights go on and off in time with the recording of their explanation. Kieran says he remembers those girls coming to him with questions about how to make that happen, and he's excited that it worked. And Jessica, making a swirling, scattered gesture, says that everything feels a bit all over the place right now. "I'm ready for something a little more solid," she says.

Datasheet: Age group: seventh grade. Content domain: science, art, technology. Collaborating teachers: Isabella, Jessica, Vanessa, Susan, Kieran. Timing: December to February (approximately three weeks total instruction and build time, due to winter break).

· 6 ·

CONTACT POINTS: THE WAYS

At the beginning of this project, as I started learning my way around the nooks and crannies of the townhouses, listening to participants and observing their work, I struggled to understand what kind of learning and knowing teachers were bringing to presence. How would I know when or if digital making and learning pedagogies were becoming enacted, or if I was simply seeing the same old stuff, but with fancy new tools? Gradually, as months ticked past, and as multiple conversations and impromptu observations accumulated, I began to notice that casual comments in the hallways, interview responses, and observations in classrooms and FabLabs connected with characteristics of 21st-century learning behaviors that I had begun to gather in the framework-assemblage of digital making and learning (Table 2). As I sorted transcripts and field notes, and kept looking at the photos, videos, and other artifacts I was collecting, including lesson plans, assessment rubrics, and other artifacts, I realized that I was encountering certain kinds of comments and activities over and over again—turns of phrases, concerns, enthusiasms, questions, classroom activities. These repetitions came to form in my mind a kind of condensate that felt like a residue of experience, like a dampness on my clothing after a passing rain shower.

To illustrate how this growing awareness of the materiality of practice affected the course of my research, recall the conversation about jazz and the industrial age that I had with Amanda, the high school history teacher. In that back-and-forth questioning of making, digital fabrication, new media, and how any of these tools mattered in the teaching of history, our interview itself began to tug at her awareness of teaching. She said, "I don't want to say you've contaminated your own study, [but] it really has made me…think more explicitly…about why I do what I do." Calling out the recursivity of the research project in this way proved important in the evolution of my inquiry, because the generative knowing that emerged alerted me to the importance of conversations more generally. This suggested to me that learning practices were coming into contact with each other. In other words, it seemed that our conversation itself was pulling Amanda into a relationship with digital fabrication and making-infused learning. In the ensuing months of my work, this notion of a relationship between practices acquired a type of stability that guided my interpretation of the stories and artifacts I was gathering. It was from these encounters, as an interpretative practice, that the typology introduced in this chapter began to appear.

The typology as a whole gathers two kinds of contact points. The Ways (illustrated in this chapter) are thought of as statements and actions that strengthened digital making and learning practices. The Challenges (illustrated in the next chapter) are statements and actions that suggested those pedagogies were weakening, or failing to gain traction. As explained earlier, I used the framework-assemblage of making and learning practices to organize what I was seeing and hearing. I wrote that the table's matrix, the relationships between its columns and rows, suggested particular relationships of practice. For example, when teachers introduced students to worksheets, Photoshop tutorials, or step-by-step instructional approaches to the laser cutter, I imagined practice acquiring the organizational affordances of traditional pedagogies; on the other hand, when I observed interest-driven learning prompts, co-learning activities, or student-led collaborations, I imagined relationships characterized by the affordances of digital materiality. Writing about, reflecting on, and discussing these relationships with the participants of the study led me to the Ways and Challenges.

The typology is illustrated with examples from interviews, conversations, and observations, both scheduled and impromptu. In this and the following chapter, I explore and categorize some of these interactions in order to figure the Ways and Challenges as *contact points*. By this I mean that between traditional teaching and emergent digital making and learning teaching, there appeared a complex interweaving of effects that I hold as materiality, a relational assemblage of affordances characterized by the substance, durability, relevance, and affect of practice. My (perhaps unintuitive) claim is that the Ways and Challenges help make this materiality available to description and further iterations of practice. In this chapter I'll explain how I identified the Ways, and then illustrate each with an example or two from the field. In some cases I'll also explain how I arrived at these interpretations, by including a brief narrative analysis; in other cases I'll simply point to clarifying aspects of the example in order to indicate where I anchored my interpretation. My hope is that as an evolving assemblage, these descriptions allow the notion of a contact point, in general, and of the Ways, in particular, to acquire traction in your imagination as a way to organize knowing and learning how to teach with digital tools and materials.

Ways: Contact Points that Strengthen Making Pedagogies

Contact points that describe a strengthening of project-based, making-infused teaching practices are called Ways. Table 4 categorizes the Ways based on their prevalence in interviews, observations, field notes, and lesson plans or other classroom artifacts, such as handouts or grading rubrics. The criteria for evaluating prevalence were, first, the number of times (as determined by line count) each contact point appeared in interview transcripts and field notes after coding and bundling for emergent themes; second, the number of different participants who referenced a particular point; third, the kind of language (for example, emotionally resonant versus matter-of-fact) that participants used; and finally, my observations of what teachers said and did when I was at the school but not directly interacting with them.

Although ordering contact points by prevalence implies a hierarchy, I am not trying to determine fine-grained value distinctions between the different Ways. Rather, I hold these lists (both Table 4 in this chapter, and Table 5 in the next chapter) as gradients; while I encountered a different prevalence of each point, there is sometimes very little difference in that prevalence between adjacent points. Nevertheless, over the entire list, there is a noticeable difference from the top of the table to the bottom. Importantly, I did not try to quantify this gradient. As well, I am not claiming that any individual participant would evaluate the contact points as they have been ordered in these tables; without doubt, the relative value of specific contact points would vary for each participant. For me, the more important goal is that a notion of contact point, generally, becomes viable as a description of practice. Given these caveats, I will look closely at the top four contact points in Table 4, and then briefly explore the lower points.

Casual Conversations

The most prevalent contact point was identified as Casual Conversations— that is to say, teachers talking with other teachers. Four subpoints were noted: direct tutorials, pep talks, project sharing, and reflective sharing. Overall, I heard and observed teachers connecting with making-infused pedagogy by talking with each other. As such, Casual Conversations contained more lines of text and a greater variety of speakers than any of the other Ways.

As defined here, Casual Conversations were primarily unplanned spoken communication between teachers. These were brief conversations, sometimes entailing no more that a passing comment, for example, a question about a setting on the laser cutter in the FabLab or a congratulatory remark about a display in the art show. Casual Conversations also appeared as longer and more focused discussions about ideas, processes, and goals. In general, the most salient characteristic of these conversations was that they were not scheduled but emerged spontaneously.

Direct tutorials. In these conversations, colleagues assisted each other with specific tools and materials. Participants told me about these conversations, and I observed them directly in and around classroom activities.

Examples.

Kieran's a great resource because he knows a lot of the specifics. If he's in my class and I say,…"Serial write to your serial monitors,"…he'll say, "Actually, serial *print*, not serial *write*." He's just a great resource to have. And he's been coming to visit frequently. (Thomas, high school science)

Thomas showed me how to [make a 3D print,] and I'm like, "Oh, that was really easy." Once he showed me how to do it, it was easier than I thought it [would be]. (Grace, elementary school science)

Vanessa told me about the project and I learned it in 5 minutes. I was like, "Oh, no way, I didn't know you could do that," and then I [thought], "Oh, I'll teach everybody." (Susan, middle school art)

Discussion. As these examples suggest, direct tutorial conversations occurred on demand and were often comprised of specific step-by-step instructions, delivered by one teacher to a colleague in response to an immediate need. The reliance on Kieran, the technology teacher and FabLab director, is not surprising, since participants acknowledged him as an expert with these tools. Isabella, a middle school science teacher, told me she felt comfortable just knowing Kieran was a few doors down the hall from her. But Kieran, even with his graduate degree in digital fabrication and interaction design, did not have a monopoly on these interventions; many other teachers helped in this way, too. For example, Grace referred to Thomas when talking about the 3D printer that had just arrived in the elementary science room, and when Susan, one of the art teachers, could not understand the workflow of a Photoshop animation project, she turned to Vanessa, a fellow art teacher.

Pep talks. Pep talks sustained and encouraged teachers as they tried a new tool or became frustrated with an existing approach.

Examples.

Kieran is really encouraging in his class. When I walk in [and] see how the girls are running the machines on their own, [it] really encourages me to not be afraid of doing the same. (Vanessa, middle school art)

[Kieran] and I overlap very happily at [the North Building] in the cafeteria,…in the morning at 8:00. He comes in and I come in, and there's a space we can actually sit down, and there isn't anybody shouting. (Amanda, high school history and humanities)

A lot of it happens in these casual talks in corners. I see [Emma, a high school art teacher] in the cafeteria or the faculty dining room. [She] comes in so excited because [a student] is doing a comic book for her Curator's Gallery project, and Emma's like, "It's going to be great." (Mia, high school art history)

Discussion. Kieran figures prominently in these conversations, too, but again, not exclusively. For example, notice that Mia, the art history teacher who is on the high school humanities faculty, told a story about encouragement offered by Emma, the high school studio art teacher.

Project sharing. This type of conversation included specific project ideas.

Examples.

It starts with this one teacher here, or this teacher over here, sharing the projects and saying, "Oh, well, that's actually really great. I could use that." And I think it's been very natural how people have learned from each other. (Mia, high school art history and humanities)

There's a certain kind of collaboration that I'm hoping for, where it's sort of more organic,…that's why the middle school teachers don't have lunch duty, [so] they have more time to connect with other teachers during lunch [and] just casually talk about something. (Vanessa, middle school art)

A lot of times I need help even figuring out what the realm of possibility is. I usually need someone with more concrete knowledge of certain technologies or certain ways of doing things to bounce ideas off of.…I almost see [it] as face-to-face blogging. (Aidan, middle school science)

Discussion. Two features of these conversations resonate: the spontaneity or just-in-time-ness (which also appeared in direct tutorials) of "face-to-face blogging"; and the suggestion that sharing is an emergent structural feature of the environment—"that's why the middle school teachers don't have lunch duty." In Aidan's case, he said he shifted to project-based learning after "talking to other teachers [and] kind of bouncing my ideas off people in the science department." Mia emphasized sharing as a learning feature: "It's been very natural how people have learned from each other." I would argue that these anecdotes describe connected or situated learning and also imply shared agency between teachers.

Reflective sharing. Reflective sharing involved a conversational partner. **Examples.**

I need to sit down and reflect on what I'm doing. And I find it's easier to sit down with somebody and talk about it, [because] that's the time when you're really willing to stop and say, "That didn't work so well." (Aidan, middle school science)

It's just nice to have somebody else to really talk through a lot of these decisions, and to sort of go along for the journey. (Mia, high school art history)

Vanessa's insight. This example comes from an interview with Vanessa, a middle school art teacher. The entire interview lasted for 1 hour and 20 minutes; the excerpt took 15 minutes, beginning with my request that Vanessa talk about a class project that had gone well. We touched on a variety of other topics as well, and then talked about an aspect of the project that did not go well. This section of the interview ended with Vanessa's insight about something she might do in the future to improve the project.

Vanessa: I recently completed a project with my fourth graders. Starting in fourth grade, they start to do these large-scale drawings, a lot of them.... They do a [stage] production called *Revolutionary Voices*,...[and] the students draw Redcoat soldiers on one side of the stage, and I have the blue coats on the other, and they're facing each other. So we talk about facial expression, and gesture, and even uniform.

The heads are always enormous, and the hands are always too small....

I've had the girls trace their bodies, [but] even if they trace, they still are not seeing the body in proportion....

One of the math teachers said, "Oh, this would've been a great collaborative project."...

Some of [the students] still had to measure, so I partnered them up, and they were just measuring each other, and really getting the data down. And then we started drawing.

A parent [said], "My daughter is loving math this year because she's realizing that you have to be creative to be good at math."...

My goal is to really exercise their way of seeing....

It's definitely more on the exploratory side....

One thing that didn't go [well]...by the time they got to drawing their hands they were very quick to just draw them, you know? I must have done 10 drawings [about] how to measure from your wrists to the top of your middle finger,...so I kept doing that, and they still were sort of rushing through the hand. And I think maybe if I had done the hand separately...maybe if I segmented the body, and then collaged it together, it might have been interesting. And I might try that next year....

Maybe if they did body parts. The head, focused on the head, and then we collaged it together, that might have been an interesting—

Me: Actually, this is—

Vanessa: I just thought of that. I just came up with that. Wow, I should have done it that way. Because then they could really focus on the hand.

Discussion and analysis. Quoting this conversation at length conveys the flavor of the work Vanessa was doing, and provides enough detail for a fairly substantial analysis. First I will characterize the conversation by point-ing to some specific features of interest, and then I will draw some general observations about the way Vanessa constructs learning and knowing in prac-tice. In this, I'm pulling from the work of Bamberger and Schön (1983) and Kasl and Yorks (2012). My goal is to show that our conversation brought Vanessa to the threshold of a new understanding of her practice.

The excerpt above can be characterized as a kind of meandering into a set of questions (What went well? What did not go well?) that emerges with new or even unlooked-for insight ("I just came up with that. I was like, wow…"). Throughout the excerpt, we notice Vanessa's willingness to explore these questions with a partner (me), and her ability to keep an open-ended goal in mind. That is, we took several detours as we talked, touching on math, creativity, scale and proportion, digital 3D design and scanning, and the dif-ferences between teaching at various grade levels. (These detours have been edited out in the interest of space.) Nevertheless, our conversation kept flow-ing toward a resolution of the questions I had asked. As such, when Vanessa arrived at her speculation about a method for drawing the hand so that its scale related to the other parts of the body (by separating the drawing tasks), her insight can be seen emerging organically from within the meandering flow of the conversation. But it appeared suddenly and, in a manner of speak-ing, in retrospect—"I just came up with that"—and yet it was aimed at the future—"I might try that next year." Importantly, Vanessa was not looking for insight; she was not trying to figure out a solution to a problem. That is, we had not approached the conversation as a problem-solving exercise. Rather, Vanessa's new way of seeing this specific event appeared as she shared it with me, as she took apart the process of drawing the Revolutionary soldiers and then speculatively reassembled it again.

Here, the emergence of *new* meaning strikingly resembles Bamberger and Schön's (1983) sense of the "historical revisionism" (p. 73) with which their participants manipulated structures of and references to meaning (for exam-ple, the bells with which they created melodies, and the invented symbol systems they used to notate those melodies). It also reprises the way in which their participants suddenly and spontaneously recognized insight after a pro-longed period of experiment and play. Bamberger and Schön wrote that their participants were "engaged in on-the-spot experimenting in response to new phenomena" and that they were "'conversing' with their materials…more like the making and shaping of coherence in the arts than like the means-ends, instrumental logic usually associated with puzzles and problems" (p. 69). That is, insight was connected to the way participants first manipulated bells to build tunes, and then created (and further manipulated) schematic representations of the bells to teach others to play those tunes. I am seeing a similar dynamic in Vanessa's manipulation of ideas about drawing, measurement of the body, scale and ratio, staging a performance, and collaborating with teachers from other disciplines—all so that fourth graders might enact relationships with the Revolutionary War and the connection of the hand to the body. In this relationship, I would argue that Vanessa's performance of her own learning and knowing, and the shape of her insight, is similar to what Bamberger and Schön present in their analysis, namely, that "unexpected insight *evolves* in the work of making" (p. 73, emphasis in the original).

I want to hold up Vanessa's insight, and the way she arrived at it, as an example of a material entanglement of practice with tools and materials. I am reminded of Elizabeth Kasl's way of knowing (*without thinking*) as she explored clay (Kasl & Yorks, 2012), and of various aspects of making-oriented pedagogy as described in the literature of maker education, particularly Papert and Harel's (1991) constructionism, Resnick's (2008) spiral of creativity, Bolt's (2013) material thinking, and Peppler's (2013) interest-driven learning. In our conversation, Vanessa built an object (a theory about why students have difficulty understanding the scale of their hands in relation to their bodies, and have trouble translating that understanding to their drawings), and iterated it by sharing it with me (by fiddling with her representation of the theory and gradually including elements of math, measurement, tracing, and performance). Her approach was open-ended and intuitive, like an unguided or playful exploration (we were not directed toward solving a particular problem, but were rather following the conversation where it led us). At the same time, this approach kept our interests accessible to us (though we touched on several tangents as we spoke, we did not trail off onto discombobulated pathways).

Finally, in Vanessa's insight I am reminded of the way learning and knowing sometimes become enacted in an artist's studio—what I've described above as material learning. In addition to resonances with Bamberger and Schön (1983) and Kasl and Yorks (2012), this further suggests that we are looking at an enacted encounter: Vanessa's insight evolves as she explores it, by surprise, not because she was looking for it. She speaks about and imagines a particular learning object that entangles *personalized making* (the Redcoat figure as a trace of students' own bodies), *materials and tools* (paint, paper, glue), and *cultural constructs* (the American Revolution), where students are learning *to be* historians and performers rather than merely *about* these things.

As described above, the interweaving of these pedagogical objects and learning objectives is among maker education's much anticipated results.

An important caveat here, mentioned earlier, is that maker education scholars primarily discuss *children's* learning, not adult learning. This suggests that in spite of the many ways that adult learning differs from youth or children's learning (Merriam, Caffarella, & Baumgartner, 2007), descriptions of project-based, making-infused teaching might be adaptable across developmental paradigms.

Doing Projects

Doing Projects referred to participants' stories about making activities in their own or colleagues' classrooms. Determined by line count, this contact point was as prevalent as Casual Conversations; however, fewer participants connected *doing* with *strengthening* their relationship to making-infused pedagogies.

Examples.

> One of the things that was most meaningful to me wasn't even [from] my own class, it actually was the Nerdy Derby....It inspired and challenged me to keep pushing resistant eighth graders to [do projects]. (Aidan, middle school science)

> The most successful path has always been to choose a project. (Kieran, technology teacher and FabLab director)

> I would like to see something like those [project-based professional development] programs being done throughout the year, but we have to provide the teachers time to do that. Is there a way to set the schedule so that for a day, a week, the students are at an internship, and the teachers are working on a project? I think that that would be ideal. (Kieran, technology teacher and FabLab director)

Discussion and analysis. Kieran's assertion that project-based professional development would be an "ideal" way to learn about making-infused teaching, and that *making things* is the "most successful path" toward changing one's practice, points to a contradiction. Participants connect their making-infused teaching practices to projects they had done: Grace linked the paperclip activity to her own awareness of tinkering as a teaching strategy (see Table 4), and Aidan referred to the Nerdy Derby as the thing that inspired him to keep pushing for project-based learning. Kieran, however, said that doing projects is an "ideal," implying a normative or prescriptive standardization.

This urge toward standardization is understandable from the one who had been hired, in part, to help reinvent teaching and learning. Simply, it was his job to teach the teachers how to use the FabLabs. Beatrice told me that Kieran's work inspired the school's move toward making-inflected teaching and learning in the first place. Indeed, many faculty realized Kieran's bellwether role, as evidenced by the conversations I saw them having with him, and by the way they relied on his expertise with tools and materials. In a sense, for Kieran, based on Beatrice's aspirational disposition, his job was to figure out how to get teachers to engage with learner-directedness. And yet, from a project-based or problem-based (sometimes known as "inquiry-based") approach (Martinez & Stager, 2013; Papert, 1980b, 2001), standardization is precisely what he wanted to avoid. That is, a hallmark of constructionist teaching and learning is that the student explores and discovers questions that matter for herself, and curriculum emerges from hands-on engagement, not from standardized objectives.

This conundrum has been described in the education literature before, perhaps most famously in the debates that pitted Deweyan progressivism against the "beaten paths" of traditionalism (Dewey, 1916/1997, p. 5). As Dewey put it at the time, the problem was that a notion of emancipatory learning contradicts itself if it becomes dogmatic. The quandary Dewey wrestled with, as the philosopher John Baldacchino puts it (2014), was how education builds and maintains a "space for interaction and transaction" (p. 71). This puzzle has not disappeared, as evidenced by Kieran's exploration of these contradictions; basically, constructionist, learner-centered pedagogy pulls toward open-ended dialog and distributed expertise, but teacher education often pulls toward a prescriptive baseline (Darling-Hammond, 2006; Goldstein, 2014; Hickman, 2011). I encountered this contradiction in Kieran's explorations throughout the year of the study, and this is why his words stood out for me here. Importantly, however, in the classroom, or with other faculty, I never saw Kieran adopt a teacher-centered, content-mandated approach—quite the opposite. Rather, I heard him wrestle with the contradiction continuously: How does one learn to hold teaching loosely, especially when the answer to the problem is so obvious? For Kieran, I would argue, the mandate *You must get a self-directed project* was felt as a troubling contradiction.

Learning to Iterate

This contact point was the third most prevalent by line count, and about the same number of participants referenced Learning to Iterate as did Doing

Projects. *Iterating* means that learners rough out concepts with whatever tools and materials are at hand, and then gradually improve on their work, for example, by progressing along Resnick's (2008) spiral of creativity. The goal is to explore a project but not get stuck on notions of perfection, or think too much ahead. In this sense, iterating resembles the time-tested saw about learning to write: All writing is rewriting. In high school, my teachers repeated that line endlessly, trying to convince us that writing our essays multiple times before handing them in was a good idea, though few of us ever did. When I taught writing at the college level, I found myself saying the same thing, with similar results. In fact, several participants reported that learning to iterate was hard, even as adults. Participants who talked about iterating usually had significant stories to tell—about the difficulties and about how good it felt to finally *get it*. Sometimes, stories unfolded over several tellings over many months.

Kieran's story about iterating. When I asked Kieran to tell me about something he had found difficult to learn, he said:

> I'm going to talk about the value of iteration and prototyping. It took me a long time to learn, and I'm still learning [it]....When I was making something in the past, I focused on just making one object, building it all in one go, perfect the first time.

> But there's a project I started last summer, called Glow Bows. It comes from noticing that students at our school love to wear hair bows, and I've been trying to come up with ways that they would find physical computing intrinsically motivating....So I hit upon this idea of hair bows that glow, that had LEDs sewn into them. So I brought it to the students, and they took it way farther than I ever would've thought, and all together we brainstormed about 80 different versions of Glow Bows.

> It was really exciting, because it got them thinking about what is possible. And so I made a hair bow with lights in it. It was super basic. There wasn't even a switch. But just from that process, I sort of realized, okay, now, what is the next step?...So then I started experimenting with different ways of attaching LEDs...[and] I finally figured that out. So I wanted to go to the next step, [but] I didn't really know what the next step would be. So I just decided, well, I knew I wanted to learn how to write C and make circuit boards. So I decided to use this project as the motivator. Then I was happy to work on that for a while and create this circuit board, but it was a hard circuit board. Nobody wants to wear a hard circuit board on their head.

> Through this process, it made me realize the power of iteration and not being so focused on making this thing the first time. I knew that was the case. I had been told that it was the case. But to actually internalize it and learn it myself, I had to do it. And in the past, even when I was in grad school, I didn't do it right, because I was always trying to make that finished project. And in the end, there was always

something wrong with it. But if you iterate—and I knew this, I was taught this, and I heard this, but I didn't really [know how to do it].

I'm so excited to finally learn this lesson, because I've seen so many of my peers in grad school that had backgrounds in technology or design, and they worked this way. They prototyped and iterated, and I was always sort of maybe a little bit jealous, because I was doing it wrong, and I knew that.

Discussion and analysis. Though not every participant had a story like this, those who did found that their experiences were transformative, at turns exhilarating and excruciating. Kieran's story is emblematic in this respect. I find it intriguing on several levels. First, as the teacher at the school with the most experience in the maker movement, as a graduate of a prestigious technology program, and acknowledged by his colleagues as an expert in the digital fabrication tools and materials at his disposal, merely having a story like this to tell is extraordinary. In fact, his colleagues might be astonished to hear that Kieran is still learning about making in such an important way.

Another aspect of Kieran's story that I find instructive is his blueprint for teaching about iterating: Get a project (Glow Bows) and start playing with it (80 different versions). Here, however, the plan is complicated by Kieran's admission that he already knew this—he "had been told that this was the case"—but he had not been able to learn the lesson. The conundrum, in terms of helping teachers learn iterating, is that the lesson seems to be unteachable. Kieran knows that "to actually internalize it and learn it myself, I had to do it." In graduate school he had been told that iterating was important, had seen his colleagues iterating, and had felt jealous and perhaps even dispirited because his own projects were not turning out so great—because he was doing it wrong, "and [he] knew that." What more could a student possibly need in order to "internalize" a lesson?

A third characteristic of Kieran's story that bears mention is the narrative arc and emotional traction it gathers in the telling. The story begins with a journey that "really took a long time"; becomes "exciting" as others (his students) join with their ideas (80 versions); takes several detours, and gets a little lost ("I didn't really know what the next step would be"); makes a few missteps ("Nobody wants to wear a hard circuit board on their head"); and finally, exuberantly ("I'm so excited to learn this lesson"), reaches a promised land ("I had been told this was the case"), leaving failure in the past ("I was always...a little bit jealous, because I was doing it wrong, and I knew that").

In fact, I heard this emotionally resonant arc in other stories about iteration, as well. For example, Aidan described learning to iterate as a "big change" for himself and his students: The "initial idea, that initial design, that initial thing that you would normally hand in and be done with is very much the beginning of learning…it's everything that comes after that makes learning meaningful and makes it real and makes it matter." Grace said that learning to iterate helped her understand her own learning process. She said that she "could not figure out how to do [a project]…[and] it was really frustrating." Poignantly recapping the power and difficulty of learning to iterate that Kieran speaks about, Grace said she had learned "That I'm just as capable as [my students] are at learning." And finally, Amanda told me that for her, learning to iterate happened when she "fell in love with an idea," "struggled and failed," and finally became "so excited" after succeeding.

My point is that each story has been carefully crafted by the participant who told it. This suggests that iterating will become an important component of future learning because, as Bruner (1994) has argued, strong stories are not only records of one's life journey, but also "recipes for structuring experience itself…[and] directing it into the future" (p. 36). In the language of ANT (Latour, 1987; Latour & Woolgar, 1979), these well-structured stories suggest that a great deal of effort is being applied to stabilize a relationship between traditional and maker-oriented pedagogies.

Experiencing Student Engagement

Although it didn't appear in interviews all that often, I've listed teachers' experiences of student engagement as the fourth most prevalent contact point because of the resonant language teachers used to discuss it, and because I observed student engagement nearly every time I was at the school.

Examples.

> The maker experience gave me more confidence about letting them pursue something they were really interested in, [and] because of the robustness in their own methods and commitments and engagement. They were as enthusiastic the last day as they were in September. (Amanda, high school history and humanities)

> I arrived in class 5 minutes late. I was afraid that I'd get there and everybody [would be] sitting around waiting for me to arrive. But they knew what they had to do, and

they just started doing it....That was where I [said], "This is it. This is working." (Kieran, technology teacher and FabLab director)

Discussion and analysis. I recognized the importance that teachers attached to student engagement in two ways: First, in every classroom, and in the hallways and at lunch tables, I observed participants committed to student engagement. In practice, even teachers who did not specifically discuss student engagement made student engagement the focus of their work.

Second, the emotional involvement of phrases like "the days that most excite me" (from Tyler, in Table 4), and "the maker experience gave me more confidence" (Amanda), describe teachers connecting practice to making *because* of their students' engagement. Tyler said that "responsive" teaching was more satisfying than a predetermined lesson plan: "Those are the best days, when my teaching is more responsive to what they need, rather than, I have this idea of something that they have to learn." Amanda drew a direct line from the ethos of the maker movement to sustained student involvement: Letting students "pursue something they were really interested in" kept them engaged and "as enthusiastic the last day [of the school year] as they were in September." And Kieran's lingering doubts about making in the classroom are wiped away when he arrives late but finds that his students "knew what they had to do"—"This is it. This is working."

As with stories about iterating, these statements about student engagement are well-constructed story maps (Bruner, 1994). That is, by articulating their students' (and their own) engagement, these anecdotes illustrate a reciprocal amplification that shows teachers exploring trajectories of practice informed by project-based, making-infused teaching. Ironically, this reciprocity might be interrupted as this movement changes teachers' position in the classroom. That is, as students begin to move along learner-centered, interest-driven pathways, teachers might come to feel less central to students' learning, and Student Engagement could become a self-limiting contradiction: *The teacher teaches herself out of a job.* This kind of reciprocally destabilizing behavior is an example of how the logic of decentering, as an affordance of digital materiality, might actually challenge the arrival of making-infused learning and knowing, especially if the structure of normative schooling cannot evolve as fast as the changes brought by student engagement. I've briefly discussed this dynamic in Chapter 3, and it will remain an important component of the narrative interpretations in the rest of the book as well.

Additional Ways of Connecting

The seven other contact points from Table 4 will be identified with minimal examples and discussion. Each was less prevalent than the four discussed above. This does not mean their value was insignificant for any individual participant, only that in the aggregate, these contact points seemed to exert less force on changing practices. This raises a point for further research: Are these Ways somehow less available to, or more difficult to deploy in practice? Or, are the effects I observed localized at this particular school?

Administrative disposition. Administrators encouraged teachers to explore, connect with, and ultimately adopt project-based, making-infused practices. This contact point refers to teachers' awareness of their administrators' desires. I have no doubt that every participant knew of the school's position; however, relatively few participants talked about it.

Example.

> From the administration's point of view, this is something important, we're moving towards a 21st-century–type of learning model, whatever it looks like. (Isabella, middle school science)

Following students' lead. Several teachers told me they depended on students' knowledge. I observed this in classrooms as well. Most participants who spoke about following their students did so in respect to digital tools. Other teachers talked about following students' lead with respect to lesson design.

Example.

> Students know a lot, enough to carry the project. So even if you as a teacher don't know how to do this particular thing, you can say, "Hey, Sally, you know, I hear you're good with iMovie. Can you show me how to do that?"…And it takes care of itself. (Isabella, middle school science)

Predisposition of the teacher. Some participants talked about childhoods filled with making and building. Intriguingly, these same teachers seemed to be wholeheartedly connecting to project-based teaching. In one case, a teacher's robust enthusiasm for changing definitions of materiality prompted me to ask specifically about her childhood. She replied that, indeed, she had grown up in a making-infused household. I find this (potential) correlation between teachers' childhood dispositions and their adult practice evocative, and will discuss it a bit more in later chapters.

Example.

I was building things as a kid, mostly with my dad in his basement workshop, where he repaired and restored antiques for sale and did other wood- and metal-working. [We were] encouraged to entertain ourselves with imaginative play…[and I] liked finding out about how things worked. Even now unjamming the copier can be a highlight of a tough day at school. (Amanda, high school history and humanities, via email)

Self-directed learning. Teachers who talked about self-directed learning were describing current activities, not recalling activities from childhood. It may be that childhood making and building predispose one to become a self-directed learner in adulthood, but I did not extend my observations or interviews to consider that characteristic.
Example.

I can teach myself how to do this and find the right people to seek inspiration, either strangers online, or colleagues who are doing interesting things. I think I've surprised myself in how, by tinkering around, I'm able to figure it out. (Isabella, middle school science)

Reflecting on experience. Personal or private reflection was not very prevalent as a contact point, though for some participants, it was powerful.
Example.

I'm feeling very reflective over the last year. I just love the fact that we can continually get better at teaching. (Kieran, technology teacher and FabLab director)

Workshops out of school. Kieran said, "The best professional development that I've been to are these immersion programs, where you're doing something for like a week." For participants who attended them, workshops were important contact points, but since so few did, their prevalence was low.
Example.

[Amber and I]…went last summer, and they kept stressing the importance of imaginative play…[and that led to tinker time]. (Grace, elementary school science)

Professional development in school. Professional development workshops during school hours were occasionally mandated by the administration, but did not appear to be very effective contact points. While some teachers acknowledged a nominal value, there was not much enthusiasm for them, and some participants who were initially matter-of-fact about the value of professional development became disillusioned by the end of the year.

Example.

> The way [PD] is mostly done…caters to a bit of an obsolete model, and then you get people who reject it out of hand because it's boring or whatever. So I don't know [how worthwhile it is]. (Aidan, middle school science)

Table 4. The Ways: Contact Points that Strengthened Digital Making and Learning (in order of prevalence based on interviews and observations).

The Way	Example
Casual Conversations	"A lot of times I need help even figuring out what the realm of possibility is.…I almost see [it] as a face-to-face blogging." —Aidan, Middle School Science
Doing Projects	"We gave them ten paperclips and they could design whatever they wanted…[and] that led to…really wanting to have more open-ended building and making."—Grace, Elementary School Science
Discovering Iterating	"It's really interesting because the paper engineering project is all about iterating and it's all about prototyping, and maybe that's why that project ended up being so successful."—Susan, Middle School Art
Experiencing Student Engagement	"The days that most excite me are where the students are incredibly self-motivated, where they're the ones driving the discussion."—Tyler, Middle School Media
Administrative Disposition	"There's an embrace of the new. They're very much into science and technology."—Amanda, High School History & Humanities
Following Students' Lead	"I don't need to be a specialist in the application,…we can work it out together. And the students are pretty into…helping their teachers along with the tech stuff."—Susan, Middle School Art
Predisposition of the Teacher	"Growing up I just wanted to be in the woods building stuff or in the basement working on projects."—Kieran, Technology Teacher & FabLab Director
Self-Directed Learning	"I taught myself Photoshop and InDesign and Illustrator."— Vanessa, Elementary and Middle School Art

The Way	Example
Reflecting on Experience	"I think that's really important for me, as a teacher…[to] reflect,…to sort of go through the choices I've made."—Mia, High School Art History & Humanities
Workshops out of School	"[The workshop] had an impact on my practice. I'm much more interested in letting kids tinker with text and making much more open-ended prompts."—Amanda, High School History & Humanities
Professional Development in School	"I think it came from a combination of professional development days and presentations that have been given to us over the last few years."—Tyler, Middle School Media Teacher

FIELD NOTES (RUBE GOLDBERG)

Before class starts, a student rushes in, yelling, "Mr. N., can we get started? It's 12:30!"

Following wind turbines, solar cookers, and a variety of simple machines, and after several weeks of parachute competitions, Aidan's eighth-grade science students were about to conclude their final project of the year: the maximally inefficient and minimally productive Rube Goldberg machine. The goal had been to design and construct a ball-drop machine with at least five steps (such as levers, wheels, pulleys, or incline planes), including a starting action, and to iterate the design until the machine could successfully complete its task two times in a row. Aidan wanted the students to do three things: build a device that demonstrated the concept of mechanical advantage; reflect on and talk about the building process itself; and apply the physics from class lectures and worksheets to describe the way their machine worked. He said that after measuring and calculating characteristics such as mass, distance, and time, "They should be able to make sense from the math." But first, the machines have to work; and today is test day.

"I'm really excited!" a student says, dropping her book bag on the floor and rushing to her teammates, who have already begun their final setup and troubleshooting. "Let me drop the ball!"

Scattered around the science lab, six teams are in position and have started assembling the ramps, levers, and scaffolding of their contraptions. The room appears about to burst; students dash to and from the materials tables with tape and glue and string, laughing and yelling at each other, and then screaming, clapping, and cheering if their machines perform properly, if the silver ball drops or bounces into a cup that swings a lever left or right, or rolls down a ramp into a pool of water, causing it to drain into the sink, or to pull a string that flips on the overhead lights. Some machines stretch long and narrow across countertops and tables jammed together, with gently sloping, linear ramps; others reach vertically from tabletop to the floor below, with steep switchback ramps that open and close weight-activated levers; and one machine is mounted directly into the wall of the student lounge outside the classroom. Behind me, Kieran appears with his smartphone, posting Vines and scrambling from one end of the lab to the other as teams announce loudly that they want him to come look at their machines.

In the center of the classroom, Aidan counts down the time remaining before the presentation runs begin. He answers a question about acceleration shouted from a knot of students huddled at the front of the room, and then begins helping another team figure out how to pop a balloon that just won't pop. As they're crouching to examine a pulley, voices scream out in unison, "It worked!" and "Yes yes yes!" In response to the generalized increase in jumping, dancing, and clapping, Aidan calls out, to no one in particular, "Hey, let's keep our voices down." To which another student yells, "Mr. N., I'm so happy ours worked!"

After the final runs have concluded, and the last silver ball has rolled off the last incline ramp, everyone breathes a little easier, and the classroom quiets down. Now it's time to get to work, Aidan says. He's already discussed the rubric, and now as he's handing out worksheets he reminds the students that they've seen these problems before, such as: Based on the formula for gravitational acceleration, calculate the difference between actual elapsed time of the ball's journey, and the expected time for an unencumbered fall; and, identify and describe contact points that reduced the efficiency of the machine, and calculate the reduction of efficiency according to the law of conservation of momentum.

Energy bubbles back to the surface as the girls grab their laptops and disperse. I hear: "What's the equation for acceleration?" "How about the unit for potential energies?" "How do you measure displacement?" and "Who's got the mass scale!?" Aidan reminds everyone that the formulas they need are still available on the classroom's networked server, and that their final work, including diagrams, calculations, and performance videos, is due, by email, that night.

I've been listening from the back of the room, occasionally taking a picture or video, and tapping into my phone—my digital notebook—as fast as I can. Now, with the room quiet and students individually engaged, I give myself a moment to reflect. Throughout the ninety-minute session, and especially during the presentation runs, the whole class had followed from one machine to the next, entirely attentive, cheering when the ball made a successful run and groaning when something went awry or fell apart. And now, with all that excitement finished, they've begun calculating momentum and efficiency from the measurements they'd made of their individual machines, and the excitement isn't over—the room hums as students move back and forth between their machines and their laptops, asking each other about mass conversion units and double-checking their equations for acceleration. Surprisingly, to me at least, the level and quality of enthusiasm and focus have not diminished. Sure, it has changed, but it didn't evaporate the instant Aidan passed out worksheets. Instead, it seemed to sink in deeper, perhaps gaining a different sort of traction, or catalyzing a grittier kind of inquiry. What was going on?

During an unscheduled observation two weeks previously, I had found Aidan in the front of his classroom, rummaging through a box of gears and wires, hobby motors, old PVC elbows, and pieces of tubing. The room was quiet, but around him the girls were working on early iterations of their machines, testing ramps and levers with glue and tape, surrounded by things propped on boards and held in place with clamps. Aidan appeared totally absorbed in what he was doing and not at all surprised to see me. As we were chatting, he pushed the box of odd parts away, picked up a wrench and pliers, and turned to something he had clamped to the table—a gear and axle combination epoxied inside an elbow join. He'd been wrestling with it for a while, he told me. "I have to get these apart so they can be reused in another project," he said. "I'm having trouble doing it, though." Adjusting his grip on the wrench and bearing down, he said, "I don't give up easily."

Class is over now and students are leaving, calling out thank yous and promising to email their assignments. When the room is empty I ask Aidan how he's feeling, and what he thinks of the session. He looks exhausted but relaxed, and says it went well; he's happy. In a previous conversation he'd drawn a connection between theories about physics and math and then connecting those theories to things that you make or build with your hands. For students to solidify their learning, he'd said, they need time to think and write about their constructs before being asked to discuss them in public. How did that apply here? Is that what I'd been observing? Aidan said he thought it was, except for the discussion that would happen next time the class met. Later, during a more extended conversation, he would spell it out in more detail: "Big-picture ideas are cemented by the making process, and by the process of do it, undo it, redo it, talk about it, learn from it, and then reflect." In fact, he would tell me, the success of the Rube Goldberg project, right there in front of him, convinced him. After reflecting on it, he'd say, "Some of these things I kind of timidly believed, and was hoping were true, but now I have evidence to really back them up, because I see girls succeed even if they're not really that familiar with this way of learning."

As I step out into the hallway I'm reminded of something that Kieran had said about the Nerdy Derby. As FabLab director and all-around evangelist for making activities, it was at his urging that the school had taken on that extravaganza, so he understandably felt responsible for its success. But one day he was late arriving down in the basement cafeteria because of a meeting in another part of the school. He told me that as he approached the basement doors, he became afraid that he'd find the students sitting around doing nothing, or worse, creating some kind of commotion that would reflect badly on his leadership, on the project, and perhaps even on the kind of learning the Nerdy Derby represented. But as he opened the doors he found that everyone was completely engaged with building and testing their cars. He said, "They knew what they had to do, and they just went right down and started doing it. That was the experience where I said, 'This is it. This is working.'"

Datasheet: Age group: eighth grade. Content domain: science. Teacher: Aidan. Timing: approximately four weeks in May.

· 7 ·

CONTACT POINTS: THE CHALLENGES

The second half of the typology, the Challenges, introduces contact points that appeared when teachers resisted project-based, making-infused practices, or pushed back against the integration of digital making and learning. As with the Ways (Table 4), the Challenges (Table 5) are arranged in order of descending prevalence, which implies but does not necessarily correlate with an assessment of any individual point's effectiveness. To reiterate, I am not claiming that contact points have fixed values, or that any acted as *de facto* stabilizers or destabilizers of practice. Rather, holding them loosely, I'm arguing that the contact points invite us to trace the emergence of making-infused pedagogies in practice.

Challenges: Contact Points that Weakened Digital Making and Learning

As with the Ways (Table 4), I will expand on and discuss the first several Challenges (Table 5). Contact points at the bottom of the list will be explored with an example, but discussion will be limited.

Content versus Making

The most prevalent challenge to project-based, making-infused teaching was a concern that making would conflict with content. This surfaced in interviews and in private conversations in teachers' classrooms, and in comments overheard in the lunchroom, hallways, entry foyers, on the sidewalks, and on field trips. Skepticism and doubt about making in the curriculum, and even outright resistance to it, was everywhere: Transcripts and field notes contained more lines of text for Content versus Making than for any other contact point, including those in Table 4.

Examples.

> You're using a 3D printer, and it looks great on our brochures, but to what end? Did it tie into something that [is] more content driven? (Aidan, middle school science)

> A big concern, whether it's with APs or math classes, [is] that they have to get to certain content throughout the year for the SATs. (Grace, elementary school science)

> What is the core content that we need students to know, that you can't strip away? That's a very tough question. (Isabella, middle school science)

> The reason this project [Curator's Gallery] was [successful], was because it stood on the shoulders of their research paper. (Mia, high school art history and humanities)

> [Field notes from a museum trip]: Vanessa and her students are exploring natural history and animal habitat exhibits to get ideas for their biodiversity dioramas. Vanessa answers questions from the students, nonstop. She tells me that she is "still trying to get my head around this project." She wants to understand the relationship between the research and what the students will build, but she wants the content to lead the build. (Vanessa, middle school art)

Discussion and analysis. Comments about the intersection of making activities and teaching for content touch on several different concerns. Isabella says that making is "at odds" with science content (see Table 5); and Aidan worries that the fancy tools might not strengthen learning, though they "look great on our brochures." Even Grace, who teaches elementary school science, wondered if making might interfere with high school preparation for standardized tests. And Vanessa and Mia, both highly invested in their students' maker projects, each held making as subservient to "research," by which they meant library research. During the study, I gradually became aware of a nonstop rain of comments that pitted making against content, and

I began to ask for more information: definitions, examples, and reflections. In countless conversations throughout the school, I heard teachers agreeing with Isabella that integrating making with content was "a very tough question," and worrying that project-based, making-infused teaching might "strip away" the "core content that we need students to know."

The concern with *content*—what it is, what it is not, and how it matters—can be interpreted as addressing a very large question, namely, what is the purpose of schooling? There are several sides to this debate: Should school strengthen established canons? Or should students establish an individualized body of knowledge, thereby challenging or perhaps even dissolving canons? Or, should the goal be to teach skills that can be applied as necessary in whatever context emerges?

This does not exhaust the curricular arrangements, of course, but it gives the flavor of the conversation we were engaged in. In a sense, participants' concern with balancing knowledge of the past with curiosity about the future reprises Dewey's (1916/1997) arguments in favor of progressivism, first formulated 100 years ago; and indeed, across educational research ecologies, this debate remains vibrant today, as Egan (2008, 2010) reminds us. But actually, at the study site, the exploration of pedagogical history and theory did not appear foremost in participants' minds. Rather, the impulse was toward action—the *doing* of teaching and learning. In fact, I rarely talked about the history of teaching or schooling with anyone while I was at the study site; rather, conversations were rooted in the desire to improve and enhance students' learning *right now*, and the emphasis was on the useful.

Teacher preference for the pragmatic is both implicitly and explicitly addressed in the literature on teacher education (for example, Darling-Hammond, 2006; Green, 2015; Kirp, 2013), so attending to the instrumental in this context might strike some as unremarkable. In fact, the argument could be made that this resistance to making represented a simple labor dispute. That is, teachers pushed back against being asked to do something that conflicted with what they'd been hired to do: to *teach something*, and to organize, deliver, and assess that something in ways that their managers understood. In this sense, perhaps this challenge (Content versus Making) is not appropriately read in the light of a debate about pedagogy at all. And maybe we shouldn't be surprised that Beatrice's invitation to "reinvent teaching and learning" was falling on deaf ears; that is, when Bradly's "Are you kidding me?" (from Chapter 4) is answered by Aidan's "It looks great on brochures," perhaps we're hearing normal workaday skepticism and nonchalance. In fact, in a conversation at a different school, a teacher told me that maker education felt like yet another shift in administrative tides that he had long ago learned to ignore.

I would argue, however, that untangling this challenge is more complex. The sheer ubiquity of the contradiction—Content versus Making—supports this claim: teachers couldn't stop talking about it. Why did it have such a grip on them? What occurred to me at the time, and has recurred numerous times since, is that the scope of the conversation was limited to participants' individual experiences, which kept us repeating ourselves and going around in circles. No one was asking broader questions, for example, how were these challenges addressed 100 years ago? What does teaching look like in schools with different learning priorities? Those conversations weren't as frequent at the school, whether by design, by disposition, by happenstance, or perhaps because there was little to no guidance from the administration. In terms of professional development, Julie, middle school divisional head, said, "We're kind of making it up as we go along." The potential correspondence here between language and action reminds me of the learning crises my art students experienced, discussed in Chapter 1, where they described their work as fragmented and then promptly fell to pieces. At the study site, might expanding the language available to the conversation loosen the grip of this conflict? This question begs a different kind of research into teacher education, which I'll return to in later chapters. In the meantime, however, it's worth mulling over this relationship: How might the resistance to digital making and learning, voiced as *loss of content*, be ameliorated by changing the terms themselves, so that content, for example, did not crash headlong into noncontent?

The Fit

How does making fit in your teaching practice? I asked this question repeatedly in interviews and casual conversations. Participants often said they didn't know how it fit, and they were skeptical about the administration's push to adopt it.
Examples.

There's no stress like project stress....It may be unnecessary to add [that] on to the already stressful life of a teenage girl. (Mia, high school art history and humanities)

You've got kids with every different ability in here, and you've got to keep that in mind. So, for some of them? It's possible, but for 80 percent of the kids? I don't know. (Thomas, high school science)

I struggle to see, sometimes, how I can use [making] in a way that's not just...jerry-rigging the curriculum around it. You want it to be something that's authentic and actually supporting the learning process instead of just making things more complicated. (Isabella, middle school science)

[The difficult part] is getting faculty to actually try and do it, which has been the challenge to integrate it into their curriculum....Some teachers are so set in their ways...what's the point of rocking the boat if their students are happy and learning? (Grace, elementary school science)

Discussion. These comments illustrate the skepticism about making-infused learning from a variety of directions—for example, in relation to student experience, curricular relevance, tools, and skills. In fact, this contact point, the Fit, overlaps with Content versus Making and with Assessment, below. As a point of resistance to making-infused or project-based pedagogy, each pushes back against changes in the space and time of practice. I would argue that when making-infused teaching entered the classroom, teachers felt a need to restructure their practice. In effect, they had to rearrange the furniture; the room simply wasn't large enough to accommodate everything. For some teachers, favorite pieces got kicked out entirely. That is to say, in the sense of change precipitating change (which precipitates further change, and so on), the entry of making wasn't neutral, and tensions surfaced. In this, we hear teachers' resistance as protecting students (Mia: "already stressful life of a teenage girl"; Thomas: "You've got kids with every different ability in here, and you've got to keep that in mind"), and the curriculum (Isabella: "I struggle to see how I can use [making] in a way that's not just jerry-rigging the curriculum around it"; Grace: "Something would have to give in the curriculum in order to integrate that fabrication component").

Assessment

Teachers spoke about changes in assessment because of shifting learning categories, and due to shifting criteria within categories. In some cases, teachers mentioned the additional work of grading from multiple perspectives. Overall, teachers were generous and sincere about assessment. Aidan said, "I really believe that most teachers don't want to grade kids in order to judge them. They want to grade kids in order to see what they're learning." Nevertheless, the introduction of making meant new demands on the practice of assessment.

Examples.

[Classroom observation]: Students are working on physical computing projects. A student wants music to guide a drawing machine. Thomas speculates that the waveform might inform the voltage. He asks, "How do you map the sound to a two-dimensional value? Frequency might control the x variable. What's another quality of sound that might control the y?" Then he asks the student: "Do you have art class this year?" Later, Thomas tells me he wonders how art plays into what the students need to know. He expected more art-oriented projects (like the music/drawing project), but students are making practical things inspired by an engineering sensibility, like a coffee cup that senses the temperature of the coffee. He tells me that he does not know how to encourage an artistic sensibility, that he does not understand it. Vanessa used to offer guidance, but not anymore. He worries that he would not know how to assess an art-oriented project even if a student made one. (Thomas, high school science)

I need to know what the student actually goes through. How easy is it to find these images and insert them here? How hard is it actually to map out this space correctly? So that I understood a little bit more about what the student was creating, so that I'm not just—I don't know what the word—not fooled, but that I can understand how much time and effort it took a student. (Mia, high school art history and humanities)

Discussion and analysis. These statements surface anxiety about a consequence of the change in instructional activities. A corollary to Content versus Making appears: If content is not the focus, what takes its place? And how will students demonstrate learning if teachers no longer have stable benchmarks? For some participants, this shift in expectations disrupted their sense of what they were teaching: Thomas wanted more "art" in his engineering class, but wasn't sure what he meant by that term. For others, the criteria of assessment itself had changed almost beyond recognition: Mia wondered how she could grade a student's project if she did not personally understand the fabrication process; and Susan and Isabella negotiated rubrics across the vastly different conventions used in science and art classrooms (see Table 5). Sometimes, teachers found that even without precipitating a categorical crisis, making-infused project learning nevertheless increased their workload. For example, in order to assess whether students understood the material relationships they'd constructed in their Prosthetic Hand projects, Isabella created an individual performance assessment in addition to her written test.

The commonality across these observations is a question about learning objectives, a key aspect of a teacher's job. "It all comes down to learning objectives," as Bradly said. Normally, lesson plans and learning units require teachers to organize the instructional environment so that objectives are clear and recognizable; but this strategy is counterproductive when learning is recognized as individual and unpredictable, as in problem-based learning. For many participants, this introduced a conflict between their current practice—enacting a normative curriculum—and learner-centered practices. As such, teachers wondered what qualified as learning in a given activity, and how that learning should be represented. I would argue that this question, at root a question of philosophy or epistemology without a clear and present consequence for classroom management or conduct, was experienced as a distraction, and sometimes as an anxiety-producing disruption. This question reprises the indeterminacies of the relationship between learning theory and pedagogy discussed above. In fact, teachers told me that they just did not know what to do about assessment, and this activated insecurities about their ability to do their jobs.

Aggregated content challenges. These first three Challenges—Content versus Making; the Fit; Assessment—might be variations on a theme, rather than separate contact points. That is, each describes changes in space and time that occur as making activities encroach on existing practices. The question is pragmatic: Given the finite space of the classroom and the restricted timeframe of the school day, when project-based, making-infused, constructionist activities are added, what gets subtracted?

The answer, I heard teachers say, was that, first of all, *content* gets squeezed. Then, to a lesser degree and in varying proportions, teachers worried about changes to the student experience, to their own experience, and about a new relationship with tools, materials, and skills. Third, teachers said that expectations around assessment had to change in order to keep pace with these other changes. I would argue that we should not be surprised about teachers' resistance to these aggregated challenges—in their already overscheduled days, these changes threaten to diminish the energy and presence they have available for their primary purpose, ensuring student learning.

Difficult Conversations

This contact point is nearly the opposite of Casual Conversations (Table 4). Here, participants spoke about making in a way that resisted it. This example is from an interview with Kieran that took place at the end of the study period, just as school was ending for the summer. This part of the conversation lasted about 15 minutes. It's presented at length because it contains several details that bear on the emergence of making-infused teaching.

Example.

Question: From the students' perspective, what do you see the students learning?

Kieran: A lot of it is a confidence in their ability to work with unfamiliar technologies, a certain amount of creative confidence and coming up with their own ideas. But there's also been a lot of math done this year.

[A math teacher] has class in the FabLab [and] he's gotten so excited. [He] just couldn't believe the violin. I've tried to say things to people in the math department, like, "Hey, you should really look at Scratch [a programming language for kids]. We might be able to do some cool projects that have to do with math." But I get the feeling [that] I'm hurting their feelings.

The math department has been really difficult to get on board with this stuff.

I'd love the opportunity to sit down with their department and say, "Let's look for ways that we can incorporate making into your classes."

Gary Stager [co-author of *Invent to Learn* (2013)] says you can fix the education system by getting rid of 50 percent of the content—either 50 percent.

I don't believe there is this canon of knowledge that everybody needs to know…. Are they going to remember all the parts of the mitochondria, or are they going to remember making a violin? What's a more powerful experience?

Question: But how do you address [that] with your colleagues?

Kieran: A few months ago there was talk around here about project-based learning, and I mentioned Gary's line. The English department said, "We could do that." Science and math, they laughed.

Math is something I can talk about because I studied mathematics, but I look at the math that sixth and seventh graders are doing, and I want to know why. Why do we teach kids to factor polynomials?

I asked the math department this year. "Why do we teach [this to] kids?"

I happened to be in the classroom when they were learning this. So I asked the teacher afterwards. I said, "What do you use this for?" I know the answer. Scientists use it. His answer was, "Oh, you use this all the time. You just don't even realize it." I called bullshit on that...

I think math, especially, needs to step back and ask themselves, "Why are we teaching this to kids? What is the goal here? And is there another way we can get there that doesn't lose so many kids?"...

Question: One of the things I've noticed here is, on the one hand, you are all very lucky to be outside some of the [high-stakes] exams and so on. You're also very lucky because you can build two FabLabs. [But] with those amazing good-luck charms come additional challenges.

Kieran: I see it as this huge opportunity.

Question: Exactly, but how do you take advantage of the opportunity?

Kieran: I don't know. The human stuff—the talking to people about these things without hurting their feelings, that's not something that I'm very tactful about. I'd like to have a conversation with them, but I probably would say something like, "Can't we just step back and look at this?"

Question: Is there a way to create an environment where you can have those [conversations]?

Kieran: Of course there is. It's not something that I have a lot of practice doing. Personally, I feel a little uncomfortable with confrontations, especially when you're talking about livelihoods to people who have been doing this for 20 years. Who am I to be like, "Hey, maybe there's another way."...

Question: But I keep coming back to this, [how do you] create the environment where these conversations can be had in a way that allows the doubt and skepticism to surface, without the fear of hurting people's feelings?

Kieran: Yeah, that's it. I don't feel like I can create that environment. I don't know. Middle management or whatever. Somebody has to create that environment. I don't feel like we're in that environment. Maybe we are. Maybe I'm just being too sensitive.

I don't feel like this is something you can iterate. I can't just go into the math department and talk to them about it and screw it up. And then, [will] I get another chance the next day?

Discussion and analysis. This long excerpt reveals some of the multiple, conflicted, and overlapping dynamics of the work Kieran is doing to bring project-based, making-infused teaching into practice. Here we find him trying to bridge a gap between current and emergent practices, particularly with his colleagues in the math department. The relationship is especially poignant; he is afraid of "hurting their feelings," but wants learning to be more relevant for students. He has the content expertise ("I studied mathematics") and he has the opportunity (the FabLab is used as a math classroom), and yet he is hesitant to pursue the conversation ("The human stuff—the talking to people about these things without hurting their feelings, that's not something that I'm very tactful about"). He might have reason to be cautious; earlier, he told me that faculty sometimes "feel like their toes are getting stepped on, or they're being watched"; and later in this interview (edited out for space), he told me about making offhand or "snarky" comments to a math teacher about student worksheets. But tact notwithstanding, Kieran also doubts that his 5 years of teaching experience give him the authority to critique teachers who have been on the job for a lifetime ("Who am I to be like, 'Hey, maybe there's another way'"). And even though he realizes that this kind of conversation is important ("Somebody has to create that environment. I don't feel like we're in that environment"), the stakes are so high that he feels nearly incapable of making a move ("I can't just go into the math department and talk to them about it and screw it up. And then, [will] I get another chance the next day?").

Kieran's realization that a difficult conversation is not "something you can iterate" is particularly compelling because it contrasts with his earlier story about learning to iterate. In that conversation he said,

> I'm so excited to finally learn this lesson, my peers in grad school prototyped and iterated, and I was always maybe a little bit jealous, because I was doing it wrong, and I knew that. (Kieran's story about iterating)

But here, Kieran has encountered a professional conflict that cuts against that triumph. That is, in spite of his overall success with bringing making-infused teaching to the school, and almost completely in contrast to his standing in the community (which has accrued in part because of learning to iterate), Kieran feels powerless to act in relation to the math department ("I can't just go into the math department and talk to them about it"). Kieran's dilemma (to confront the math department or not) is at the threshold of becoming a crisis; as such, it underlines the importance of difficult conversations more generally—having them, resolving them, suppressing them, or not having a space or mechanism for them.

Other participants spoke about this sense of conversational powerlessness, too: Susan said, "We were never really talking amongst each other"; Vanessa told me, "There's no one saying okay, these are the skills we want to address"; and Isabella said, "I don't think I've had a meaningful conversation with [that administrator]." In these voices, we hear isolation and fragmentation that contrast and potentially undermine the community empowerment that resonated in Casual Conversations. In a variation on this theme, one participant told me that she avoided conversations about making because she was skeptical of the whole movement. In an interview that touched on a wide spectrum of ideas and technologies, from quantum mechanics to 20th-century literature to advanced contemporary art, Emma, a high school art teacher and the head of the art department, said that she felt peripheral to the conversation going on around her, as if she was on a different "wavelength" from her colleagues.

This leads me to two speculations: First, the emergence of digitally infused maker-oriented teaching, with its wider problematic of digital materiality, might be slowed or even halted if conversations about the processes and structures of teaching do not happen in a way that promotes growth and trust, even or perhaps especially if resolutions cannot be reached. And second, when these two contact points are taken together (Casual *plus* Difficult Conversations) the power and importance of conversation becomes clear. That is, I would argue that if making-infused pedagogies are to take hold at the school, open-ended conversation is crucial. This should, of course, come as no surprise: We learn by talking with each other, and when talking together is suppressed, learning can be impeded. From the perspective of how the *absence* of conversation affects organizations, Latour (1996) suggests that the demise of a cutting-edge, French public transportation system, and the institutional bureaucracy that supported it, traces at least in part to the lack of spontaneous conversations between engineers, public relations executives, corporate leaders, and politicians; as such, Latour argues, there was not enough relational density among the various actors and stakeholders to avoid the technical snafus, performance misunderstandings, and cost overruns that eventually killed the project.

Additional Challenges

As with the Ways, the other six Challenges I've identified here (Table 5) will be illustrated with an example, but discussion will be limited. Based on line count and the number of participants who referenced these categories, each was less prevalent than the four already discussed. And to repeat, I'm not suggesting that participants found these challenges insignificant, only that in the aggregate, these contact points seemed to exert less force on changing practices.

Lack of time. Teachers spoke about time as a challenge in different ways: the lack of personal time for learning new skills; the lack of classroom time for projects to evolve; and a diffused pressure brought on by being overscheduled more generally.

Example.

> The struggle is the time issue. We need to give teachers the time to just play with the stuff. It's not just the time. You need a specific intersection of a bunch of times. You need the time when teachers are free. You need the intersection of that to be with the time that the tools are available. You need that to be intersected with the time that the teachers are motivated to actually do something. (Kieran, technology teacher and FabLab director)

Predisposition of the teacher. Predispositions played a role in how teachers talked about their practice. But whereas teachers who gravitated to making pedagogies talked about building skateboard ramps or working in their grandfather's tool shed, here, teachers told me that they learned better with direct instruction rather than exploratory sessions, or in lecture presentations rather than in learn-by-doing participatory sessions.

Example.

> My inclination as a learner is more of the "type A." I like lecture; I like lots of information. (Isabella, middle school science)

Lack of expertise. Some teachers felt challenged by either a specific or general lack of expertise. These concerns did not appear very often, perhaps because teachers expected that tools in the FabLab would be explained, or because they assumed students knew how to use them.

Example.

> With digital technology moving as quickly as it is, you don't really know how anything works all the way through. You then don't have the fluency or the expertise in order to help [students] deal with their frustrations. (Aidan, middle school science)

Loss of control. Anxiety about losing control in the classroom overlaps with several other challenges. First, it contradicts a primary assumption about teaching, namely, that teachers clearly and efficiently organize learning objectives and manage their classrooms. Secondly, it pushes against Following Students' Lead (Table 4). Third, Loss of Control might amplify Lack of Expertise, or feeling overwhelmed by the Lack of Time to prepare for class.

Example.

> [Making-infused teaching] centers around how comfortable you feel with the possibility that things may go differently, and relinquishing your control a bit. This school really encourages innovation, [but] I'm actually very cautious, and very controlling, so it's difficult for me. (Isabella, middle school science)

Rethinking the curriculum. This final challenge might be thought of as a container for the others, a conceptual drawstring pulling them closer. It directly reprises the administration's commitment to "rethinking teaching and learning," but it presents a nearly insurmountable conflict. That is, "rethinking" practice is arguably a precondition for deeply engaging learning-by-doing pedagogies. But practice, as an enacted community-wide process, is beyond individual agency. As such, asking for an individual evolution in practice without at the same time working toward systematic change as a community might be an incoherent request. By this view, a significant impediment to digital making and learning pedagogies appears from within the learning ecology itself.

Example.

> Everything's got to be different, even starting with grouping kids by age. I think that we can start to group kids by interests, and there'd be a whole lot more play going on, to help them discover their passions and then sort of nurture those. As far as what it would actually look when they're walking around? I'm sure it would be very messy. Maybe seem a bit chaotic. (Kieran, technology teacher and FabLab director)

Assembling the Typology of Contact Points

I am encouraged by the way these lists of contact points appear flexible yet stable enough to accommodate much of what I encountered during the study. The question that remains is whether the typology as a whole enables me to hold practice in play without collapsing these dozens upon dozens of stories into binary oppositions. Table 6 consolidates both categories, the Ways and the Challenges, into a single list, but this move might obscure the descriptive potential of the typology if it oversimplifies the complexity that has just begun to be explored. In fact, Table 6 surfaces apparent contradictions when some of the Ways parallel some of the Challenges, rather than simply opposing them. For example, Administrative Disposition, from the Ways—*being told what to do*—echoes Loss of Control, from the Challenges—*not having the autonomy to direct teaching agendas and activities.* How can these two essentially identical contact points both stabilize and destabilize? This entanglement is, of course, an everyday irony of living with complexity: Sometimes you love the rain; sometimes you hate it; the rain, however, remains indifferent. Indeed, the indifference of the contradiction itself might signal the typography's success, if binaries can be held open and unresolvable. And yet, the risk remains that sorting and cataloging experience into thematic unities will quiet the dynamic relationships that I'm trying to describe, thus causing practice to fall beyond the reach of either analysis or participatory action. My goals for this study are to learn how teachers come to participate in the enactment of digital making and learning teaching practices, and to understand how (or if) their teaching changes in the process. Does the typology help me reach these goals? To approach this question from a slightly different direction, in the next chapter I'll gather narrative interpretations of several specific teaching practices, and read them through the typology. As Law (2004) has cautioned, however, especially with respect to the way simplistic rubrics dispose researchers to clean up the mess they encounter, thereby making an even bigger mess, in this application of the typology, the goal is to hold analysis somewhat loosely. That is, to deploy the weather vane analogy again, I want to know if the typology of Ways and Challenges can help detect which way the winds of digital making and learning are blowing, but without stifling that wind in the process.

Table 5. The Challenges: Contact Points That Weakened Digital Making and Learning (in order of prevalence based on interviews and observations).

The Challenge	Example
Content vs. Making	"There's content we want to teach them and skills as well, and that can be at odds with the type of learning that digital fabrication involves."—Isabella, Middle School Science
The Fit	"I need to know more about the whys about it....Right now it's a method without a point."—Amanda, High School History & Humanities
Assessment	"And Isabella kept saying, how many points is it going to be worth in your class, [but] we don't really grade on points in here."—Susan, Middle School Art
Difficult Conversations	"As far as working specifically with teachers, we didn't have enough planning time. So we were never really talking amongst each other."—Susan, Middle School Art
Lack of Time	"I don't have the personal time I need in this area....It's hard when you're a full-time teacher to put in what the course needs, [which is] preparation time and planning time." —Thomas, High School Science
Predispositions of Teacher	"We've got a group of teachers that are feeling adventurous,... but they're a minority, to be frank. Most of the teachers at this school are pretty set in their ways."—Kieran, Technology Teacher & FabLab Director
Lack of Expertise	"With digital technology moving as quickly as it is,...you don't really know how anything works all the way through [and] you then don't have the fluency or the expertise in order to help [students] with their frustrations."—Aidan, Middle School Science
Loss of Control	"Well, that meant giving up control. Right, there's one thing teachers want, it's control of their room."—Amanda, High School History & Humanities
Rethinking the Curriculum	"Everything's got to be different,...even starting with grouping kids by age. I think we can start to group kids by interests, and there'd be a whole lot more play going on."—Kieran, Technology Teacher & FabLab Director

Table 6. The Ways and Challenges: Contact Points Between Changing Teaching Practices.

The Ways *Strengthening digital media making and learning practices*	The Challenges *Resisting digital media making and learning practices*
Casual Conversations *Sharing and learning together*	Content vs. Making The Fit
Doing Projects *Engaging in individual practice*	Assessment *Recognizing the multiple shifts in teaching that are implied by evolving, making- infused practices*
Discovering Iterating *Releasing expectations of perfection*	
Experiencing Student Engagement *Vicarious enjoyment of empowerment*	Difficult Conversations *Not talking with each other about skepticisms, anxieties and concerns*
Administrative Disposition *Being told what to do*	Lack of Time *Feeling overwhelmed by requirements*
Following Students' Lead *Giving up control to others' interests; emergent curriculum*	Predispositions of Teacher *Holding to modes of learning from earlier in life, namely individualized study or nonparticipatory lecture-based learning*
Predispositions of the Teacher *Holding to modes of learning from earlier in life, namely making-infused play*	Lack of Expertise *Inadequate technical know-how with the specific tools and materials in makerspaces and FabLabs*
Directed Learning *Disciplined individual study or learning via tutorials or expert lectures*	
Reflecting on Experience *Individual, meditative, consolidation of learning*	Loss of Control *Not having the autonomy to direct teaching agendas and activities*
Workshops Out of School *Attendance at extracurricular maker education workshops*	Rethinking the Curriculum *Recognizing that changing individual prac- tices imply system-wide structural changes*
Professional Development in School *School-based workshops*	

· 8 ·

MUSIC, ART, ENGINEERING:
ENACTED ENCOUNTERS

In this chapter I'll use the typology of contact points (Table 6) as an interpretative guide to understand whether and how teaching practices are adapting to, integrating with, or resisting digital making and learning pedagogies. What follows are narrative vignettes of events and conversations I observed and participated in. I've crafted participants' stories so that a comparative analysis might call on features from the typology of Ways and Challenges. As discussed previously, the typology was gathered from what participants said and did while at school. In this sense, it might be loosely held as a catalog of teaching and learning configurations.

These vignettes were constructed with Laurel Richardson's (2000, 2002) conventions of autoethnography in mind, particularly, first-person point of view, chronological unfolding of the plot, scene descriptors, and reported speech that conveys a sense of presence and attachment while "[meeting] literary criteria of coherence, verisimilitude, and interest" (Richardson, 2000, p. 931). I'm guided in this use of narrative as an interpretative device by several examples from cultural studies, including Maxine Greene's (1995) evocations of fiction and poetry to explore the role of imagination in education; Steven Best and Douglas Kellner's (2001) use of Thomas Pynchon's 1973 novel *Gravity's Rainbow* to grapple with postmodernism; and Katherine

Hayles's (2012) analysis of data structures as narrative constructs in the epic poetry of Mark Danielewski's 2006 novel *Only Revolutions*. And from the field of science and technology studies, which might be closer to the milieu of my study, at least in spirit, another major influence is Bruno Latour's (1996) *Aramis, or, The Love of Technology*, a sociological study that investigated the collapse of an innovative urban rail system in France, told almost entirely in dialogue with a novelized, whodunit plot structure.

Interlude: A Lunchtime Scenario

This first vignette was constructed from field notes entered into my research journal immediately after the event occurred. There was no audio recording, so the scenario should not be taken as a transcript. Direct speech is indicated by italics rather than by double quotation marks. As a small story (Chase, 2011) that relates an unfolding event that happened in a specific locality, for a particular community—in this case, a teacher telling a story about teaching to an audience of teachers—I am aware of the various ways this construct invites bias and distortion. But I'm not after an objective window on an external reality. Rather, I hope the structure and content of the story will suggest, or make available, an "ordering of experience" (p. 421) that gathers some of the pragmatic indeterminacies of digital making and learning to our attention.

Scene

One afternoon in April I arrived at the North Building cafeteria to find lunch well in progress. As I walked in, an assistant administrator who also taught music waved me over to her table, where several other teachers and staff were already eating and talking. She was clearly excited and wanted to tell me a story. People budged sideways to make room at the table, and I squeezed in beside her. She apologized to the group for telling the story yet again, and began:

A group of eighth graders had come to the office earlier that morning to ask if they could get into the music room to work on a song, and she had given them permission to use the School of Rock room. *After all, music making is making too*, she said, turning toward me. I agreed.

She let them in the room, the students got to work, and she returned to her office. Just before lunch she went back to find them working on piano and percussion arrangements. They were ecstatic, she told us, *Though they had some work to do on their harmonies.*

As she was standing at the doorway of the music room, another student appeared, carrying a violin made of wood. Holding it up for all to see, the student explained that she had made the violin in the FabLab over the past several weeks and that, finally, it was done. With a huge smile, she dragged the bow across the strings and played a few notes of a children's song.

In the music room, everyone was astonished. And at the lunch table we were surprised as well, and filled the space between us with *oohs* and *aahs. She made a violin in the FabLab?* someone at the table exclaimed.

Without pausing, the storyteller said, *She was just about in tears, she was so happy.*

Around the table, I heard exclamations of approval and encouragement, especially from people who had just joined the table and had not heard the story in an earlier telling. The administrator turned to me and said, *That's really what all this making is about.*

Interpretation

This scenario illuminates some of the work that was going into shifting teaching practices from existing paradigms. Here, several contact points from the Ways point toward strengthening connections with project-based, making-infused practices, and at least one contact point from the Challenges seems to indicate resistance or at least to minimally destabilize that strengthening. To begin, I'll identify the contact points and describe the work I observed.

First, the story as a whole appears as an impromptu, casual conversation, identified as the most prevalent way of linking to making-infused teaching (from Table 4). We might say that the story was initiated and shaped primarily by the students in the music room and FabLab, but I want to consider it as encountered at the lunch table, because that was the only aspect of the event I directly observed. Further, the focus here is on the relationship of teachers to teaching practices, not on their students. For instance, as the storyteller spoke, listeners' responses (for example, the *oohs* and *aahs*) shaped her performance, which further shaped responses from the audience, and so on, recursively. Following from this amplification, the scenario appears to strengthen the collective commitment to learner-centeredness and making. That is, as a project-sharing pep talk (a sub-category of Casual Conversations), digital making and learning expands to include music as a material and form of making (*music making is making too*), and by the introduction of a new kind of object (a digitally fabricated violin). The surprise at the appearance of this new object, as figured by the questions and interruptions when it was mentioned, suggests that these teachers might suddenly have considered making in a new light, perhaps imagining themselves and their practice affected by digital making and learning pedagogies in a way they had previously discounted.

Secondly, the conversation as a whole (the telling of the story and the audience reaction) translated a direct experience with student engagement into an emotional testimonial in support of digital making and learning, which was explicitly acknowledged and applauded. Third, the storyteller's asides directed to me (*that's really what all this making is about*) could be taken as a strategic linking with my pseudo-administrative status within the school. Finally, the entire scenario, with its implicit emotional investment and payoff, was set in motion by an interest-driven student project—in other words, the administrator followed the students' lead.

Looking only at contact points that strengthen maker-oriented practices, we find that the storyteller has enlisted four of the Ways: Casual Conversation (in the form of a Pep Talk); Experiencing Student Engagement (students writing their own pop song and making their own musical instruments); Following Students' Lead (the episode began with a student request); and, finally, perhaps to a lesser extent, Administrative Disposition (she was an assistant administrator, and her references to me leveraged what everyone at the table knew—as a researcher, I had the head of school's explicit permission to be asking about project-based, making-infused teaching and learning). I would argue that identifying these four contact points indicates that maker-oriented teaching was stabilizing, or gaining presence at the school. Going further, we might wonder if lunchtime scenarios like this one were shaping the collective experience of knowing, as an action, perhaps disposing teachers to hold making-infused learning as normative. As such, it seems reasonable to suggest that as such conversations become more commonplace, existing practices and making-infused practices will interweave further, leading to the normalization of maker pedagogies across the curriculum.

This is where some messiness appears, however. A closer look at the conversation suggests that the first analysis might be too neat. What initially appears as a simple strengthening of maker-oriented teaching and learning might also contain some resistance to that strengthening. In the Challenges, Loss of Control was identified as a point of resistance. This point has appeared here as the speaker's comment about the girls needing to do *some work to do on their harmonies*. That is, in spite of following her students' lead and encouraging their interest-driven engagement, there remains something about the experience that drags back a little (perhaps an urge to control or manage the students' work?): Something about the event falls flat. This might be stating it too strongly, but the point remains—why say anything about a shortcoming?

As discussed, this contact point from the Challenges (Loss of Control) goes to an important affordance of traditional pedagogies: They center on the figure of the teacher, who is accountable for what happens in the classroom, which makes standardization of content scalable, and theoretically achievable. Julie, the middle school head, admitted that since teachers had by and large been trained to stay in control of lessons and learning objectives, asking them to hold loosely to outcomes in a makerspace was deeply challenging. Aidan told me that, to some of his colleagues, making-infused education looks "almost like moderated or controlled chaos, where kids are up out of their seats…[which] sometimes looks a little funky to people who aren't used to that." As such, I would suggest that the storyteller's comment implies at least some resistance to fully adopting maker-infused teaching, or at least some skepticism about simply letting students explore their interests entirely on their own terms. Perhaps it springs from a teacher-knows-best stance, even if only vestigial or only enacted in the comment itself. Nevertheless, there it is, muddying the clarity of the analysis.

This muddiness, in fact, points to a strength of the typology. As I've shown, the work of connecting teaching practices with digital making and learning was happening in different ways throughout the school, but not uniformly, and certainly not under the direction of any individual actor. As Julie had explained, the administration's approach was to "make it up as we go along"; and as Bradly had admitted, coaxing new practice from the faculty was frustratingly slow ("I still see people lecturing for 75 minutes, and I'm like, 'Are you kidding me?'"). In the lunchtime scenario, teachers explored interconnections via their closely attended practice. That is, these teachers cared about their students' well-being, and expected to be involved in nurturing that well-being, even to point of spending their lunchtime sharing strategies and stories. Not only do we glimpse the empathy and power of their engagement at this cafeteria table, we also glimpse some of the internal contradictions they're experiencing. Frankly, the advent of new arrangements of tools excite them, but the new pedagogies those arrangements afford worry them. In other words, the evolution of practice was not a straight-ahead progression. If the typology of Ways and Challenges is useful here, I would argue, it's because we can chart some of these contradictions onto the narrative without collapsing it into a clean reckoning, or noncontradiction. This ability to deal with indeterminacy, as a structural feature of the event we're trying to understand, shows us maker pedagogies simultaneously stabilizing and destabilizing at the school, an interpretation that enables, or makes available, a robust description of intersecting and interweaving practices.

Two Art Teachers and an Engineer

The paradox of an indeterminacy that increases stability appeared elsewhere as well. An example comes from the practices of two art teachers and an engineering teacher. A comparison draws connections that highlight a characteristic of digital making and learning's new ethos: teaching as an activity that is distributed between human and nonhuman actors, where the teacher and the materials are symmetrically agential in bringing practice to presence.

Vanessa's Material Insight

The first vignette comes from an episode related in Chapter 6 to illustrate Casual Conversations. It concerns an insight arrived at during an in-depth interview with Vanessa, a middle school art teacher. In Chapter 6 I argued that the way Vanessa came to her new understanding about her teaching resembled material learning, introduced earlier as a kind of learning and knowing that is recursive and co-emergent with play and exploration. In Chapter 3 I likened material learning to Vygotsky's (1978) notion of a child's gesture that inclines human beings toward symbolic tool use. And in Chapter 6's interpretation of Vanessa's insight I called on presentational knowing, or knowing without thinking, as described by Kasl and Yorks (2012), and on Bamberger and Schön's (1983) reflective conversations with materials, to explore how Vanessa's insight matters to making-infused practice. I'll briefly reiterate that episode so that its salient details are available to the other two narratives.

Vanessa. A middle school art teacher with more than 10 years experience, Vanessa wanted the school's makerspaces to be used across the curriculum. An insight into achieving this goal emerged from a story about helping fourth graders understand the scale of their bodies—feet, hands, head—in order to draw pictures of themselves as Revolutionary War soldiers for a stage presentation. My conversation with Vanessa took several detours, touching on math, creativity, scale and proportion, digital 3D design and scanning, and the differences between teaching at various developmental levels. At one point, Vanessa displayed some frustration about her inability to control aspects of the project, such as interactions with faculty from different content domains, and particularly with the way her students drew their hands. She said, "I must have done 10 drawings [explaining] how to measure from your wrists to the top of your middle finger....So I kept doing that, and they still were sort of rushing through the hand." Later in our conversation she found herself speculating about a way to fix the problem, so that the hand remained in proportion to the body. As she puzzled the implications of her new idea, she suddenly became excited, saying, "I just came up with that!...I might try that next year."

Vanessa's insight is an example of knowing that appears suddenly and organically, from within the meandering flow of one's work with a material. In this case, it emerged from the material of our conversation, becoming present as we explored it. That is, Vanessa was not looking for insight; we had not approached the conversation as a problem-solving exercise. Rather, her innovation appeared as she turned ideas over in her head, as she was sharing them with me. I am reminded of the way knowing sometimes occurs in an artist's studio, for example, when a flow state (Csikszentmihalyi, 2008) has been reached, or when, after prolonged grappling with a difficult problem, insight suddenly emerges (Irvine, 2014). Here, an object—a way to teach drawing—was shaped by its evolution, and its form appeared by surprise. For Vanessa, the result amplified the entanglement of personalized making (the Redcoat figure as a trace of students' own bodies), materials and tools (paint, paper, glue), and cultural constructs (the American Revolution), to open a space where students might learn to be historians rather than about isolated topics.

Thomas's Assessment Conundrum

This second vignette was first reported in Chapter 7 to illustrate a difficulty with assessment that teachers mentioned as a Challenge to making-infused pedagogies (Table 5). It comes from an observation that was not audio recorded. As with the lunchtime conversation, speech is italicized rather than enclosed in double quote marks.

Thomas. Formerly a chemistry teacher, Thomas had been asked by the school leadership to teach a project-based engineering elective for high school seniors. He told me that the students had surprised him with the diversity of their projects: a box that played music based on the Dow Jones average; dice that would Tweet the high roller's score; a thermos that sensed the level of the liquid inside; and an umbrella that lit up in the rain. But Thomas was concerned; unlike AP physics and honors chemistry, the assessment rubric was not clear, and he didn't know how to evaluate these projects—were they useful enough? Fun enough? In class he asked a student, *Do you have art this year?* Later, he wondered how art played into what students needed to know. Most projects seemed inspired by an engineering sensibility, like a coffee cup that sensed the temperature of the coffee, and he told me that he didn't know how to encourage an artistic sensibility, that he didn't think he even understood it. Vanessa once guided him in these questions, but now he was on his own. And he was exhausted. *I am struggling a little bit*, he admitted. *I'm going to assist 11 kids in building their own projects, and they have no idea what they're going to do. So that's me making 11 projects.* I asked him what he needed in order to be ready for the next iteration of the class. *A one-year sabbatical*, he said.

Emma's Quantum Curiosity

This final vignette is drawn from an interview with Emma, head of the art department and a high school art teacher herself, with 20 years teaching experience. Of all the participants I interacted with, Emma had the most eccentric collection of curiosities to offer the nascent curriculum taking shape at the school—science, art, technology, history, and language—but she voiced a hard-to-pin-down resistance to maker-oriented pedagogy. This interview was not audio recorded; instead, I took notes on a yellow pad of paper as we spoke. As above, direct statements are italicized.

Emma. On a bright spring day, in her airy studio classroom on the top floor of one of the townhouses, in front of huge windows overlooking leafy treetops, with dappled reflections sparkling on the crown moldings and high ceilings above us, our conversation cascaded across a free-ranging menagerie of wonders, touching on the invention of the telegraph, Boo Radley's tree, Dennis Oppenheim's Mickey Mouse virus, string theory, President Garfield's assassination, QR codes as student art, Maya Lin's Vietnam Memorial, and the moral imperative for teaching high school girls about quantum entanglement.

Afterwards, I wrote in my field notes that the interview had been one of the most engaging of the entire year.

Emma told me that she avoided conversations about making because she was skeptical of the maker movement. She said she felt peripheral to the conversations around her, as if she was on a different *wavelength* from her colleagues. Among her objections was the belief that educators should start with an idea, or a movement between ideas, and explore tools in relation to that movement. But, she said, conversations about making too often began from the tools. Her impatience with her colleagues' infatuation with the FabLab was palpable: *Start with the idea, then go back to the tools,* she said.

To illustrate, she showed me a semester-long student project. Beginning with an artwork held by a famous museum, the student explored and responded with her own drawings, sculptures, digitally mediated composites, and a series of ink prints on fine paper. The process was informed and alternately accelerated or slowed down by an evolving dialogue with her peers and her teacher—i.e., Emma. Sorting through the student's multipart pictorial responses, Emma explained that the student had learned *how to think, to take risks, to have the courage to keep going, to get herself unblocked.* Gesturing at the variety of art the student had produced, Emma asked me, *How do you Google that?* When I asked how she might explain what she was doing to the math department, she laughed and said she didn't know. *You have to be a little embarrassed,* she said. *That's when you know you're on to something good.*

On leaving the studio, it occurred to me that Emma's passion and curiosity offered a challenge to the maker conversations I'd been charting across the school. Why had it taken until the end of May to finally sync up with her for this brief, unrecorded interview? On that point, Emma said, *Yeah, I blew you off.*

Losing Control to Gain Traction

Each of these narratives enlists similar contact points in order to enact and resist making-infused practice. From the Ways, these include Casual Conversations, Doing Projects, Following Students' Lead, and Discovering Iterating; and from the Challenges, Assessment, Difficult Conversations, and Loss of Control. First, we should recognize that each practice was fully invested in a project-based learning trajectory that prompted engagement in long-term, iterative learning and knowing. Vanessa's fourth graders followed their Revolutionary War figures across content domains to end up in a stage show at the end of the fall term; and Emma and Thomas's high school seniors committed themselves to semester-long explorations of making and remaking. Secondly, each vignette emphasizes the lead of the students, though to a different degree. Emma explicitly and enthusiastically encouraged her students' artistic responses, and then followed alongside them. Vanessa closely attended to her fourth graders' learning in order to puzzle through the challenges they encountered, though she did not encourage individual pathways, for example by prompting students to follow their own fancy in the design of their stage avatar (by constructing a dinosaur, for example, or something other than a Revolutionary War soldier). And Thomas, wildly successful in helping to launch independent learning trajectories, became discouraged when he couldn't keep up with his students in the way he thought he should.

The salient point here is that each teacher encountered similar configurations of practice, based on the contact points identified, although no two practices were identical in content, age group, outcomes, or the tools and materials available. This leads me to ask what made each teacher's response so different? What was it about these practices that gave each its distinctive affordances? That is, in these assemblages, the courses variously known as elementary art integration, creative engineering, and advanced high school fine art, all situated in an ecology that privileged project-based, making-infused pedagogies and had invested in the tools and materials to support those pedagogies, how am I to understand the various trajectories I observed?

This surfaces another point of comparison and highlights a contrast. Each teacher encountered Loss of Control, and each responded differently. Yet each also recognized, at least implicitly, that Casual Conversation mitigated the challenge. For Vanessa, her inability to control the drawing process found voice in the undirected flow of our conversation; Emma said that student empowerment came from a meandering dialogue that carried her and her students close to embarrassment; and Thomas, surrounded by runaway student engagement, found the need to retain control exhausting and nearly debilitating, especially in the absence of Vanessa's conversational guidance. What kind of learning and knowing is going on here? Each teacher appeared to be stumbling through their practice, discovering it as they encountered it. It occurs to me that each was dealing implicitly with the paradox of collective or distributed agency, an affordance of digital materiality that is supposedly calling school reform toward a new ethos or new culture of leaning. Who's in charge? Who sets the course? These teachers each replied differently. Vanessa went with the flow to serendipitously arrive at an answer; Emma let herself drift with and through multiple channels of potential, confident that answers would appear, spontaneously and just in time; and Thomas discovered suddenly that he didn't understand what was going on—how could he assess the learning and help his students if he wasn't in control? Each teacher recognized that releasing to the flow of practice could amplify student engagement, though it might also invite uncertainty or anxiety. With less subtlety, the dynamic I observed might be described as one where to lose control is to gain traction. This clarifies the conflict. Teachers aren't supposed to lose control, but every teacher longs for more engagement. Here, the art teachers give over to the contradiction and become emboldened; the engineering teacher, on the other hand, struggles, and wants to escape, wondering if "art" might reinvigorate him, even as knows he doesn't understand what he means by that idea.

This paradox is similar to the one explored in the Lunchtime Scenario: the indeterminacy of stabilization and destabilization occurring together. But in relation to Vanessa, Emma, and Thomas, losing control to gain traction also reminds me of Aidan's chaotic classroom where good learning looks a little "funky to people who aren't used to it"; Kieran's age-agnostic classroom where "there'd be a whole lot more play going on…very messy, [and] maybe seem a bit chaotic"; Beatrice's need to refuse "roadmaps" in order to "reinvent teaching and learning"; and Julie's empathy with teachers' anxiety over the "ambiguity of not having everything mapped out": She said, "it's hard for us to transition to this place where we don't know where we're going exactly." Further, losing control to gain traction reminds me of the paradox of decentered embodiment as an affordance of digital materiality, where the appearance of diminished individual agency enhances the potential agency of the collective. Is this what these teachers are experiencing?

One way to get at this dynamic is to hold loosely to how any individual teacher's agency is described. Frankly, charting my observations of each teacher across the territory of his or her practice suggests no other sensible conclusion: Too much was going on for any one individual to reasonably claim responsibility for it all. True, there was a teacher (Vanessa, Thomas, Emma), but also true, there were lots of teachers (Thomas taught Grace; Kieran taught everyone; Vanessa used to teach Thomas), and students (who were leading and teaching their teachers), and administrators (pushing, pulling, and cajoling teachers to join them on the path to digital making and leaning). As well, there were tools, materials, chaotic calendar schedules, pressures from parents (whose outdated notions of education had to be remediated), and those convoluted, labyrinthine townhouses, with all their architectural oddities and surprises. More to the point, these teachers themselves were aware of the collective and cooperatively emergent nature of their role in the practice that gathered around them—that's why the lunch schedules had been arranged, so they could talk with each other.

Now, to be sure, no one specifically articulated decentered embodiment in the way I've gathered it here—after all, it's a term I invented while working on this book! But that's not precisely the way I'm pursuing this question of agency. Rather, I'm pointing to the iMac handle, where you feel the change in the relationship even if you can't articulate it, much less specify the materiality of that relationship. Considered further, in fact, the kind of agency I observed appears similar to material learning, which you'll remember is my term for what sometimes happens in art studios or creative workshops, where learners give over to tools and materials in order to synchronize their individual directedness with the affordances of particular relational assemblages—clay, tempera paint, photography, poetry, or code. In this, I'm moved to describe the teaching I observed and participated in as an enacted encounter with materiality.

In arriving at this phrase, *an enacted encounter with materiality*, I feel a snap. Unexpectedly, there's a falling into place, an ordering of impressions and sensations, a satisfying thump, click, release.

When I teach art, writing, or creative coding, I play with different ways of articulating this phenomenon of order achieved, or relational stability, but the actual sense of it appears to be fundamentally extralinguistic, like what a potter feels when the clay centers on the wheel, or a mathematician senses when the proof works, or a poet when the poem tells you that it's done. In studios and seminar rooms I coax students towards the *snap*, never knowing if or how it'll appear, or how to explain what they're looking for before it comes up on them. The challenge, for me, is to coax them to keep working until they feel it for themselves, in their bodies. Snap. That's the word I use, because I like the crisp way it bursts from my mouth, and the shape of it on the page.

In this particular case, the snap happened as I was teasing and tugging impressions from my notes and transcripts, as I was writing memos, emails, and the initial interpretative reports that preceded this book. I don't know why this phrase works so well for me—*enacted encounter with materiality*—at least not consciously. Perhaps it's because it connects two notions of agency that otherwise exclude each other. *Enact* implies multiple actors coordinating multiple kinds of work, but to *encounter* something is to come upon it by surprise, implying a different kind of directedness. Combining these words suggests multiple actors doing something together in a way that is both focused and open to serendipity. But further, *materiality* implies entanglement with the affordances of tools and materials, the relational assemblage of matter, duration, relevance, and affect that I've described in Chapter 3. Taken all together, these terms, this phrase, makes agency available as a relational assemblage that paradoxically but accurately describes the teaching I observed.

The Language of Interpretation

At this point in the story, I want to pause for a brief digression on the role of writing in the way I'm telling it. Landing at this phrase, *enacted encounter with materiality*, which feels utterly accurate to my experience during this study, introduces an anomalous artifact, one that needs to be called out. As indicated in Chapter 4 and elsewhere, the methodology that guided this study rests on a set of assumptions and strategies that invite interpretation as co-emergent with activity in and with materials. In this instance, that implies that the material of the book itself, which is language, is a co-actant in the research process. This recursive and puzzling relationship begs a pragmatic but ironic question: Where are these interpretations coming from? From data collected at the study site? From the literature reviewed in this book? Are they internal echoes from my inadequate attempts to translate what I cannot put into words?

This self-referential critique of language encompasses writing as a research activity, following Richardson's (2000, 2002) evocation of ethnography as a creative practice. Earlier, I discussed this idea in the abstract, but with the arrival of this phrase, the abstraction keys to a specific object, or artifact (the phrase itself), so it seems prudent to discuss it again. To be certain, I might have stumbled onto a different string of words, because there's arbitrariness to material learning, after all, but since this particular arrangement of syllables resonates so strongly, I will stick with it, and hope that by making the process of its manufacture available to your critique I might engender your trust, or at least a suspension of your disbelief. In fact, it might yet turn out that this is not precisely the right language. To keep some options open, therefore, I want to briefly explore the language of actor-network theory, in case I need to poach from its rich and varied lexicon.

Fenwick and Edwards (2012) claim that "ANT's language can open new questions and its approaches can sense phenomena in rich ways that discern the difficult ambivalences, messes, multiplicities and contradictions that are embedded in so many education issues" (p. ix). This focus on the *language* of research is an overriding concern of ANT scholars. In their ethnographic study of neuroendocrinology at the Salk Institute, Latour and Woolgar (1979) observe that laboratory results are founded on the particularity of scientific language, an insight that launched the field of science and technology studies (STS) and began a cascade of neologisms, like "actant, network, translation and intermediaries" (Fenwick et al., 2011, p. 110). That is, from the beginning, ANT has focused on how *description* constructs the world in particular ways. As such, one goal of ANT-inflected research is to question the language that method itself relies upon. For example, in her study of virtual reality technologies in Danish fourth-grade classrooms, Estrid Sørensen (2009) argues that her "vocabulary and metaphors contribute" to understanding "the network pattern of relations" in the school (p. 85). She writes: "The metaphor of fluidity allows us to think about technology as changing and varying. It teaches us that changing and varying processes can also be stable, and that stability may lie elsewhere than in immutability and control—that it may lie in the process of change" (p. 85).

Earlier, I introduced John Law's (2004) argument that research requires nuanced, varied, and messier language. The problem with social science research, he writes, is that it tries to clean up and smooth out the inconsistencies and contradictions it finds. But the world is not like that: "Simple clear descriptions don't work if what they are describing is not itself very coherent. The very attempt to be clear simply increases the mess" (p. 2). In his opinion, a more powerful approach includes "metaphors and images for what is impossible or barely possible, unthinkable or almost unthinkable. Slippery, indistinct, elusive, complex, diffuse, messy, textured, vague, unspecific, confused, disordered, emotional, painful, pleasurable, hopeful, horrific, lost, redeemed, visionary, angelic, demonic, mundane, intuitive, sliding and unpredictable,… each is a way of trying to open space for the indefinite" (p. 6).

ANT's description of the *indefinite* in ways that hold it open to practice is why Fenwick and Edwards (2012) "believe that ANT offers truly important insights about the process and objects of education" (p. ix). But ANT's neologisms and unfamiliar word usage require researchers (and readers) to keep adjusting their footing in order to keep their balance in an unfamiliar terrain. Up to this point in the book I have not deployed much, if any, of the specific and precise terminology that ANT researchers have introduced, though a concern with the efficacy and suitability of the words I'm using is obviously on my mind. A glossary of ANT's conceptual terminology is beyond the scope of this book, and perhaps even antithetical to ANT's commitment to emergent relationality. On this point, Fenwick and Edwards (2012) have suggested, "It may be accurate to think of ANT as a virtual 'cloud,' continually moving, shrinking and stretching, dissolving in any attempt to grasp it firmly" (p. ix). These caveats notwithstanding, some key ANT terminology that has informed my thinking include:

Actant. Jane Bennett (2010) defines actant as "a source of action that can be either human or nonhuman; it is that which has efficacy, can *do* things, has sufficient coherence to make a difference,…alter the course of events" (p. ix). In effect, Latour's (2005) word makes available a conundrum at the center of science and technology studies, or STS; namely, that empirical appraisals of complex ecologies require researchers to suspend predispositions toward who or what participant or object in a given assemblage has the agency to act. Rather, ANT researchers are admonished to simply follow the actants (as if it were simple!) and trace the associations they encounter.

Materiality. This word resonates with ANT researchers as "a way of thinking about material…as a continuously enacted relational effect. The implication is that materials do not exist in and of themselves but are endlessly generated" (Law, 2004, p. 161). This sense of materiality is broadly consistent with the descriptions I've already explored in the book.

Network. For ANT, *network* refers to a relationship between actants. That is, ANT does not refer to or distinguish between digital and nondigital networks as such, but holds all networks as "an assemblage or gathering of materials brought together and linked through processes of translation, that together perform a particular enactment" (Fenwick & Edwards, 2012, p. xiii).

Network effects. ANT conceptualizes actants as assemblages, following Deleuze and Guattari's (1987) sense of relational unfoldings of more or less stable potentials, as I've discussed previously. A *network effect* asks, in a sense, how objects hold together when everything around them is changing. By analogy, consider that table in front of you—how did it come to presence in the precise way that you now experience? In addition to tools, materials and craftsmanship, a robust answer to that question would have to chart an extensive catalog of other relationships, including branding, labor and economic markets, and even the historical contingencies that produced the notion of table (and the house to put it in). For ANT, "all objects, as well as all persons, knowledge and locations, are relational effects" (Fenwick & Edwards, 2012, p. xv).

Symmetry. The complexity generated by holding everything of interest as a network effect requires grit and honesty from the researcher. That is, where does interpretation end? Where does the researcher cut the network relationships and decide that this or that component of an assemblage falls outside the sphere of interest? First, ANT researchers realize that the cut itself is an arbitrary relationship that must be called out. Second, to manage some of that arbitrariness, and to hold research accountable to the assumptions it builds upon, ANT investigators assume that all relations are more or less equivalently agential, until proven otherwise. In other words, ANT begins by adhering to "the principle that the same kind of explanation or account should be given for all the phenomena to be explained" (Law, 2004, p. 164). *Symmetry*, in this instance, means "human and non-human elements [are] treated equally" (Fenwick et al., 2011, p. 96).

Translation. To address questions about cultural or technological systems, ANT researchers ask how particular assemblages hold together, and how they fall apart. The tried and true method for doing ANT involves suspending preconceptions about particular actants and simply listening and watching as networks reveal themselves through the associations, or trails, that actants leave behind them. *Translation* is "a process whereby two actors become related in such a way that one actor borrows some of the other's strength" (Blok & Jensen, 2011, p. 173), in order to establish or disintegrate an association. To put it another way, translation is "what happens when entities come together and connect, changing one another in the process of forming links" (Fenwick et al., 2011, p. 98). As such, it is only "through translation [that] actors associate with other actors to form joint vectors of agency" (Koyama, 2009, p. 26).

With these basic definitions, then, in the language of ANT, the typology of contact points can be described as a catalog of translations that build and unbuild network effects between actants—teachers, administrators, students, FabLabs, makerspaces, and the multitude of tools and materials encountered in those spaces. With the narrative vignettes in this chapter, and the interpretative coloring I've layered over them, I'm attempting to describe maker education with the kind of complexity that the literature of ANT has made available in its analyses of complex technical systems, as I've previewed above. My hope is that this exploration of the language of ANT, even if cursory and incomplete, will clarify my interpretative process by drawing your attention to the question of language. I don't claim a pedigree as an ANT researcher, but deploying its language here helps me articulate some of the conundrums I found myself confronting during my study.

Condensate

Law (2004) cautions that simplistic rubrics tempt researchers to clean up the mess they encounter, making an even bigger mess. I would argue that, in this chapter, the typology of the Ways and Challenges holds together because it lets the mess stand. That is, enlisting the typology here did not produce simplistic readings of complex events, but rather multiple and indeterminate descriptions. In fact, the typology precipitated at least two somewhat nonintuitive findings.

First, to gain traction, teachers are losing control, which implies that, rather than a purposeful activity, teaching is the situated enactment of a collective that invites surprise, affect, and even embarrassment. Not only do these descriptions counter normative expectations of teaching, they also appear self-contradictory, even fuzzy. Things are moving opposite to themselves, simultaneously coming into presence and going away. What might be gained by an interpretative move that amplifies such a blurry trajectory?

My reply again recalls Mol's (2002) study of arteriosclerosis. In her final paragraphs she gathers her contradictory and indeterminate analysis of medical practice to a conclusion by refusing to conclude, close down, wrap up, or extinguish the questions she had been exploring from page 1. What is arteriosclerosis? She keeps open the possibility of not knowing. More precisely, she shows that arteriosclerosis isn't one thing but many, for many different reasons—a choreography of overlapping ontologies implying separate but overlapping treatments, risks, benefits, costs, histories, genders, and social hierarchies, among other things. Forcing a collapse of those overlapping ontologies, she suggests, might entail enormous cost. In the hospital, she writes, doubt and confidence alternate, but the question of *what to do* is always foremost in the minds of the surgeons, clinicians, pathologists, and patients, as well as every other stakeholder caught up in the ebb-and-flow enactment of medicine. In medical practice, she argues, almost counterintuitively, doubt is pragmatic because it keeps options open. And as long as illness is cast as *living with* disease, there is the chance that something else can be done to bring the *good* of healthy living to presence. In the hospital, the question is how to grapple with doubt, to live with it, to hold it open so as to not extinguish the fuzziness that it makes available. "Somehow we must come to terms with the fact that we live in an underdetermined world, where doubt can always be raised. Somehow we must learn to understand how it is that, given this possibility, we can still act" (p. 165). In medicine, what to do remains a call to action.

And in schools: What to do? How to educate? To teach? How can we know that we've taken the right path? As I followed participants and watched their work unfold, these questions were foremost in my mind. But in writing about the study, including this book, I could not puzzle my way out of the conundrum I'd encountered—what good could come from this paradoxical indeterminacy enframing teaching? Then, unexpectedly, after completing the first draft of this book, I encountered Mol's (2002) study. In fact, she is not the only one praising doubt (for example, Law, 2004, who holds doubt at the foundation of his method assemblage, and whose work was already interwoven with mine). But for whatever reason—the way she keyed doubt to practice, perhaps?—I found in her book an echo of how my interpretations had ordered my impressions, and a suggestion about why indeterminacy mattered: to keep options open. In schooling, perhaps as much as in medicine, what to do relies on sustaining openness.

In remaining open to the indeterminacy, I encountered what initially appeared as evidence of teachers' participation in, or refusal to participate in, digital making pedagogies. As such, it seemed, teachers talked about what they did as teachers. But as I attended to their words and actions more closely, their comments and behaviors took on added complexities. Suddenly, it occurred to me that teachers were not in control of their practices. Rather, as Latour and Woolgar (1979) had described scientists at the Salk Institute, teachers worked with multiple human and nonhuman actors—faculty colleagues, students, administrators, the tools and materials of the FabLab, video lab, maker space, and classroom—to enact network effects that *looked like teaching*.

The appearance of this second, surprising, and unintuitive idea recasts individual agency as a choreography of assemblages. Instead of watching teachers push and pull on their practice with intentionality, or purposefulness, I began to understand their work as a collective translation of network effects—that is, practice was pulling and pushing on them. As such, the notion of contact points between practices suggested that practice be considered a thing in itself, and the collective activity of the school an entangled choreography of different but related things. In turn, this abundant *thingness* cast pedagogy as a materiality, and teaching, or the actions of the teacher, as an enacted encounter with that materiality. And then further, keeping the language of ANT available suggested symmetry between actants, or in this case, between teachers and practice, and implied descriptions of teaching practice without requiring a teacher at its center.

While this second finding initially appeared even stranger than the first, the typology of contact points invited such a description because of the conceptual and pragmatic shift that tools and materials are apt to exhibit. As illustrated with the stepladder analogy in Chapter 3, at first the typology appeared as a descriptor or indicator of what teachers did, assisting the work of interpreting observations, as a stepladder assists in the work of organizing cabinets and plates in the vertical dimension. But then a shift occurred, and the typology appeared as a material that actants used to build their practices. That is, Aidan connected to the "realm of possibility [by]...face-to-face blogging"; Grace connected with tinkering because of the paperclip activity; and Susan connected to iterating because of a paper-engineering project. At the same time, Isabella pushed away because "the content we want to teach... can be at odds with the type of learning the digital fabrication involves"; and Thomas said, "I don't have the personal time I need....It's hard when you're a full-time teacher to put in what the course needs" (these examples are from Tables 4 and 5). In these and so many other statements and actions, including the vignettes in this chapter, teachers invoked Ways and Challenges to move toward or away from digital making and learning. In other words, the typology was not only an indicator, like a weather vane, but also a tool-material, like a hammer or wrench, a roll of tape, or a bag of nails. This vacillation in the ontology of the Ways and Challenges raises another question: If an effective making-infused practice relies on sustaining such indeterminacies, how can we keep the contradictions in play when teachers and practice swap and share agency?

This might be where the Möbius strip becomes useful. Just as a twisted band of paper must be held loosely in order to enact its puzzling topology—so that binary relationships might appear both separate and identical—the metaphor of the Möbius strips suggests that the typology of contact points is capable of sustaining relational complexities if it is held loosely. This arrangement recalls Law's (2002) notion of fractional coherence, a way to gather multiplicities without collapsing the assemblage into a singularity. It also reprises Lakoff and Johnson's (1980) ontological-substance metaphors, where abstractions are mapped to physical objects to help us handle slippery effects. For instance, in their example, mapping *mind*, an abstraction, to an object in the world, such as *machine*, yields metaphors that point to the physicality of thinking, such as *We're crunching the numbers,* and *I'm just not wired that way.* For Lakoff and Johnson, these word-maps are the critical tools and materials that enable us to talk to each other across the chasms of our irreconcilable life-worlds.

Similarly, the typology casts binary oppositions as stable relations: Teachers and practices are symmetrical actants *and* teachers are individual craftspeople. Or, teachers are losing control *and* gaining traction. In other words, by not demanding one-to-one alignment of these overlaps, by not insisting that teaching (or preparing to be a teacher) is only one thing, the indeterminacy holds certainty at bay and keeps our options open. This, I would argue, is a necessary ingredient in the on going conversation about what to do in education, especially today as the affordances of new digital tools and materials imply new relationships of empowerment for knowers and learners.

My goal in chapter has been to read these narratives of practice through the emergent typology of Ways and Challenges: Do these terms, paradoxes and contradictions hold up? Do these narratives stick together? I would argue that they do, though not in a simplistically linear way. That is, to my mind, the actants described here, these multiple assemblages of multiple actors, agencies, and modes of knowing (human and nonhuman; individual and communal; interior and exterior), suggest that digital making and learning is coming to presence at the school as a dynamic fluctuation, an oscillating stability, or a stable wobbling. This would be a third finding to weave in with the first two—teachers lose ground to gain traction; and teachers and practice, as symmetrical actants, work together to enact network effects that look like teaching. But frankly, in the midst of so many observations and spontaneous conversations, it was impossible to grasp whether practices were moving toward or away from digital making and learning, like trying to determine whether the tide is coming in or going out by watching the waves for just 5 minutes. And while I'm confident in the pragmatic usefulness of the typology as a tool, we might need a different kind of gathering, or mode of analysis, to get a grip on *how* digital making practices were translating knowing and teaching. In the next two chapters I'll construct and explore another narrative, but one that's more robust, like a denser weave, or a thicker condensate, in an attempt to trace the fine-grain detail of a single practice, of one teacher's learning trajectory.

· 9 ·

HISTORY AND RECONCEPTUALIZED OBJECTS

This chapter tells a story about Amanda and her practice. She is the high school history and humanities teacher whose work has been discussed several times in the book. I selected her practice as the focus for this chapter because of the pedagogical moves I observed during observations in her classroom, during interviews, in casual conversations in the hallways, in faculty meetings, and from dozens of other impromptu interactions. To my mind, these moves reprised characteristics of the ethos or new culture of digital making, learning, and knowing as gathered in the framework-assemblage (Table 2), even though she did not use the tools and materials in the FabLabs or makerspaces. As such, she and her practice presented an opportunity to question the question that launched this study: Does learning to teach with the tools and materials in makerspaces and FabLabs change teaching? In this instance, teaching seemed to be changing, but the tools weren't being used. This paradox invited closer exploration.

As in Chapter 8, the story constructed here follows narrative inquiry methodology that positions the writing process as interwoven with the writing product (Britzman, 1995; Chase, 2011; Richardson, 2000, 2002; Riessman, 2008). To be clear, the following is an interpretative and analytic construct derived from my experience, not a documentary report of phenomena *out there*. I recognize that describing the messy, decentered assemblages brought to presence by human and nonhuman actants is difficult, but I am persuaded by the sociomaterial literature of ANT and narrative inquiry to make the attempt. In this, I am trying to bring into view a complex phenomenon—a teaching practice—in a way that invites coherence from the entanglements that comprise it: teachers and ways of teaching, administrators, students, tools, materials, classrooms, makerspaces, widely separated school buildings, and changing schedules. As such, the sense-making on view here is combinatory: In writing it, I am hoping to understand it.

Amanda's Practice

Amanda's contributions to this research have been discussed above, for example, with multiple comments illustrating the Ways and Challenges (Chapters 6 and 7), and with her story about the Jimmy Heath concert (Chapter 4), where she drew a comparison between the foundations of the industrial age and today's postindustrial era, which helped me clarify the direction of the study. My goal here is to describe her practice in a more holistic way than these previously reported anecdotes have been able to provide. To construct this broader vignette I have pulled from two in-depth interviews, two classroom observations, one humanities team meeting, numerous casual conversations in the hallways, stairwells, and lunchrooms, and written materials Amanda provided, including handouts she gave to students and email communications directly with me. In addition, Amanda has read versions of the narrative and has discussed it with me, helping to shape it along the way. While this is not to claim that the narrative represents some disembodied truth to experience (nothing of the sort, actually), it might go some way toward ensuring that the story of her practice, as a collaborative construct, feels broadly accurate to both her and my experiences.

Background

Amanda teaches upper-school history and humanities. She is in her mid-fifties, of Anglo-European descent, and has taught at the school for 16 years. Teaching high school was not her original goal, however. Rather, after completing a Ph.D. in church history at Union Theological Seminary in New York City, she expected to return to college and postgraduate teaching and research. Instead, she crossed paths with the leadership at the school and discovered that they shared compatible needs and goals: The school needed a history teacher, and she needed a job.

For a short time at the beginning of her teaching career, Amanda taught both religion and history, but for the past 14 years she has taught history exclusively. Her courses focus on ancient world civilizations for ninth graders, modern world history for tenth graders, U.S. history for juniors, and China, as an elective, for seniors. About 12 years ago she was on the team that rebuilt the ninth-grade curriculum and subsequently integrated English, world history, and art history into humanities, a year-long multidimensional course. Amanda told me the goal of the course was to build a "foundation of both content and skills for all the ninth graders,…so that…by the time they finish ninth grade, everybody's got a common standard. [For example], when you say 'read,' what does that mean? When you say 'take notes,' what does that mean? When you say 'look at evidence,' what does that mean?" To achieve that goal, Amanda told me, the humanities faculty as a whole—two English teachers, two history teachers, and an art history teacher—collaborated closely so that students encounter overlaps between subjects, and so those overlaps might amplify and accentuate the basic skills they are expected to learn. In practice, this meant that teachers coordinate their schedules so that transitions between learning units are aligned, and so that conflicts between assignments, tests, and projects are minimized. Due in part to the reorganization of the school's schedule during the year I conducted this study, among other challenges, however, this minimization of conflict remained an ideal rather than an achieved operating principle.

Curator's Choice/Curator's Gallery

A major element of ninth-grade humanities, and certainly *the* major project of the year, was Curator's Choice/Curator's Gallery. This 13-week, multipart research and exhibition collaboration was designed and coordinated by Amanda's colleague, Mia, the art history teacher. The rest of the humanities team—two English teachers (Earl and Barbara) and two history teachers (Amanda and Mark)—were deeply invested in it as well. The project launched at the start of the spring term, just after winter break, with students choosing an artifact from the ancient or medieval world—for example, a devotional statue from early Greek Christianity, a decorated war helmet from pre-Renaissance Europe, an ink painting from Song Dynasty China, or any other object that resonated with the student, as long as it could be found in the collection of the nearby art museum where art history class was held once a week.

After students had chosen their objects, they began researching them from an art historical perspective, keeping present in their minds the literature and world civilizations history courses they were taking simultaneously. The first goal—the Curator's Choice part of the project—was to write a research paper discussing their individual objects in light of a theme they had established as a group. That is, not only were they to consider their objects as discrete artifacts, they also needed to construct a conceptual link between all the objects in their group, and this link had to sustain and inform their research and writing. The second task—the Curator's Gallery half—was to aggregate what they had learned about their own objects with what the group knew about each others' objects and design a museum exhibition that interpreted the entangled relationships between them.

Throughout the project, students worked individually and in groups to accomplish these broad-scope tasks, balancing fine-grained knowledge of the objects they had chosen with an evolving understanding of how embedding those objects in rich material contexts contributed to learning. At the conclusion of the 13 weeks, each student group built and presented a prototype gallery or museum display to demonstrate what they had learned. On the final day of the project, the groups displayed their galleries for students from the lower grades, as well as for teachers and administrators, in an open, convention-type event. Visitors—or "patrons"—wandered from exhibit to exhibit, taking notes on the clarity and innovativeness of design and presentation, and then ranked each project according to whether they would "fund" it as an actual museum installation.

The year I observed the project, these prototype displays included cardboard and wooden models, gallery floor plans, video documentaries, 3D immersive videos, websites, interactive electronic games, and reproductions of objects made from materials as diverse as clay, paper, found objects, chocolate, wax, 3D prints, laser-etched plastic, and wire. Some groups wore costumes interpreting their objects or the historical period they came from. Other groups gave out souvenirs, including 3D-printed replicas of ancient Roman coins, a laser-etched wooden griffin brooch, and small cardboard Buddhas. As with other projects I observed at the school, an outward-facing disposition was encouraged—how does your work make the world a better place?—and one group had gone as far as to integrate a charitable donation box for the World Wildlife Fund into their museum concept and presentation.

Curator's Choice/Curator's Gallery is an important part of the humanities course because it helps the ninth graders build a learning foundation, a set of shared understandings about how to approach their learning. Amanda called it "somewhere to start." She told me that "one of the things that made Curator's Gallery so wonderful [was that] it had months [to build] a kind of long-term engagement and commitment and willingness to grapple." For her, "content is factual, interpretative material that is cognitively based...stuff educated people ought to know because...it is going to make people into better, more reflective citizens." But to engage content, one needs certain skills. For Amanda, these skills are what enable students to *do* learning. She said,

> This course is as much about how to [do]—that is to say, someone hands you a text, something printed and written, what do you make of it? How do you wander into it?...And then by the same token, any kind of evidence,...look at that chair,...what does it tell you? It can tell you things by [its] style...by the material it's made of. It can tell you [if] it was manufactured, [or if] it was handmade. And so we try to think about skills...in a more meta level, in the sense [that] we want kids to begin to think not just about stuff they do in school but anything that's evidence.

Grappling with evidence to build arguments is the ultimate goal. On this, Amanda was clear: "It's not simply enough to say, I know what it says....What do you think about what it says? What does it mean to you? Can you connect it to something else—how will you put it in historical, literary, artistic context with some other piece of something that comes to you?" Her goal, and the goal of the humanities team, is to encourage students to "become more thoughtful, more insightful, a little bit more self-aware of themselves as interpreters." To that end, teaching history focuses on the present: "I care about content, but the whole point of learning about 5th-century or 6th-century Athens is because it informs what we do now," she said.

Classroom Practice

In her classroom, Amanda drew on contemporary life to encourage students to connect their studies with day-to-day experience. For example, during a discussion about Roman economics in the 2nd century B.C., to illustrate conflicts between farmers, patricians, and the government, Amanda asked students to think about their own buying habits: "What's cheaper? Sweaters made in China?" In another class, during a discussion of the Tao Te Ching and the importance of properly structured relationships in Chinese culture, she asked why teachers do not wear jeans to school and "go around blasting Jay Z all day." To which one student replied, "Because it would mess up the flow." As the discussion evolved, she prodded students with "Say more," and "Where else have we seen this?" In response, students connected Laozi's notions of filial piety and stable relationships to their own experiences of always sitting in the same chair around the dining room table, and by recalling that school admin-istrators have always met them at the front door before and after school with a handshake—a tradition that has been in place since the school's founding.

This notion of connectedness between cultures and across ages was fur-ther accentuated by Amanda's fully embodied performances in her classroom. During the class sessions I observed, she spoke and gestured continuously, moving from the whiteboard to the center of the room, to the video display screen, and back to the whiteboard, asking questions, soliciting responses, probing for deeper thinking, and engaging both the outgoing and the quiet students alike—all while drawing a diagram on the whiteboard piece by piece, with different color markers. Every now and then during her circuit of the room she would return to her computer and change the image on the display screen—and then set off again around the room, asking what the style of the emperor's bust implied about what people thought of him. At times it seemed I was watching a dancer enacting an elaborate choreography. At one point during a freewheeling discussion of Roman society—about the wrenching economic impact of Diocletian farming policies on land use—Amanda took a powerful but awkward stance, feet spread apart, torso twisted one direction, head the other, and said, "Look, why do you think I'm standing this way?" Later, I asked her about the energy of the performance, and she said, "It's part of my practice…it's not unconscious, I do it quite deliberately." Another time, she told me, "I hope that by the different methods I use it gives them [a] handle on [the content]; that is to say, they look at a picture, watch me move, maybe move themselves, and…[it] gives them the chance to write, gives them the chance to make with their hands, which we do with the studio art people."

Amanda emphasized embodied, multimodal learning when she talked about her favorite material in the classroom: paper—that is, photocopied handouts of the historical documents that are required reading in her class. "I really want people to be able to write on [the document] and color it in, and…fold the pages, and do stuff that you just can't do online," she said. For example, in the classroom, she asked students to retrieve their handouts, saying, "Please, please, please write on the text." And, "Did you write back to the document?" Leaning over one student's notebook, she said, "Thank you. That's a beautiful dialogue. It's talking to you." And to the room at large, she said, "When someone is talking to you, what do you do? Respond." Amanda told me, "I am still pretty much, I confess this, tied to the text. I love reading and I love kids working with documents."

Digital Tools and Materials

In reference to the role of other materials in her classroom, such as the tools of digital fabrication—laser cutters, 3D printers, and electronics—or the low-tech DIY materials often found in makerspaces, such as cardboard and paper, beads and ribbons, glue guns and scissors, Amanda was less enthusiastic, though not closed-minded. At the beginning of the school year she said, "I'm not sure what it means for education. Right now, in my life, right this minute, [the maker movement] has the ring of gadget about it." But she was not dismissive; rather, we talked at length about how, or if, FabLabs might change schooling:

> I think there's probably something behind it. It's not there yet, and I'm not there yet, but this has the potential, given that it is a story, and I know what happened when mass manufacturing moved in and displaced the individual craftsman—it was cataclysmic, both in a disastrous sense, right, it undid the status of the craftsman—[but] at the same time, it made enormous goods available to people, literally. Like manufactured clothing and decent plates to eat off of, and people didn't get so sick. You ever try to get a wooden plate clean?…And when you're not sleeping on straw any more, you don't get so many bugs.

Historicizing the maker movement within a narrative about modern manufacturing, and recalling the way computers were used before the birth of the internet, she said:

> I understand enough historically about the home computer—[it] was a gadget, and it didn't do much either. I was in college when this stuff all happened. So I remember [computers] didn't do much. Give me my typewriter, for god's sake. But eventually it became clear that this was a portal to something much bigger and much more powerful, and once…you could get somewhere on one of these things, there was somewhere to go, then it became worth going. Right? Why buy a car if there's no road?

Referring to her earlier example of analyzing how a chair becomes meaningful because of its materials and style, and whether it was made by machine or by hand, Amanda explained that when students look deeply at an artifact, "they're going from the object to the idea." This method of inquiry emphasizes the history of objects and the use to which culture puts them. Her job, as a historian, she told me, is to excavate meaning from what people value: "What

I'm doing is using objects to then dig back to the process and how they got made." As such, her role is to "get [students] to look at objects and get to the idea." The problem with the maker movement as currently configured, she said, was that it encouraged a reverse motion—from idea to object—which doesn't prompt the kind of analysis she wants students to learn how to do. "For the kids…[it's] not just about the making of the thing, to me that's the fill-up on the end, that's not really the point. What about conceptualizing back to object?" In other words, for Amanda the emphasis in ninth-grade humanities should be on *how* objects mean, and this is what she found lacking in the school's push to integrate the maker movement more generally in classrooms—at least as she saw it at the time. Summing up her skepticism, she said, "It's a method without [a] point."

And yet, Amanda refused to dismiss the possibility that, in fact, making might eventually become important to her teaching. For instance, taking the perspective of her students, she said, "The idea that they get to generate [objects] from their own desires is really exciting to me." And continuing to puzzle the question with me, she referred to the invisibility of mass manufacturing—"I don't understand or haven't appreciated the process of building that [store-bought] barrette." To elaborate, she recalled a jazz concert at a public park and the conversation afterwards (described more fully in Chapter 4) about jazz as a performance of living and breathing, and the MP3 recording as what is left over from the living and breathing. "We're in a manufacturing age where this [object] is evidence of some unseen process. We're about to make the process seen, and we're about to think about the object as [the] recording at the end of the jazz." At the beginning of the school year, toward the end of our first in-depth interview, after pushing and pulling with me on the meaning and potential of the maker movement in schooling, Amanda said, "I get the feeling that…I'm going to be thinking about creating [objects]."

Two Meetings: Hallway and Humanities

Toward the end of the school year, two interwoven episodes helped me tie together these observations and conversations with Amanda. Both episodes derived from the Curator's Choice/Curator's Gallery project, and both spoke directly to the most prevalent Ways and Challenges identified and discussed above, namely, Conversations (both Casual and Difficult), and Content versus Making. One was a hallway encounter between Amanda and an administrator, where reactions to the just concluded Curator's Gallery exhibitions sparked a heated conversation; the other was a humanities team meeting led by Amanda, held just after the Curator's Choice/Curator's Gallery showcase, where the project as a whole was critiqued by the teachers who had organized and shepherded it to completion. Neither event was audio recorded. With the hallway meeting, I have narrated the dialogue to give context, so direct speech is italicized rather than enclosed in quotation marks.

Hallway Conversation

On a rainy Friday in the middle of May, the ninth graders presented their exhibit prototypes—the Curator's Gallery half of the project, the culmination of 13 weeks of work. Spread out across the fourth floor of the North Building, occupying most of the classrooms, the media lab, the student lounge, and the hallways, groups of students—some dressed in costume—set up trifold poster boards, computer monitors, iPads, and elaborately constructed wood and cardboard dioramas that included 3D-printed scale models of museum goers, laser-etched jewelry, comic book stories, websites, and immersive, animated video walk-throughs. The excitement was palpable; I watched imaginative gallery spaces come to life in each corner of the building while the girls zipped from table to table, buzzing and anxious about the patrons soon to arrive. As I scouted the space, students checked with friends about last-second adjustments to their displays and hurriedly repaired mechanical or digital models that had stopped working. Many were practicing their speeches, clarifying the language they would use to discuss the objects they had chosen, and refining their team strategies—who would go first, who would go second; who would explain the overall gallery prototype, who would identify each individual object; how they would hand off the speaking duties among themselves, and how they would gather new visitors. Some groups had clearly practiced in advance, but others were scrambling to get ready as show time approached. A few minutes later, seventh and eighth graders and teachers and administrators arrived, and each Gallery group began pitching their projects, trying to win votes and secure funding for their team's exhibit.

After the event had ended and the girls had disassembled their displays, a group of teachers and administrators stood together in a loose semicircle in the carpeted hallway at the top of the stairwell, chatting casually about the scope and flow of the event and about the immensity of the project as a whole. Everyone was excited, and I heard the phrase "the bar has been raised" several times. One of the most enthusiastic was Cecilia, curriculum director for the school. She said again and again how impressed she was with the students' work, and that the enthusiasm and preparedness and depth of knowledge were exactly what the school, as a whole, needed more of. The other administrators and teachers agreed, adding their own congratulations to the humanities team, most of whom were standing there, too. Amanda, responding to the praise, said, *Yes, it's very exciting, but it [the project] ate a lot of content.*

From the other side of the semicircle, Cecelia immediately said: *What do you mean? That was the content! They were totally engaged and owned their learning!*

Amanda replied: *Yes, but they didn't get to China.*

But that doesn't matter! Look at what they did get to! Cecelia fired back.

At that point, conversation stopped abruptly and the group rapidly dispersed, some to catch the bus back to the townhouses, some to teach their classes. The flare-up had quieted the conversation, but Cecelia (whom I followed downstairs) was still excited. On the third floor landing we crossed paths with Mia, the art history teacher and overall organizer of the Curator's Choice/Curator's Gallery project, who was working her way up the stairs, against the stream of traffic. Cecelia stopped and congratulated her: *How wonderful!* she said. But Mia was distracted by something forgotten upstairs, and was rushing up and then back down to the street to catch the bus. She quickly excused herself, saying thank you and laughing, and then disappeared.

The stairwell was empty and hushed, the deep carpet having absorbed the echoes of everyone's departure. Cecelia turned to me on the second-floor landing and said, *Do you believe that about "content"?* She turned back again and walked directly into the administrative offices, sat down, and began talking with one of her North Building counterparts. I followed through the door and sat down beside her.

This is the learning we want, she was saying. *This is integrated knowing.*

Her colleague turned toward her, and the two began sharing pictures of the event from their phones, talking about what the students had said, and commenting on what they had made. Cecelia pulled a fistful of laser-cut Buddhas from her pocket and pointed to the 3D printed Roman coins her colleague had collected. *Did you noticed the sarcophagus made of white chocolate,* she asked, holding up a photograph on her phone. Cecelia said that the girls owned their knowledge, and that when she had asked them about the "big picture," they had dropped their rehearsed speeches and spoken eloquently and authentically about their projects. Both administrators agreed that this was the kind of learning the school needed, and then Cecelia replayed the conversation with Amanda about content, which her colleague had not heard. Cecelia, still incredulous, said to no one in particular, *Yeah, you lost teacher-controlled content, you mean.*

A little while later, downstairs in the entryway of the building, Cecelia's excitement had ebbed, but she remained somewhat agitated. She showed me her pocketful of Buddhas again and snapped a picture of the wood-cut griffin pin I was wearing. She admitted that Amanda's comment had set her off, but she did not regret her reaction. Mostly, she was happy she had come uptown to participate in the event—the rain that morning had almost kept her away, she said. Then, in a more reflective mood, she told me that she wondered how to address the combination of tools and techniques available to students and faculty, and how to leverage the power of the learning that seemed to keep bubbling to the surface. She talked about the range of reactions she gets from faculty, about how she feels in their language an interest but not yet a commitment to understanding the changes that are coming in education. She also wondered how the school's increasing reliance on and integration of these new tools and methods would intersect with the changes in standardized tests and (in her words) *other vectors of learning that are outside the school.* And further, she worried about how to make conversations about these new expectations vibrant. Actually, she told me, she was not quite sure how to even get the conversation going—that is, how to bring the discussion around to the issue of *content* in a way that opened everyone to new possibilities about the changing role of teachers.

To illustrate, Cecelia reminded me of one of her favorite gallery prototypes upstairs. The model had been constructed in the shape of a circle, and should the project be "funded," future viewers would experience the exhibit by following a circular route through the galleries. When she had asked the group why they had chosen that particular design, they told her they wanted to reference a clock because they had been struck by the way each of their objects had been influenced by its place in time. Cecelia said they had constructed a physical metaphor about culture as an unending series of continuances and segues. But I protested that the girls had certainly not said that themselves. Cecelia said: *No, they hadn't. But that's where the teacher needs to step in with something to add in order to extend the conversation.*

As I said good-bye to Cecelia—and hurried to a coffee shop to record these events while they were fresh in my mind—I was troubled. At several points in our conversation, I had wanted to interrupt: The cursory way in which Amanda's comment about "content" was being discussed did not accurately reflect what I knew about her teaching; and in fact, perhaps the whole controversy (content versus not-content) needed to be reformulated and critiqued. But I knew that saying such a thing would have crossed the line. That is, inserting myself into the conversation with Cecelia and her colleagues in order to defend Amanda in that way would have been out of character with the research I was trying to do. And yet, I did not understand how Cecelia and Amanda could be so close to each other in spirit and mind, yet apparently so distant in language. In fact, I asked myself, what was the purpose of Amanda's comment? Where had it come from? In my observations to that point, Amanda and her practice had seemed quite fluid in their treatment of content, especially in the insistence that the study of history had to be applicable to today—for example, by keeping Greek and Chinese history anchored in students' daily lives. The conundrum, for me, was reconciling what I thought I knew about how her teaching intersected with making and learning practices, with her public articulation of that intersection. In some ways, what had just unfolded did not make sense.

Humanities Team Meeting

A few days later, I sat in on the humanities team debriefing, where Curator's Choice/Curator's Gallery was discussed and critiqued. The meeting began in the basement cafeteria at the North Building, but because of the cacophony brought by the arriving ninth graders—who would soon find out which team had won the most patronage for their gallery prototypes—we moved to the school counselor's office, a small room off the corner of the cafeteria that doubled as a green room, costume closet, and set storage area for the school's theater group. At the perimeter of the room and stacked to the ceiling were racks of flamboyant Victorian costumes, exuberant in their bright colors, and furniture piled on top of furniture; a bank of makeup mirrors stretched along one wall, festooned with plump, frosted bulbs and draped with scarves and cloaks. We sat in the center of it all, surrounded by tall bookcases filled with black three-ring binders, which wrapped around us in a semicircle, the brooding darkness of their cheap wood-grain veneer keeping the backstage chaos of the room at bay. A vibrant throw rug in the center of our circle established a kind of boundary for our conversation, and we pulled up to its edges with whatever seating we could scavenge—office chairs on castors, short stools, and overstuffed armchairs with gilded Queen Anne legs, which Amanda called "vaguely Louis." Amanda, leading the meeting, asked Mia to recap the project.

Mia first thanked her colleagues for the support and enthusiasm they had shown throughout the previous 13 weeks. Then, reading from loosely organized notes, she talked about her strategy for announcing the winners of the "patrons'" votes. After tabulating the comments from student visitors and teachers, she had decided to award six prizes, with a special mention to the group who had connected their work to a community concern by taking up a donation for the World Wildlife Fund. She said that responses from the ninth graders themselves had to that point been enthusiastic; the girls were incredibly proud of their work, and their comments and reflections, based on feedback forms collected since the event had happened, were constructive and positive. In spite of this, she said, she expected some complaints about poor table positions and maybe some other "sore loser" remarks, but didn't expect any serious disagreements or dissension about which teams had won the most votes.

At that point, Amanda asked for comments and questions from the team. The discussion that followed touched on some of the challenges that project-based teaching and learning present, which have been mentioned above, such as the time crunch and scheduling difficulties, but primarily focused on the place of "content" in the humanities curriculum and how projects like Curator's Choice/Curator's Gallery fit overall learning objectives. I am reporting the meeting at length because it speaks to the question of how teaching practices connect with digital making and learning pedagogies. Like the hallway conversation detailed above, the meeting was not audio recorded. In this instance, however, rather than narrated dialogue, the following paraphrasing is derived from the notes I took during the meeting, and presented without further embellishment.

Transcript (paraphrased).

Amanda: Agreeing that scheduling everything that had to be done was challenging, nevertheless, what has been learned?

Mark (history teacher): He wants to examine the project's genesis; he thinks the humanities course as a whole needs to catch up to the project; he refers to Cecelia's comment about integration and the goal of education; he wonders about rolling back content and about how the rest of the team might take a more active role in the project.

Mia: She would welcome more participation from the team, perhaps to help with deadlines.

Earl (English teacher): He wonders about skills; how teaching skills fits.

Mia: Knowing the deadlines in advance would make scheduling easier; reinforcing deadlines would help manage stress levels, keep the focus on positive energy.

Earl: But skills as a work period would disappear.

Amanda: It's a question of management. Stress is resolved because of time management.

Mark: The stress gets out of hand; the project becomes a permanent negative because there is so much stress; stress suppressed the "aha" moment.

Amanda: Next year, the student personalities change significantly; there will be different psychological challenges.

Mia: The project ended on a positive note; students were forced to reflect; they learned how to manage stress.

Mark: He wants to be more familiar with the project; he has heard 80 percent positive and extremely positive feedback from students, but they still want it to be tighter; perhaps it could be shortened by 2 weeks; they might roll back the history component.

Mia: It was long this year because of the 8-day cycle; she could not have done it at all without the support of Kieran (FabLab director), Tyler (video teacher), and Emma (upper-school art teacher), but their schedule was too tight as well; every aspect of the project needed more time.

Barbara (English teacher): The creative component spiraled out of control; students put so many hours into it; it used to be a poem but this year it became statues, books, games, videos, and digitally fabricated trinkets; this year the content of the course became less important.

Mia: That was because the ninth graders no longer have a dedicated art class.

Mark: He questions how the humanities team might allocate time for workshops; he thinks they should consider doing that to ease time constraints; he asks if Emma [the high school art teacher] gets her ninth-grade art class back next year; he has heard that the FabLab will be fully staffed next year.

Barbara: They should also consider changing the creative component from an art project to a poem.

Amanda: Perhaps the project can end a week earlier next year.

Mia: (agitated) I cannot do that, because of the pressure from AP art history for the upper-class students.

Amanda: It's a question of scope and sequence; it's a whole year question—about visualizing the entire year, not just part of the year.

Mark: How about tweaking the English creative project [which is separate from history and from art history]?

Barbara and Earl: That's not possible, because our project covers content.

Amanda: Let's delay this conversation until June, when next year's schedule will have been finalized.

Barbara: We are losing class time while Mia and art history are getting more time.

Mark: We need to focus on the big themes; what is integrated, what isn't; not whose project it is; it's psychological—it's how we think of it; if the project is art history, it's Mia's; if it's world civilization, it's ours.

Barbara: But it is still loss of content for English.

Amanda: Let's chew on it in June; we need the facts of the new schedule.

At the end of the meeting, Mia thanked her colleagues again for their support and for their feedback, and said they had helped her learn a lot about managing such a complex project. Mostly, she said, she was thankful to the students for putting so much of themselves into the work; they were the ones who triumphed. Then the team went back into the cafeteria, where the entire ninth grade had now assembled and was anxiously waiting to learn of their patrons' decisions. As expected, pandemonium erupted when the winners were announced, but no trace of animosity or jealousy among the girls was overtly visible. Certainly there must have been some disappointment in the room, as Mia had suggested there might be, but the support and enthusiasm of the girls for each other, and for their teachers—and of their teachers for them—were by far the most salient features of the assembly.

Highlights and Expansion

Reading certain aspects of Amanda's practice in light of the Ways and Challenges extends the validity of the typology as an interpretative tool. Three episodes of Amanda's practice will be highlighted, including her attendance at an out-of-school workshop, her story about iterating, and her encounter with the conflict over content. One episode will be expanded: Amanda's sense of text as a material. Each of these is interwoven with the others, but to this point in the book, each has been introduced in isolation; threading them through each other will help describe the dynamic push and pull Amanda's practice experienced as it made contact with digital making and learning.

Highlight 1: Workshop Out of School

Amanda first described her attendance at a workshop out of school during our initial interview. She attended the workshop in the summer of 2013, just before the study period had begun. As discussed in relation to the Ways (Table 4), attending workshops outside of school was one way teaching practices came into contact with maker education pedagogies, but it did not appear as particularly prevalent according to my interviews and conversations. Kieran, however, told me that "the best professional development that [he had] been to are these immersion programs, where [attendees are] doing something for a week." The workshop that Amanda attended is one of several summer institutes where teachers explore a range of digital and analog tools and materials in collaboration with other teachers in order to make projects they find personally interesting. While there, Amanda worked with two other teachers who were also novices with the tools and materials on offer; one was Isabella, a middle school science teacher at the school and a participant in this study; the other was from another school in a different part of the country. Amanda and her partners decided to create t-shirts that illustrated the digestive system. About the experience, Amanda said:

Oh, it was really fun…and what was great about it was the conceptual stuff, the play during the day, which was most of what we did,…[but] I was clueless, but because I care about the body, it was really interesting to me.

When I asked Amanda about the impetus for attending the workshop in the first place, she said that Kieran had suggested she might enjoy it, and that Cecelia, the curriculum director, had encouraged her to go. Amanda told me:

I said to Cecelia, who was picking people to go, I said, "You know, Cecelia, I have no idea what I would do with this, and I'm going to be twice the age of most of the people there." And she said, "I don't care." And I said, "You understand, I really don't know what I'm doing with this." She said, "No, I don't care."

In the end, though, Amanda found the workshop to be more than simply fun. Indeed, as discussed above, for her, the ideas about practice that were introduced continued to ripple through the school year. During our second in-depth interview, at the end of the study period, Amanda spoke again about the workshop: "[It] had an impact on my practice." And, in terms of how she thought about the work she was asking her students to do, she said, "I'm much more interested in letting kids tinker with text, and [I'm] making much more open-ended prompts." Intriguingly, she saw the most pronounced changes in her U.S. history course rather than in the humanities course, that is, despite the prevalence of making and doing activities in the Curator's Choice/Curator's Gallery project.

Highlight 2: Discovering Iterating

Another measure of the importance of the workshop appears in Amanda's story about discovering the value of iterating, identified in the Ways as a prevalent contact point between current and emerging teaching practices (Table 4).

At the beginning of the study (October 2, 2013), Amanda said:

What was interesting to me about [the t-shirt project] was the holes we fell into… [and] what that revealed to us about our process, and how we fell in love with an idea and then built it, and then created two more problems, and then had to unbuild it.

At the end of the school year (May 29, 2014), she returned to the t-shirt:

I was so excited about [the t-shirt]. Not because of what it did, though that was cool, but because of the experience I had of struggling and failing, struggling and doing something else....And that's the part that I think made the biggest impact on me this year as a teacher, was being much more open [and] willing to let alternative things happen in my classes.

I have argued previously, particularly in my analysis of Kieran's story about iterating (Chapter 6), that learning to iterate was difficult to attain, but once learned, a transformative experience for participants. Amanda's story reiterates this interpretation. In the 8 months between these two statements, Amanda had started to notice iteration in a tactical way; it became something she did, a material part of her practice. Here she has described a pedagogical turn—"being much more open" and "willing to let alternative things happen." This suggests a kind of teaching that begins with relinquishing mastery and invites a shift in agency. In other words, by holding herself open to alternatives, the teacher is no longer the center of the practice. This reprises aspects of the digital making and learning framework-assemblage— for example, digital materiality's affordance of decentered embodiment—and points toward Following Students' Lead in addition to Discovering Iteration (Table 4). One way to say this is that the Ways are gathering allies among themselves in order to steer Amanda's practice toward the new ethos of digital making and learning. Strengthening this interpretation is Amanda's changing awareness of how learning and knowing gets done: "We fell in love with an idea and then built it, and then created two more problems, and then had to unbuild it." To me, this indicates that digital making and learning has connected with her teaching, translating it, suggesting that practice is evolving.

Highlight 3: Content Versus Making

In Chapter 7 the Challenge Content versus Making was identified as the most prevalent point of resistance to linking existing practice to digital making and learning. As discussed, this conflict occupied more lines of text in transcripts and field notes, after coding for thematic coherences, than did any other contact point, including the Ways in Table 4. Additionally, almost every primary participant talked to me about their struggle to balance content with making, or with skills, and many background participants did so as well. Clearly, during the year of this study, a preoccupation with content was abundantly present at the school.

For Amanda, this conflict over content appeared no less acute, though her articulation of what content *was* and what it *was not* had a very different flavor—more complex, more nuanced—from most other participants. At our interview at the end of year, she answered my question about content with a clear delineation: "Content is factual, interpretative material that is cognitively based...that is to say, literally historical, factual material." She went on to say that "good high school teaching includes some cognitive content stuff educated people ought to know because...it is going to make them into better, more reflective citizens." As discussed above, this emphasis on action in the world was a consistent concern for Amanda, and indeed for the school. When I pointed out the role of interpretation as a component of such effective action, she said, "[That's] also content...maybe more heuristic content, but it's content. It's stuff I'm teaching that I could ask you to write an essay about and expect you to furnish it out of stuff from your head." Importantly, at least for this discussion about teaching practice, and especially considering the previous discussion about iterating, Amanda leavened her certainty about content as an internal construct made from an outside world—"historical, factual material" that is "from your head"—with two additional components that she considered critical for strong learning. The first was skills. She said:

> Say somebody hands you this [book], you [have to] know what to do with it....So in that sense, the *skill* is decoding text....Now, maybe [it's] not easy, right? Give somebody Faulkner for the first time—okay, that's going to be hard. But in the sense of historical material, people should be able to wade into a newspaper or an informational text and pretty much be able to read it and figure out what's going on.

The second point was capacity:

> Then the [other] thing that I also want to teach is what I call capacity...that is to say, the strength to pick up this book, the interest to say, "Hmm, I wonder what this says? I think it's worth reading."...If you never challenge kids, they never know what it's like to feel satisfied. They don't know what it's like to get through that sort of thing, they'll shy away from it, and you haven't built their capacity.

For Amanda, these three elements—content, skills, and capacity—formed a balanced tripartite structure that she encountered as an unfolding entanglement of history and present-day engagement, as I observed in her classroom and in our conversations. That is, the question about making and doing crowding out content was not, for her, the issue. Rather, she saw teaching as a multiple practice with an indefinite shape, which addressed the overall-ness of a student's learning journey (at times, with the teacher as an active leader or guide). She said:

> Whatever else you've done [as a teacher], you hope that by the time you graduate them, [students] know a few things, so they're not ignorant. You hope that they know how to do a few things. And then you hope that they have the capacity to want to.... It isn't just about content in the sense of stuffing their heads with stuff, it's also about teaching them how to *do* stuff, explicitly.

Watching Amanda teach, and observing her interactions with students, colleagues, and administrators, encourages me to understand her statement about the relational intermingling of content, skills, and capacity as a form of material iteration. That is, Amanda understands teaching like a potter understands clay, or a painter, paint. For each, practice is an encounter with material that is enacted through relational entanglements with self and others, both human and nonhuman. In this entanglement, new objects emerge, sometimes as if by accident, sometimes without thinking, and sometimes as if from the material itself—that is, without any human agency at all. In Amanda's case, the iterated material is the *content* that is being learned. And that material has a complex interwoven structure that is dynamic and multiple. In this, I am reminded again of Elizabeth Kasl's experience with the clay (Kasl & Yorks, 2012) and of Bamberger and Schön's (1983) conversations with materials. A complex, relational sense of multidimensional, material presence fuels learning and knowing in these examples, and I can describe a similar dynamic in Amanda's practice.

Earlier in the school year, Amanda had used the metaphor of a knot to describe the content of a learning unit on Roman history that explored the role of Theodoric ("a Goth, but he considers himself a good Roman in the 5th century"):

> It [the curricular material about Theodoric] was a knot with colored string. You know, the strings were all knotted up, as they should be, that's how real life is, but [students] could follow the strings well enough to untangle.

This following of the thread was what mattered to her, and to be able to do so, and to *want* to do so—these things were what she wanted her students to learn. She suspected that what would stick with her students, though, was a *feeling* of knowing, so that was her focus. For Amanda, the *material* of content was a feeling of knowing. She said:

What you really learn in high school is what you learn about yourself. The part they're going to remember isn't about Theodoric. I bet if you looked at them now, half of them wouldn't remember what Theodoric even was. But I hope in my wildest dreams as a teacher, what they get to keep forever is what it felt like. "How do I go back there and get that feeling [of knowing]?" That's what I want.

Expansion: The Materialities of Teaching

Holding content as a hybrid cognitive material—the feeling of knowing, a knot of colored string, a conversation with text, a dance—is significant for several reasons. For one, it must be said, this is not a misstatement or random formulation; throughout my association with Amanda, I observed her wrestling with these ideas many times, in multiple ways, deeply, sincerely, and with a commitment to improving her own teaching and her students' learning. Secondly, it evokes the notions of materiality as a relational assemblage that increasingly pervade the research and scholarship on education and digital media networks (Davidson, 2011; Hansen, 2015; Hayles, 2012; jagodzinski & Wallin, 2013; Koyama, 2009; Latour, 2013; Sørensen, 2009). And third, it opens a line of inquiry into teaching as a material practice, or as an enacted encounter, as described with respect to constructionist artistic development (Bolt, 2013; Burton, 2000; Papert & Harel, 1991), transformative or presentational knowing (Kasl & Yorks, 2012; Yorks & Kasl, 2002), and reflexive, conversational, or metaphorical knowing (Bamberger & Schön, 1983).

Amanda's take on the materiality of learning might be traceable to the maker workshop she attended one summer, to her Ph.D. studies in church history, to her tinkering in her father's furniture workshop, or to something else. But regardless, content as materiality—a kind of physical cognition with certain affordances, namely, a feeling of knowing—is clearly important to her. To the point of the study, though, what, actually, does Amanda *mean* when she evokes these metaphors to describe her teaching? More importantly, what is she *doing* with this material that might be changing her practice?

To approach this question, I want to consider a comment Amanda made about the way my interview questions had become a spur to her learning. In our final in-depth interview, she said:

This is something that's evolved, and I think it's taken time to evolve and…I'm not sure it would have evolved had we not started talking about it. I think, in a way—I don't want to say you've contaminated your own study—it really has made me think more explicitly and more intentionally about why I do what I do. In conjunction with the maker movement, that's what [I'm] doing with text, which maybe everybody else knows, but they didn't make it explicit—it's just coming to me now. I mean, not right this minute, but this year.

Two characteristics of this statement resonate. First, far from "contaminating" the study, as Amanda feared, her comments alerted me to the powerful work that certain kinds of conversations were having for many of the study participants, which I eventually identified as Casual Conversations. Amanda was not the first to tell me that my questions strengthened connections with maker education, but she was the most direct. Indeed, I had already noted and written about this in my field research journal by the time this conversation with Amanda took place. And second, and more importantly, this is where we hear Amanda both becoming aware of a new kind of (textual) materiality and linking that materiality with making. That is, the statement reveals a connection between two ways of thinking or rethinking practice that is explicit and transformative. As such, the comment argues for the notion that Amanda's practice is gathering a contradictory or fractional coherence from two binaries that often oppose each other: the material and immaterial, the substantial and insubstantial, the content and noncontent. This is precisely the kind of making-inflected characteristic of learning and knowing that digital materiality makes available to a fully realized new culture or new ethos of digital making and learning. This conclusion is strengthened by Amanda's statement that the idea has been evolving throughout the year, perhaps beginning with our conversation about jazz as breathing and recording as evidence of breathing. At that time, Amanda said, "I get the feeling that something else is about to happen...where instead of deciphering objects...we're about to reconceptualize the object."

· 1 0 ·

THE FEELING OF KNOWING

Asking for a Response

In October 2014, I emailed Amanda to ask if she would read the narrative of her practice that I had constructed (Chapter 9) and discuss it with me. I explained that her continued participation in the study was important because, as a test against validity, her collaboration in constructing the vignette would help assure its accuracy. I also told her that after many months of living with the accumulated artifacts, field notes, memos, and transcripts collected during the on-site period of the study, I kept returning to the stories, metaphors, and experiences she had shared with me. Consequently, certain aspects of the study had been derived from her practice, as when a mist consolidates in rain, and a methodological problem had arisen. That is, while she had given me her permission to quote her in this report (by signing the Informed Consent), I had not foreseen this emergent emphasis on her experience when I had asked her to participate in the study. On that point, from the perspective of narrative inquiry methodology (Chase, 2011), the density of minute personal details *required* me to ask for her further consent, because what I was writing and the way I was writing it went beyond the scope of a signature on a piece of paper. But more important than this methodological requirement, in terms of the study itself, I had a different question: Would Amanda's interpretation of my interpretation support or contradict *my* tentative conclusions? Either way, it seemed to me, the recursive and emergent dynamics of our collaboration would strengthen the study.

In a face-to-face conversation in December 2014 we talked about the path the research had taken since the on-site portion of the study had ended that previous June. I told her about the typology (i.e., the Ways and Challenges—though she had not read it yet) and described how I had characterized teaching practices as material constructs that only partly depended on any individual teacher's intentional agency. We briefly discussed narrative inquiry, actor-network theory, posthumanism, and the new materialism of digital making and learning pedagogies. On points of methodology (for example, narrative inquiry and ANT), Amanda was interested but admitted not having the expertise to comment (her own doctorate had emphasized different trajectories). To my request for further collaboration as a point of both validity and collaboration that went beyond informed consent, she readily agreed, assuring me that she was comfortable with whatever I might write. On points of digitally infused, maker-oriented pedagogy as a framework-assemblage, however, she was curious and uncertain, especially about notions of posthumanism and new materialism and their challenge to the traditional pillars of humanism. As with our many conversations during the previous year, our discussion in that meeting was wide-ranging and engaging; at its conclusion, Amanda agreed to read the draft of the narrative I had written.

Amanda's Response

A couple of weeks later, by email, Amanda wrote that aside from a minor error of fact (regarding a point of Roman history she had discussed in her classroom while I was observing), the vignette conformed to her own memories and understandings of her practice. She also wrote, "The importance of casual conversations, and other direct interpersonal exchanges, to the development and enhancement of teaching practice directly squares with my experience."

About the hallway meeting after the Curator's Gallery project, she wrote:

> I must admit, I don't recall making the comment about...the students not getting to China. But I admit I do feel pressure both to engage the freshmen with the global geographic areas/cultural traditions the humanities course includes... and also to build their skills and capacities as learners, which the iterative,

independent, collaborative, constructivist work of the Gallery project does. So it's entirely likely [that] in that moment, at the end of a long process and close to the end of the year, I voiced frustration with that pressure.

On the disagreement with Cecelia, she wrote:

I regret that my remark caused Cecelia's irritation that day, and suspect she, too, feels considerable frustration…with the slow, halting pace of curricular and pedagogical change. She and I have talked this year about some innovations in the AP U.S. history course…and, while I'm sure we differ about some of the particulars, I think we share a commitment to a broadening view of teaching and learning.

About the humanities team meeting, she wrote:

The team meeting…is exactly where, in my teaching life, some of those issues get worked out, with the friction that process entails. As you saw, the team includes divergent points of view, each of which is…represented in the curriculum…

In follow-up emails, Amanda and I discussed the potential for pedagogical change along some of the parameters I had noted. When I asked her to reflect on how the project-based, making-infused environment at the school might be affecting her practice, she wrote that the question was "intriguing," and that "two examples leapt immediately to mind."

The first was a new ninth-grade humanities project that integrated cooking, video production, and history. It was developed by Mia and Mark, her humanities team members, and had been implemented for the first time in the fall. Each student researched a recipe from the time period they had been studying, and then made a video of themselves preparing it in their kitchens at home. Students were prompted to demonstrate "not only how to prepare the dish but also its social and historical location and context." The culmination occurred right before winter break, when students brought their dishes to school for the Roman Breakfast Banquet in the North Building cafeteria. Amanda wrote:

The project wasn't directly my doing, but its invitation to connect the textual and the material I would like to think is a fruit of my leadership. I am feeling increased freedom to make metaphors this year, and am feeling fresh energy to treat old topics in new ways in the classroom.

Amanda's second example approached the question from a different angle. Instead of describing a project she was excited about doing, she wrote about a project she would most likely be prevented from doing. Recently, the school leadership had decided to mandate an end-of-year social justice objective in the eleventh-grade advanced placement U.S. history course—a course that was already hampered by too many curricular requirements, according to Amanda. That is, though other faculty had said that they did not feel pressured to teach to a test (because high-stakes testing was largely nonexistent at the school), some aspects of the curriculum were nevertheless beyond their control. Due to its implications for college applications, the AP U.S. history course was one of these exemptions. The reason the mandate upset Amanda was that she already had an idea about how to end the history course that coming May, and the social justice project would disrupt those plans. Amanda wrote: "I am involved in resisting a controversial proposal to take the final 3 weeks of the course, after the exam on May 8, for a... social justice activism project." Importantly, she wrote, she did not oppose social justice projects. Rather, she had wanted to give the students time for something else at the end of the year—something that was not teacher- or school-directed. She wrote:

> My hope for that time was finally to set the students loose on U.S. history topics of their choice, to invite each student to dig around in an area she wants to know more about, then share her learning and her questions and connections....[T]he goal [was] to offer them a treat after a hard year's work,...[but] it looks as though that [won't] be possible this year; we'll see what the future holds for years to come.

Responding to Amanda's Response

Several aspects of Amanda's response bear on the question about whether and how digital making and learning, or project-based, making-infused pedagogy is gathering presence here. Two episodes from her response will be characterized in some detail—the hallway conversation and the social justice internship in history class. But first, broadly speaking, it is notable that Amanda thought the narrative construct itself accurately brought her practice to presence; she wrote: "There's nothing I would disagree with in how you've constructed the narrative so far." As mentioned earlier, this is not to claim that the construct is somehow true to phenomena outside of or pre-existing my observations, but rather to point to a concordance in two observers' accounts. With respect to describing how learning and knowing are enacted, from an ANT disposition, this concordance implies an overlapping descriptive framework and a kind of stability (Latour, 1996). From Law's (2004) discussion of mess in relation to method, I would argue that this stability implies a gathering of presence; simply, there is something here. This seems a good place to start.

Iterating in the hallway. Amanda wrote that she did not explicitly remember her comment about "not getting to China," though she allowed that it sounded like a release of frustration. This confirms the confusion that I wrote about in my field journal at the time. That is, the enthusiasm (and heat) of Cecelia and Amanda's disagreement did not *make sense*. But it was *sensible*—everyone in that circle at the top of the stairs felt and responded to it (for example, the conversation went silent, the group rapidly dispersed). The distinction is one of meaning versus affect, a particularly difficult binary to hold onto, at least in humanist terms (for example, Cartesian presumptions of a mind/body split still animate much of the friction between what and how we think and feel about knowing [Clark, 1997, 2011; Damasio, 1994, 1999]). For a participant on the periphery (me), the episode was confusing; but for participants at the center (at least for Amanda), it resonated differently. Perhaps rather than a deep disagreement, like a fissure opening up, the episode was a momentary fluttering of attention and anxiety, like a release of geothermal pressure, as Amanda suggested, or a ripple in a pond. Amanda's empathy with Cecelia's frustration about the "slow, halting pace of…change" supports this conclusion: They do not disagree with each other. In fact, rather than reading the scenario as a challenge to making-infused learning, perhaps it implies a strengthening; the faculty here enacted a powerful connection between an emergent pedagogy (that is, Curator's Choice/Curator's Gallery was an open-ended inquiry-based project that relied on interest-driven, passionate engagement) and a receding practice, perhaps even a vestigial practice (for example, teaching that foregrounds clear-cut learning objectives and the assumption of accomplishing specific curricular goals). That Amanda does not remember the "China" comment, but nonetheless feels bad about the fallout, supports the speculation that the grip of pre-established learning objectives is loosening, and with it, robust ecologies of learning are gathering around digital making–infused teaching. As such, perhaps the conversation in the hallway surfaced this dynamic, and everyone felt the friction (at least for a moment) that bringing it into presence had released.

In terms of explaining the way in which this contact point between practices came to be enacted here, at that particular moment, I am pulled again to the Möbius strip. Keeping present its curious topology that holds binaries in play, I arrive at the following description. This casual conversation in the hallway at the top of the stairs in the North Building, on a rainy day, immediately after the conclusion of a 13-week multimodal learning project, assembled a fractionally coherent object from opposing multiples. Meaning and affect, content and feeling, collapsed into each other, producing an object that is extremely challenging to enact in schools (as evidenced by the vast skepticism teachers expressed around the Challenge I've called Content versus Making). The fact of its appearance, as an emotional outburst, testifies to the energies expended in its production. Perhaps excitement in the final seconds before its arrival amplified a recursive loop of focused attention that expanded out of control, like audio feedback, generating an outburst that dispersed the actants that had contributed to it. These were many: Amanda, and her sense of content, skills, and capacity, articulated as the feeling of knowing; Cecelia, and her frustration with the slow pace of change; the carpeted stairwell, and its electric atmosphere of the just concluded exhibition; the students, 20 teams of girls with their bundles of cardboard models and costumes leaving whirls and eddies in the air as they streamed past us and through us on their way downstairs; the faculty, a close semicircle of bodies at the top of the stairs, jockeying to voice enthusiasm and support; the rain outside, calling awareness to the buses downstairs and the impending need to rush away. Each of these actants, and others, traced divergent arcs through the time and space of these few moments, with varying degrees of intensity and urgency, colliding and then careening onto new orbits, momentarily stabilizing, perhaps, or spiraling off sideways. And then Amanda said, "But they never got to China," and Cecelia snapped back, "But look at what they did get to!"

In what kind of learning and knowing are these actants collaborating? The difficulty of articulating this tempts me to erase the complexity by hitting the delete key. I am reminded of Walkerdine's (2007) difficulty in describing the relational dynamics of boys' and girls' video game play; and of Sørensen's (2009) difficulties with the recalcitrant language of Enlightenment materiality in her study of virtual environments in Danish elementary classrooms. Both researchers grappled with disruptive metaphors, but they did not give up. In this case, with the hallway conversation, I play with writing—they agreed, they disagreed, then they agreed again—and with concluding that the fireworks were ignited by random temperaments and personalities, a to-do about nothing. But this dismissal rings false; something else was going on. Casual Conversations were the most prevalent way of strengthening digital making and learning practices, and I have argued that Casual + Difficult Conversations were critical ingredients in holding technological binaries open (following Latour, 1996; and see Feynman's 1999 discussion about why the *lack* of difficult conversations was a proximate cause of the *Challenger* disaster). Here I would add that the space of the hallway played a role, too: Flare-ups happen if ecologies support them, but what happens next is relational and indeterminate. In this densely interwoven, warmly confrontational space, however, the multiple actants involved included the comfortable hush of the carpeted stairwell.

A social justice conundrum. The introduction of a social justice requirement in the eleventh-grade advanced placement U.S. history course presents another example of the push and pull of digital making and learning pedagogy. The emergence of this example is unexpected, and casts this research itself as a material learning process.

Amanda first told me about the proposal for requiring the eleventh-grade social justice internship when we spoke in early December 2014. She said that the idea had been dropped on her without much warning, and that she did not have much recourse in opposing it. She agreed with the leadership about the value of a social justice project for the eleventh graders, but she did not understand why it had to happen during advanced placement U.S. history. In fact, she said, she was excited about those final few weeks of her course because after the AP exam, she wanted each student to expand on the expertise she had acquired during her year of studying, "to dig around in an area she wants to know more about, and then to share her learning and her questions and connections, perhaps in a conventional research paper if that's her choice, or also perhaps in some other form." In this, Amanda was planning to integrate and even celebrate maker-oriented learning. From the Ways I can identify Doing Projects, Following Students' Lead, Student Engagement, Discovering Iteration, and Self-Directed Learning in her plan. As well, holding the Möbius strip diagram in my mind, I would argue that Amanda was beginning to play in a field of expertise (for example, the study of history) by letting it slip fluidly between binary positions on continua that she had openly begun to question (for example, text as material, object as process, document as agential, knowing as individual and distributed, as interior and exterior). In this she rooted the *feeling of knowing* to a dynamic slippage between content, skill, and capacity, the key components of the relational assemblage she knew as teaching. In an email she wrote: "The goal…[at end of the course was] to offer them a treat after a hard year's work, a reward of pleasure and play, to experience scholarship as freedom and joy."

During our conversation I could tell that Amanda was distressed. She said she felt herself about to cross a threshold in her conceptualization of practice. I recalled our discussions about the maker movement, tinkering, iterating, student engagement, open-ended problem-based learning, and other related strategies relevant to digital making and learning pedagogy. Her resistance to the leadership's plan came from disappointment, she said. In fact, she told me, she might resign if the leadership did not reconsider their decision.

What are we to make of this situation? Judging by the sound of Amanda's voice in December and the tone of her emails after that, the disagreement over the social justice project was far more serious than the conversation in the hallway could ever have been. And so might be the consequences—a teacher's resignation because of a disagreement with school leadership would ripple across multiple domains: the curriculum, her colleagues' relationships with the leadership, students' relationships with their teachers, not to mention the effect on Amanda's livelihood.

The details are confusing, too, resembling a collision between two firmly held mandates that have gone out of their way to collide. How did a commitment to social justice crash into enthusiasms for making-infused pedagogy? Both are valued by the school as educational goods: Social justice activism is explicitly articulated in the school's mission statement, in the socially aware projects emerging from the FabLabs, in science and engineering classes, and even in the second grade's Invention Convention. And the enthusiasm for making-infused teaching and learning was abundantly present, from the head of school (who wants to "reinvent teaching and learning") to most of the participants in this study. But neither of these mandates precludes the other. In fact, in other instances, they complement and complete each other; for example, scholars and educators of digital making and learning explicitly articulate the connection between FabLabs, makerspaces, the internet, and social justice, or democratic empowerment (Blikstein, 2013; Ito et al., 2013). As such, there is no obvious configuration of learning and knowing that irredeemably points to this conflict; at least, not that I observed after a year at the school.

The Feeling of Knowing

(How) does a public argument between a teacher and an administrator help move practice toward open-ended encounters with materiality? (How) does a collision between two strongly situated educational goods move practice away from such encounters? These questions are open and likely to remain so, at least in terms of this study. That is, outside of further interviews or observations, or a new study, I am left with speculation and confusion. Without expecting such a result, it is perhaps appropriate that the last findings in a research study about open-ended teaching and learning remain open-ended. That is, not knowing what happens next suspends cause-and-effect instrumentalism. Without a conclusion, we cannot collapse causes with effects. Perhaps we find ourselves drifting into new configurations of learning and knowing, instead. This would reprise Bradly's observation that a tools-first mentality closes off the potential for effective teaching—a closure that he interrupted in workshops by suggesting that teachers put away the iPads and use paper and pencils, often to the surprise and disbelief of his participants. As well, the suspension of cause-and-effect instrumentalism echoes Kieran's story about iterating as the most important skill for makers to learn, because keeping the learning process in suspension coaxes new solutions to presence. In effect, perhaps knowing nothing more about either the hallway conversation or the social justice conundrum gathers attention on the enactment of digital making learning and knowing as practice, which is directly aligned with the inquiry project overall.

Fragile emergence. Before addressing some pragmatic implications of digital making and learning pedagogies as encountered during the study (which I'll do in the final two chapters), I'd like to suggest a corollary to the proposition that open-ended inquiry energizes teaching and learning (a correspondence that is prevalent in the literature of maker education; for example, Martinez & Stager, 2013). The example can be found in Amanda's reframing of her practice, a *way* of teaching that emerged from how she *does* teaching. It occurs to me that her grappling with the assemblage she holds as content + skill + capacity fuels her dance with knowing, her conversation with text, and her exploration of history as a knot of colored string. As such, she has reconceptualized the object of teaching as the feeling of knowing. Amanda, as the teacher accompanying the gathering of this particular practice, has opened to a notion of materiality that holds theories and things as equivalent. Her practice—and her grasp of these dynamics—suggests that describing practice as an enacted encounter with materiality does seem to have an effect, at least here with her. That is, as a history teacher without a particularly strong attraction to the FabLab, she wants students to make *things*. She knows her practice is changing, she says, because she feels "fresh energy to treat old topics in new ways," which has led her to advocate for students to "experience scholarship as freedom and joy."

The caveat is that the potentials for knowing and learning that Amanda is exploring are fragile and very difficult to hold, and can be whisked into oblivion, into nonpresence, by an errant wave of the hand, or by a single actor's decision. In fact, holding practice as Amanda does requires positioning materiality as relational, and that requires a turn that has not yet been articulated among teachers or teacher education, perhaps because it implies upending centuries of Enlightenment and humanist cultural norms. As such, the assemblage that excites Amanda is bound to be excruciatingly difficult to enact and, no doubt, exceedingly rare as well. In fact, Amanda is skeptical of these ideas, even as she enacts them in her dance with knowing. Perhaps this goes, in part, to what is happening in the AP U.S. history class: The leadership does not recognize the thresholds of learning and knowing that Amanda is crossing because they do not know what to look for; because they presume that a history teacher who does not use the FabLab is resisting the head of school's mandate to reinvent teaching and learning; and because when the only *material* in a classroom is paper handouts about Roman history, the *materiality* of pedagogy is invisible.

Backwards and upside-down. The questions at the heart of the study ask how teachers learn to use the tools and materials of digital making, and how (or if) learning to do so changes teaching. In Amanda's case, these questions are backwards, or upside-down. That is, she has not learned to use digital making tools and appears to have little interest in doing so, yet her practice is changing in ways that are consistent with the ethos of digital making and learning pedagogies. For example, she tinkers with text, but does not play with cardboard, glue, or crayons. Rather, she makes metaphors with dance and history. She speaks to documents, and they speak back. She has reconceptualized the object of content as a cognitive/affective hybrid. In every sense that matters, Amanda is fully engaged with the new ethos of learning promised by the digital making and learning movements. But the leadership's eyes, focused on 3D printers, electronics, computer programming, gaming, robotics, and so on, do not see her.

Ironically, Amanda told me that she "think[s] about [teaching] in conjunction with the maker movement, that's what [I'm] doing with text." And that she feels "much more open [and] willing to let alternative things happen in [her] classes." And she suspects that the entanglement of food, video production technologies, and social history in the Roman Breakfast Banquet was connected to her "leadership" because, though that project was not initiated by her, she is "feeling increased freedom to make metaphors this year."

How do we describe this entanglement of digital making and learning enthusiasms in a non-maker practice? Does *making* matter to Amanda, even though she does not *make* (in the sense defined by maker education)? For example, she spoke enthusiastically about learning to iterate at the summer workshop she attended (where she "fell in love with an idea and built it"). This is similar to what other teachers said about maker-infused learning. Has this affected Amanda's practice, too? In fact, Amanda has told me that she thinks it has.

But to that point, can Amanda's maker-transformation (in a non-maker way) be attributed to one summer workshop, even when combined with her childhood memories of repairing furniture in her father's garage? Perhaps doing the Ph.D. at Union Theological Seminary contributed. Or talking regularly with Kieran. Or learning to manage the conflicts with the humanities team. Or experiencing her students' excitement about the feeling of knowing. But there's something else, too. Amanda focused on material conversations in her teaching ("Did you write back to the document?"), and on the narrative connotations of materiality in culture ("You ever try to get a wooden plate clean?"). In this respect, as I've suggested, Amanda and her practice stood out from the others I encountered, though I don't know how they attained their trajectory. As such, can we hold building with text and metaphor as equivalent to tinkering with 3D printers, Arduino microcontrollers, or sewing machines?

Questioning Focus

This gathers Amanda and her practice closer to us, but I want describe it with language that might as yet be unformed. Following Law (2004), I would argue that we not make a mess of these complexities by rushing to simplify them; and following Mol (2002) I would argue that leaving a little room for mess invites doubt, and keeps our options open. And following Amanda, let's not minimize the bumps in our journey by paving them over with pretty words: That is, in "a knot with colored string...the strings [are] all knotted up, as they should be, that's how real life is."

In the teaching practice that surrounds Amanda, that she accompanies, participates in, collaborates with, curates, the maker ethos of open-ended inquiry-based learning and knowing is strong and vibrant, and becoming more so. What is missing from this practice, in maker terms, is a robustly enacted encounter with the tools and materials found in FabLabs and makerspaces. But holding this as a rejection of digital making and learning pedagogy, ironically, would validate maker education's diminished sense of materiality, and further obscure the material learning that precipitates innovation. This is because Amanda and her practice—their enacted encounter with materiality—respond to some of the most difficult challenges facing schooling today, namely, those coming from digital materiality and its affordance of decentered embodiment which cast us on trajectories of knowing and doing that entangle self/other, object/subject and individual/citizen in ways that none of us have yet come to fully understand. The practice that holds Amanda in motion at this school enacts these opposites as open and in relationship with each other, irresolvable and irreducible in their complexity. In relation to the many other practices I encountered during this study, I would argue that this one has traveled the farthest into the conceptual, pragmatic, and situated space of digital making and learning. While I am skeptical that I know precisely how such a thing has come to presence, I would argue that the narrative about practice offers an interpretation that interweaves metaphor with learning. Rarely in my experience as an artist and educator have I met and worked with someone who plays with analogy and story as freely, wittily, complexly and enjoyably as Amanda. This, I would speculate, opens an inquiry into how making metaphors informs teaching. This precipitates a further question to maker educators: Where are the stories? Why do we entertain so many questions about how tools work, constantly Googling projects that our students might make, but attend so rarely to the stories our tools want to tell?

· 11 ·

WHAT WAS LEARNED

This study began with the desire to learn how, or if, teachers' use of digital making tools and materials affected their practice. As it turned out, the assumptions embedded in that simplistically linear proposition threw me a curve as soon as I tangled with the complexities of day-to-day practice at the school. In this chapter I'll summarize what I've learned. First, I'll review the connections and resistance I encountered. And second, I'll highlight some of the missed and approaching opportunities for teaching and learning in makerspaces and digital media labs that I observed.

Summary of the Study

Enacting Digital Making and Learning Pedagogies

With the typology of the Ways and Challenges (Table 6) I sought to identify digital making and learning pedagogy by holding teaching practices as entities, or things, or as enacted materialities, and by attempting to trace associations between existing and emergent ways of teaching. This sense of practice was derived from closely attending to what participants were saying and doing. As a description of teaching practice, and how teaching changes, I linked the emergence of digital making and learning to the literature of various learning and knowing traditions, including maker education, art education, and digital media learning—which is also known as situated or connected learning (as described in Chapter 2); and to a notion of digital materiality and its affordances that I derived from new materialism and new media theory (described in Chapter 3). To aid in collecting and interpreting observations and interview data from the study, the first finding of the research was a framework-assemblage of digital making and learning pedagogy (Table 2), which I've referred to throughout the book. The idea of holding practices as an overlap between traditions, and the framework-assemblage as an indicator that enabled me to notice those overlaps, led me to describe practice as flowing back and forth across the thresholds between different traditions. This approach was derived from dispositions that included sociomaterialism, narrative inquiry, and actor-network theory (as discussed in Chapter 4).

As I listened to participants describe their teaching, and followed them here and there across the territory of their practices, comparing what I observed at the school with the framework-assemblage of digital making and learning, it occurred to me that points of contact between practices began to consolidate as actants in themselves. As I attended more closely, poring over transcripts, memos, emails, and other documents, these contact points became the Ways and Challenges (which I've illustrated with multiple examples and narratives in Chapters 6, 7, and 8). As such, I was able to describe the stabilization of digital making and learning at the school by pointing to Casual Conversations, Doing Projects, Discovering Iterating, Experiencing Student Engagement, and so on, leading me to argue that the Ways (Table 4) gathered and made available open-ended, learner-centered, constructivist, material-focused teaching.

At the same time, other contact points pushed back against that stabilization, consequently diminishing digital making and learning practices. The Challenges (Table 5) included skepticisms about Content versus Making, about the Fit of making-infused pedagogy, of difficulties with Assessment, a Lack of Time, and anxiety about Losing Control. Overlaps and contradictions between the Ways and Challenges were not precisely delineated, but the typology as a whole became useful as an indicator of the emergence and dissolution of digital making pedagogies. This indeterminacy, the simultaneous stabilization and destabilization, I argued, held opposing binaries open and unresolved, thus making complex descriptions of teachers' actions available to interpretation. In Chapter 8 I demonstrated how such indeterminacy might work in practice by interpreting an event in the cafeteria and three different teaching practices. At that point I suggested that the typology, by not collapsing under an attempt to simplify the complexities of those practices, made further complexities of practice available to description and, potentially, to enactment.

Finally, as an example of a technical tool, broadly speaking, I argued that the typology was subject to the evolutions and shifts demonstrated by tools more generally, where initial extensions of agency become tool-based dependencies, and then secondly, actants, materialities, or relational assemblages with their own specific affordances, which are then available to participate in the enactment of an ecology. In Chapter 3 I illustrated this recursive and emergent, world-makes-world relationship with the stepladder analogy, and by pointing to selections from the literature of cognitive science, new materialism, and human development. In the case of the typology, I argued that it initially appeared as an *indicator* but became an *activator* of practice. The shift occurred when I was able to describe contact points as bending, warping, or entangling digital making and learning pedagogy with more traditional pedagogies. Overall, I did not find a way to determine which contact points did more or less work during any particular encounter, and I argued that holding the typology open and unresolved did not diminish its value or usefulness. In this, I pointed to the Möbius strip as a metaphor for understanding practice. As a figure that requires a light touch and continuous movement in order for its topology to be enacted, it occurred to me that the Möbius strip made available a kind of relationality that resonated with how I used the typology. Another way to say this, perhaps, would be to describe the emergence of digital making and learning practice by using John Law's (2002) term *fractional coherence*, or, as I might prefer, a dynamic, *oscillating stability* that remains in flux from day to day.

Oscillating Stability

To be clear, with this term *oscillating stability* I am not describing digital making and learning at the study site as alternating between stability and instability, but rather that the kind of stability I observed was an oscillation, like a standing wave. The cliché *change is constant* approaches this meaning but does not capture the notion of fluctuation between identifiable parameters. That is to say, I want to describe the *way* that digital making and learning was coming to presence as a dynamic fluttering, or wobbling, between traditional practices, maker ecologies, and learning ecologies suffused with digital materiality. In response to this oscillation, teaching practices might be described as adopting or resisting digital making and learning along the dimensions mapped by the typology of Ways and Challenges. The learning dynamic that I am trying to describe suggests that we need a different kind of language to gather the complexities that digital making and learning is bringing to presence in schools and other educational ecologies.

Evidence of contact. Throughout the study, I observed digital making and leaning stabilizing at the school. Examples include Vanessa's arrival at an unexpected insight while reflecting on learning; Kieran's and Tyler's enthusiasm about experiencing student engagement; Aidan's conviction about the value of projects in the classroom, especially the immersive week-long Nerdy Derby; and Grace's description of how she and her teaching partner, Amber, began to think about the value of making and tinkering in their second-grade science class. These and other examples reported throughout the book reprise some of the characteristics of digital making learning and knowing catalogued by the framework-assemblage: for example, a pull toward open-ended, interest-driven learning; a shared agency; a diminished place for lecture or direct instruction in favor of hands-on exploratory engagement. As well, perhaps more enigmatically, they also describe teachers as holding practice a little loosely, listening to materials, or going with the flow, which are attributes of a way of learning I've called *material learning*.

Evidence of resistance. I also observed digital making and learning practices becoming destabilized, as described by the Challenges (Table 5). Chief among these points of resistance was teachers' skepticism about how to integrate content in maker activities. In fact, Content versus Making contained more lines of text, and more individual conversations, than any other contact point, including those from the Ways (Table 4). Examples range from Thomas's concern about covering his engineering curriculum ("Well, that's interesting, but man, I've got to get through my curriculum"), to Vanessa's confusion about the Biodiversity Diorama project and her desire that content take precedence over building and designing the physical structure of the diorama, to Isabella's skepticism about how digital making and learning diminishes science learning ("What is the core content that we need students to know, that you can't strip away? That's a very tough question"), and to Aidan's fear that making might obstruct meaning ("My skepticism and my fear is about getting to meaning"). Beyond these, examples of other resistance points included Mia's concern that the stress of project learning might be counterproductive for teenage girls, Grace and Aidan's discussion about rethinking the curriculum, and Kieran's story about the difficulty of talking with his colleagues about making learning more engaging and relevant. An additional but hard-to-pin-down resistance to maker-oriented pedagogy can be identified as the desire to avoid talking about it altogether, as Emma said: "Yeah, I blew you off."

Choosing Doubt

What kind of learning and knowing was enacted in these callings on contact points? How might we describe it? I have written about stabilizing and destabilizing, but that might be the wrong metaphor. What does it mean to hold a teaching practice as stable? A table or stepladder can be steady, wobbly, or falling apart. If I cast practice as furniture, what do I gain? What affordances are made available to my narrative, to my interpretation, when I ask the assemblage *stepladder* to arrange the assemblage *practice*? I would argue that this question about metaphor is actually about the ordering of knowing and learning, a question that needs to be asked of every action configuration we encounter, but rarely is. Mol (2002) maintains that asking *what to do* always invokes doubt, begs debate, and opens possibilities for new trajectories. *What to do* is a question of action in and with the world, about how to live, how to *do* learning and knowing. It is a question of practice. In this book I've been trying to figure the practice of teaching by casting doubt on my choice of metaphors. That is, to explore teachers' learning, I learned to doubt the figure of the teacher, which opened me to the arrival of the contact points. Now, to offer some kind of explanation for how I think the contact points worked as actants that translated practices, I'm back again to doubt. Perhaps another metaphor: Let's do the Ways and Challenges as a gathering of new materialities and maker paradigms.

How the Ways Worked

In listening to participants and watching them teach, I noticed a preponderance of surprise. That is, again and again, participants reported or I witnessed connections with or the arrival of insight emerging unintentionally or without foresight. For example: the arrival of the FabLab violin that had everyone at the lunch table oohing and aahing; Vanessa's meandering through the problem of hands and bodies in Revolutionary War avatars, until she exclaimed, "I just came up with that....Wow"; Grace and Amber's astonishment from the periphery as their second graders made flowers, jewelry, or wire glasses from paperclips, which made the notion of tinker time available; and Tyler's excitement on recognizing that when his students were "driving the discussion…[his] teaching [was] more responsive." Similarly, for Kieran and Aidan, surprise arrived when they found their students fully engaged and nearly oblivious of their absence from their classrooms, leading Kieran to exclaim, "This is it. This is working."

How the Challenges Worked

The enthusiasm I heard in participants' experiences of make-to-learn moments of surprise, where student engagement gathered around explorations of materials, machines, and imaginative projects, and where teachers themselves reported their own expansion of engagement, begs the question: What are teachers resisting when they invoke skepticisms about content, the fit of making, their contrary predispositions, or the difficulty of talking with colleagues about maker-infused pedagogy? Why would any teacher reject the passion-led learning that so many researchers have observed in digital making and learning ecologies, and that was clearly abundant at the school? It is difficult to imagine arguing *against* student engagement.

Resistance

The question *What are teachers resisting?* highlights some of the challenges that digital making pedagogies face in schools. Based on what I've learned here, I would suggest two responses.

The first is that teachers are resisting a challenge to their professional identity. That is, teachers depend on content—in Amanda's words, *"factual, interpretative material that is cognitively based"*—to tell them what to do, because that is substantially how they define themselves as teachers. Accordingly, teachers resist distractions even if leadership mandates those distractions, and even if they themselves recognize that the goal is to benefit learning. Perhaps because teachers are buffeted by so many challenges during the day-to-day tsunami of their complex work, changing their most basic job description—why they were hired—activates pushback.

The second is a fear of losing control, a Challenge that was not very prevalent in interviews or conversations, but which I argued might be significant because of the way it amplified other anxieties. In fact, from a teacher's perspective, loss of control, and especially *inviting* the loss of control that digital making and learning practices precipitate, would be a distraction worth resisting.

While this rather simple explanation of teachers' resistance fits with my observations and what I heard participants saying—e.g., *digital making and learning is a distraction that challenges my professional identity*—it leaves me wondering how (or if) digital materiality's decentered embodiment complicates the situation. As aggregated with and amplified by Loss of Control, teachers' anxieties over the loss of content might feel like losing a sense of purpose—e.g., *If I'm not teaching content, what am I doing?*— precipitating a more existential crisis. I would argue that this is more significant than the distraction explanation, and more difficult to defuse, because adult relationships with purpose and the transformation of purpose are more complex than the questions that children or youth encounter (Kasworm, Rose, & Ross-Gordon, 2010; Kegan, 1998; Kroger, 2006; Merriam et al., 2007). It also makes available a description of maker education that could be useful in understanding what's going on in this school. That is, in a sense, digital making and learning describes a teacher who is no longer *teaching*, because teaching as an action has transitioned from that of an agent who makes stuff happen in the classroom to being a facilitator, manager, or coach on the sidelines, like someone riding a swirling wave of overlapping relational actants working collectively to enact learning and knowing. This is what I observed with Kieran and Aidan. Beatrice realized the scope of disruption: "How do you change your role from the center of the universe to the facilitator, the encourager, the inspirer, the affirmer? It's big." But crossing those thresholds has little to do with content, exactly, at least as traditionally defined, *and* everything to do with how teachers position themselves in relation to their institutions and careers.

This might be crucial: Digitally networked ecologies privilege co-learning as an enacted relationship with action in and with the world, and with iteration driven by interest and curiosity, potentially rendering the teacher at the front of the room invisible. But teachers who participated in this study had not been, by and large, prepared for this new trajectory. Kieran said, "We've got a group of teachers that are feeling adventurous,…but they're a minority, to be frank. Most of the teachers at this school are pretty set in their ways." His administrators tended to agree; Cecelia recognized that teachers were worried, and Julie said, "People have to be willing to deal with some ambiguity, because things aren't all mapped out." Beatrice, whose vision of a reinvented ecology of learning and knowing had led the school to this threshold, said, "We cannot be afraid to disrupt what has been same old, same old, year after year. But the challenge is, how do you get your faculty to develop that same mindset?"

It occurs to me that this might in part explain how the notion of content gathered such power to describe and order practice. These disruptions changed teachers' relationships with knowledge as an object, something they once possessed and were obligated to share. Amanda recognized the encroaching need to "reconceptualize the object," and didn't obsess over content. But nowhere else did I encounter as robust a description of purpose. Beatrice understood what the FabLabs and makerspaces, and the hiring of Kieran, had started. For her, the problem was that teaching had long been organized around the teacher's ability (and responsibility) to "dictate the pace and the direction and the volume of work that needs to be done. [But] technology just wiped it all away." In the ensuing upheavals, participants redefined practice day to day as best they could, and frankly, they did a good job. Bradly insisted that everyone had to begin by recognizing all the great work they were doing, saying that maybe "the Shangri-La is almost here." Nevertheless, the possibility of such a radical decentering was unexpected, and did not fit teachers' definitions of teaching. It might be that participants latched onto *content* as a substitute word for what they felt was changing but didn't know how to articulate.

This interpretation is consistent with the nominal loss of control that one feels when entering a new territory of whatever kind, that sense of being a little bit lost or disoriented. Perhaps such uncertainties, if amplified by digital materiality's radical decentering, are felt as weakened ownership of (Amanda's) "cognitively based" material, which releases a cascade of anxieties. How might this dynamic translate a learning ecology? Perhaps as: Making does not fit, assessment does not make sense, there is no time to learn these tools, and so on. This explanation for why teachers resist digital making and learning in their classrooms at least makes available some empathy for teachers' sense of disruption. Perhaps too, we recognize the contradiction that confronts them: They desire the student engagement that appears within reach, if they can grab onto digital materiality without completely losing their balance.

Here I am reminded again of Amanda and her practice. For her, content was not singular but multiple: content + skills + capacity = *the feeling of knowing*. Amanda said she did not *understand* the way her role in the classroom was changing, but she wasn't overly discombobulated by those changes, either. In this sense, her tripartite schema helped her stay balanced. In fact, gathering Amanda's example before us, the challenge that I've called Content versus Making takes on increased density; in addition to resistance bred from distractions and even, potentially, an existential crisis, we might understand teachers as resisting the expanded space of knowing itself. That is, where once *knowing* was tucked away inside our heads, separated from messy body-based feelings and manual skills, today it is breaking its Enlightenment-era boundaries and oozing across thresholds that used to be inviolable. For example, in the conversation about content, some teachers talked about skills, but no one talked about feeling, at least not in the way Amanda did. Was that topic off limits? Could it be that another affordance of digital materiality (which we might also hold as a consequence) is a surplus of feeling, as Hansen (2004, 2005) has implied, and an increased movement toward interest-driven, passion-based learning, as digital media and making scholars have argued (Gee, 2013; Ito et al., 2013; Martinez & Stager, 2013; Peppler, 2013). Could it be that as digital making and learning activates relational knowing, it pulls affect onto the field? If so, teachers have yet another reason to resist making-infused learning and knowing—feeling, as content, is unthought and unthinkable, at least according to established norms. This might be another way that Amanda keeps her balance—she makes metaphors in dance, with her body, thus turning embodiment into a tool for metaphor making.

Emma, the head of the art department, and the practice she curates, might gather resistance a little differently. She was by far the most adamant of all the participants in her rejection of maker education. She even rejected the study itself, by refusing to meet with me until the very end of the school year. Ironically, of course, this happened simultaneously with a practice that vigorously enacted robust and unpredictable making and building; her students constructed a 12-foot-high Boo Radley tree in the lobby of one of the townhouses, posted digital QR code poetry in the stairwells, and created fashion statements from recycled materials. Nevertheless, Emma said she stayed away from the school's enthusiasm for digital making and learning. Why would this be? Based on the resonant intellectual landscape of our interview and the vast diversity of tools and materials on offer in her art room and displayed in the school-wide art shows, one might expect her to be a leader in the integration of digital materialities in learning and knowing. But instead, she was skeptical about what she felt as a narrow application of making in the curriculum—like putting lights on a box, she said. In Emma's case, I wonder if her already embodied and decentered trajectory of learning and knowing—her celebration of unpredictable iterations; of following the students' lead; her passion for the moral necessity of enacting science and art and history and culture as an entanglement of being; her active decentering of herself in relation to teaching (for instance, by telling students to ditch projects if they go off the rails, and to ignore what she tells them)—I wonder if Emma found making, as currently described by maker education, and as articulated at the school, a *negation* of learning and knowing. That is, by her view, the valorization of an isolated *making* might be held as gathering ignorance and even canceling curiosity in an instrumental and overly designed pursuit of knowledge—where predetermined outcomes focused on skill acquisition rather than on how to take risks, have courage, get yourself unblocked, and other critical lessons that are difficult to bundle into a project that teachers can search for on Google. That would explain, to an extent, her skepticism of this research project, as well as her dismissal of the school-wide enthusiasms for maker-infused teaching swirling around her.

What is a maker educator (or maker administrator) to do with practices such as Emma's? In this particular learning ecology, at this school, the administration's attempts to gather Emma's practice to the mission of "reinventing teaching and learning" seems almost laughable. She's already done it. How would Julie's "making it up as we go along" pull Emma into the conversation? Outside a firmly enforced mandate from Beatrice, that would seem to be inadequate, as would most other project-based initiatives that I observed. For example, I doubt that even the Nerdy Derby's extraordinarily immersive, week-long racing project would gather Emma's enthusiasm, if only because the object of the learning has already been determined—students are building cars, to race on a grooved track. But for a teacher who holds it as a moral imperative that high school girls learn about quantum entanglement, collapsing the *action* of knowing, that unpredictable unfolding of world-makes-world relationality, into car racing, parachute dropping, diorama building, or even Roman Breakfast Banqueting, all of which are predetermined products rather than a pulsing exploration of practice that might end in embarrassment, would seem a terrific diminishment of potential. Why would she waste her time?

Near Misses and New Approaches

In addition to teaching practices that clearly advocated for digital making and learning, such as Kieran's practice, or that campaigned against it, such as those with anxieties about losing content, or that ignored it altogether, as in Emma's art room, I also observed blurry trajectories, where what I observed and heard was difficult to map. I think of these as near misses and new approaches, where the indeterminacy was too great to be interpreted as either a coming together or pulling apart of practices.

Near Misses

For example, one afternoon in the North Building FabLab, I spoke with Susan, the middle school art teacher, about her students' use of the laser cutter in a sixth-grade art project—pop-up nameplates cut from paper. Each sixth grader had created a three-dimensional interpretation of her name in such a way that it stood up on its own. These were painted or otherwise decorated with sparkles, buttons, beads, string, and ribbons. Some were bright and fanciful, barely readable, overflowing the paper base they sat on; others were more restrained in shape or color. Despite the uniformity of object-ness (they were all neither more nor less than pop-up signs displaying the student's name), I noticed that some students had used the laser cutter while others had used hand tools such as X-acto blades in making their work. When I asked about this, Susan told me that students in Vanessa's sections had used the laser cutter in the FabLab but her sections had not, because she had not yet learned to use it herself. In her class, students had cut their nameplates by hand. Although Susan considered this a deficit on her part, I suggested that it offered the chance to talk about how laser cutters and X-acto knives made different materialities available for dialogue, and might prompt further iterations of making. For example, the smoothly precise cuts of the laser juxtaposed against the slightly ragged or jumpy edges of the handheld knife suggested (to me) stories about craft work and machines, cottage industries and the industrial age, one-of-a-kind-ness and mass manufacturing, and I imagined enacting a rich and expansive conversation along these parameters that might empower the sixth graders to open their concept of making and naming, just as a start. Susan, however, said that no such conversation had taken place. This, I would argue, was a missed opportunity for pushing toward a make-to-learn materiality, where talking about the affordances of the tools available at the FabLab might have gathered new stories and metaphors, and perhaps even a new ecology of empowerment. While what actually happened didn't appear to weaken connections with digital making and learning, it certainly didn't strengthen them either.

A second example from the FabLab involved Kieran's sixth-grade technology class. As we discussed the semester and looked at student projects that used the tools on offer, such as the 3D printers, the vinyl cutter, and the laser cutter, Kieran told me he was dissatisfied. One of his goals was for students to engage with the machines in order to achieve a measure of expertise with them. To reach that goal, he prompted them to make things within each tool and material domain—such as a musical instrument with the 3D printer, or a fold-together cube with the laser cutter. Kieran said he was happy with some projects but unhappy with others. For instance, when students wore their 3D-printed earrings around school, he knew they had been motivated to engage; but when they made simple copies of fold-together cubes from online patterns, he realized that they had not gained enough traction in the lab to sufficiently explore the tools. As we paged through some examples on his computer, he said that he did not know how to account for such a wide diversity of successful and lackluster results. In response, I asked about the conversations that had occurred around the projects, and similar to Susan, he said there hadn't been any. This, again, seemed a missed opportunity for learning, and again I would argue that asking students to grapple with how particular machines afford certain kinds of stories opens those students to both conversation and further iterations of learning. This again is a question of materiality. In this case, I suggested that asking students about a gift that each fold-together cube might contain would gather their attention to the way the laser cutter and other materials, for example, wood versus colored plastic, enact different orderings of experience, potentially amplifying their interests in their work. How they might "wrap" a gift to a friend, a parent, or a grandparent?

A third example of a missed opportunity came from the Biodiversity Interactive Diorama project, a collaboration between seventh-grade science and art teachers, where students researched ecological problems such as habitat fragmentation, extinction, urbanization, public policy and the legal implications of environmental degradation, the value of biodiversity to the food supply and medical care, and the aesthetic value of nature. To present their findings, students created dioramas. Their completed projects reprised scale models of gallery exhibits one might find at a natural history museum, made with wood, cardboard, plastic, and various types of fabric, and populated with figures of animals, trees, rocks, and humans cut with the laser cutter or made with the 3D printers, or with clay or painted paper. Some of the dioramas were outfitted with lights or buzzers or small motors and moving parts, and others included videos on iPads inserted into the walls of the gallery or at the side of the display. Despite the variety of materials and range of topics, however, neither the girls nor their teachers seemed to have broached a conversation about how any particular material or configuration of material related to research problems or findings—how certain kinds of problems might be made more available or present with one material rather than another, or with particular colors, textures, or electronic components. Admittedly, the conceptual and material sensitivity that such a conversation would require has probably not been part of a seventh-grade curriculum before, but I would argue that the making and learning ecology that is emerging at the school perhaps makes it possible, if the opening for the conversation itself can be perceived.

But as with the sixth-grade nameplate project, these teachers and students missed an opportunity to expand their enactment of knowing and learning because they didn't realize they were leaving part of the story untold. Isabella's end-of-project assessment notes, which she shared with me, support this interpretation, suggesting that through the doing of the project she had become aware that an "applied materials exploration" might have enhanced students' learning by encouraging them to better "represent desert, trash, rough surfaces." This interpretation is also supported by the teaching team's self-assessment debriefing session (which they shared with me as an audio recording). There, in addition to discussing time management, the lack of time, student engagement, and the overall authenticity of the experience, Kieran critiqued the way technology seemed to be simply "slapped on" because the narrative value of "interactivity was introduced too late in the project." Similarly, Susan lamented two students' impatience with material explorations, explaining that even after showing them various ways of making "fire for slash and burn…[such as] layers of color and clear acetate with colored tissue…the next thing I knew they had printed out a picture of fire from the internet and just stuck it on there." In their brainstorm about potential solutions to these issues, the team touched on broadening fabrication skills, introducing mixed media, or paper engineering, or using paint and glue in different ways. They also discussed the hazard that, as Jessica worried, the work might become "too crafty, or too slick." As such, I would argue that even as an opportunity might have been missed, there are hints here that a new way of holding and perhaps amplifying materiality in teaching is approaching. If this were to occur, it would be a strong indication of a digital making and learning ascendancy at the school.

New Approaches

An example of a new approach to maker education, where the materiality of learning might be described as approaching a phase transition, as when water condenses to become ice, occurred in Isabella's seventh-grade Prosthetic Hand project. Here, students built a hand-like appendage that can lift an empty soda can. The materials on offer included cardboard and rubber bands, as well as other craft materials. In addition to objectives drawn from seventh-grade biology standards, Isabella said she also wanted students to demonstrate their understanding by building a hand—where elements of their construct would share characteristics of a biological hand. When one pair of students suggested cotton balls in place of bone, however, Isabella understood that something was missing, or at minimum, that the students were not connecting science content with the materiality of the hand. I would argue that Isabella's awareness of the way materiality might contribute to learning, what Lakoff and Johnson (1980) call a structural metaphor, is an instance of an approach that might strengthen the ethos of digital making and learning in her teaching practice.

A second example of a threshold-crossing approach to making-infused learning occurred in the lower school makerspace, where a group of third and fourth graders explored basic electronic circuitry by passing Ping-Pong balls between them. The teacher arranged the girls in a circle around the large table in the center of the room and then gave each a Ping-Pong ball, explaining that no one could hold more than one Ping-Pong ball at a time. She then picked up an extra ball from a box on the table and immediately passed the one in her hands to the girl on her right. That girl passed the one she had been holding to her right, and so on, until all the Ping-Pong balls had shifted one position and the "extra" ball had been removed from the circle. This, the teacher explained, was the way electrons behaved in a circuit, the kind they had been making with batteries, paperclips, and light bulbs.

This activity is an example of Lakoff and Johnson's (1980) combination orientational-structural metaphor, where the position of one's body in space helps order ideas about experience, making those ideas available for constructing meaning. In this activity, the embodied and relational organization of bodies and Ping-Pong balls made available a materiality (the flow of electrons) that was not sensible, or not able to be experienced directly. That is, the girls stood shoulder to shoulder, eagerly anticipating the approaching "extra" Ping-Pong ball, wiggling their bodies in anticipation of making the handoff, and then taking their turns at enacting the shift, sometimes clumsily, sometimes dropping the ball, and then laughing, cheering, or groaning as they watched the wave of "energy" continue around the circle. Whether or not this metaphor for the materiality of electric current catalyzed deep learning about electricity, for example as described by electrical engineers or physicists, is less important than the potential that embodiment as a way of knowing became present and available for future metaphor making. For example, for these fourth-grade girls, the affordances of standing shoulder to shoulder in a circle passing Ping-Pong balls to your friends casts electricity as friendly, participatory, collective, relational, and funny. This doesn't seem like a bad way to begin a relationship with a new material. And as with the Popsicle sticks and rubber bands of Isabella's Prosthetic Hand, I would argue that this activity in the makerspace suggests that new learning opportunities are approaching.

A third example of a new approach happened in a class on computer programming that was attended by both high school seniors and faculty. In this experimental, noncredit elective, both students and teachers gathered to learn Processing, a computer programming language. In the sessions I observed, the leader, a data-visualization expert who taught computer programming at the university level, led the group through exercises and independent projects that varied in complexity but were tailored to individual interests. During these class sessions, high school seniors raised their hands alongside Cecelia and Bradly and other teachers, and everyone shared their work in order to help each other understand the code. Throughout these sessions, the teacher approached participants as equals, even to the point of encouraging the high school students to correct their teachers' mistakes. This example, perhaps even more directly than the first two, reprises an eagerly anticipated outcome of the new ethos and new culture of digital making and learning, namely, that all learners are co-learners, without prejudice for status or expertise. In fact, I remember becoming intensely aware of a new configuration in the learning ecology: Teachers and students engaged and attended together, exchanging and sharing struggles, frustrations, surprises, and success, together, without obsessing over preconceived expectations or road maps—no one was getting a grade! They were having fun, and it was hard. The lessons were challenging, risky, and rewarding, but doing the learning together blurred boundaries and invited a crossing of thresholds that felt exotic and perhaps even a little indecent. Teachers struggling alongside their students? What's going on here!? From the back of the room, I recall thinking to myself that if maker education could reliably coax such boundary crossings into presence, we might truly be on the threshold of new trajectories of learning and knowing, perhaps even leading to significant reformulations of schooling.

· 1 2 ·

AFTER RESEARCH

How the findings of this study matter in practice depends on whether digital making and learning is held as an educational good in a given learning ecology. In fact, an assumption of the value of digital making and learning has been explicitly central to this book. But based on many conversations with teachers who were skeptical of it, I don't think its worth or efficacy can be assumed ahead of time for any particular school, even if school leadership or an enterprising teacher has established a makerspace or FabLab. That is to say, simply agreeing with the underpinnings of constructionist artistic development and socially centered learning—the assumptions of Dewey's progressivism, Piaget's constructivism, Papert's constructionism, and Lowenfeld's developmentalism— does not presume effective *practice*, or offer much guidance in the enactment of maker pedagogies in a specific classroom. Further, the assumptions of these 19th- and 20th-century traditions are knotted up in the complexities of digital networks and new media materials that are basic to the emergence of 21st-century teaching. Simply, the maker movement and socially centered learning depend on the internet and other digital networks. As such, digital network dynamics, including digital materiality and its peculiar affordances, need to be theorized as thoughtfully as any other aspect of maker education. On the basis of these caveats, then, I would propose the following:

Implications for Practice

First, to establish digital making and learning pedagogies, teachers, administrators, students, parents, school staff, and other actors with close community involvement would be encouraged to become aware of the overlaps and contradictions presented by contemporary and historical learning traditions, including the explicit expectation that making-infused learning will lead to student empowerment and interest-driven, passion-fueled learning, and even might require a redefinition of teaching. Based on what I observed at the school profiled here, stakeholders should realize that digital making and learning might be understood as broadly antithetical to schooling. To educate itself on the potential for disruption, leadership might initiate exploratory opportunities for faculty and other participants to become familiar with the history of digital making and learning, with its goals, tools, and materials. I would argue that such opportunities take various forms, including reading and discussion groups, online symposia, guest lectures, and faculty presentations, as well as hands-on workshops that engage participants with the tenets of digital making and learning.

Second, during the introductory period, when making-infused learning and knowing begins connecting with school culture, leadership would be encouraged to deflate expectations about high-tech machines such as laser cutters, 3D printers, and CNC routers, among others. This is not to say that schools should not buy such tools. It is, however, to argue that an association of maker education with FabLab should be discouraged. Not only is digital making and learning not primarily about these fancy tools, it might not be even remotely about them. To accomplish this recalibration, discussion groups might begin with marshmallow towers and walks in the woods, and by privileging dialogue about how expanded materialities make new metaphors available for conversation, making, and doing.

Third, digital making and learning and *knowing* is about new configurations of materiality that are taking hold across a broad spectrum of cultural domains. As such, leadership might encourage faculty to explore the paradoxical territory that decentered embodiment brings to presence, and even to ask what it means to teach without teaching. While such notions would likely appear esoteric or obscure, there is reason to suspect that enacted encounters with digital materiality generate learners who are familiar and even deeply comfortable with these paradoxes, at least in children and youth learning environments (Gee, 2013; Ito et al., 2013). I would argue that teachers who work in digital learning ecologies be encouraged to explore this kind of know-ing in a way that induces them to become such learners themselves.

Fourth, teacher education might benefit from an emphasis on material learning as a way of knowing and, importantly, as a way of *doing* teaching. Material learning holds content acquisition as a feeling of knowing that emerges from and with enacted encounters with materials, where insight or innovation arrives sometimes as if by accident, by surprise, or as if from the materials themselves, whether those materials be paint, clay, cardboard, bit-maps, 3D polygons, vector data, or virtual reality immersions, or documents from the Revolutionary War, poetry from the Han Dynasty, or a bacterial smear in a petri dish. While this recommendation runs counter to notions of teaching as an intentional, human-centered activity, and to teacher education that grounds practice in narrowly cognitive terms or instrumental best prac-tices, I would argue that a robust enactment of digital making and learning—as a way of knowing—is an aspirational trajectory that holds serendipity, flow, and conversations with materials as a more important educational good than standardized outcomes and scaffolded content.

Fifth, exploring material learning in schools and teacher education pro-grams suggests that, as a matter of teacher professionalism, attention be gath-ered on how tools order experience, or in other words, how tools tell stories. This runs counter to training based on *what* tools do, or what *you can do* with a particular machine. Rather, more emphasis might be placed on the narra-tives that tools and materials make *available* to learners. As such, metaphors would be foregrounded. In this I am thinking of multimodal poems and stories where one kind of experience can be analyzed and mapped onto other kinds of experiences—visual, aural, tactile, olfactory, gustatory, and kinesthetic, in addition to literary or linguistic. In this, I'm arguing from the proposition that metaphor making is a primary component in meaning making, whether conceptual (Lakoff & Johnson, 1980), methodological (Law, 2004), or spa-tial (Sørensen, 2009). Following art education traditions of material dialogue (Burton, 2000, 2009), the goal would be for teachers to make the extralinguis-tic materiality of practice available to their teaching.

Sixth, and finally, in instituting any of the above, school leadership and teacher educators are encouraged to prioritize safe conversation zones where critique and disagreement can be entertained without penalty or bias. Enact-ing such an ecology requires time (an intersection of different *kinds* of time, as Kieran said), as well as trust and goodwill. I would argue that opening spaces where binaries can be kept in play without collapsing them into singularities (such as on the Möbius strip) is important for establishing digital making and learning's new ethos of learning: We disagree with each other...Great! Let's keep talking. In support of this claim I point to the finding that, in this study, digital making and learning practices became stronger in casual conversations and weaker when difficult conversations were foreclosed. As such, creating and maintaining time and space for authentic conversations about learning will strengthen teaching and learning across the curriculum.

Further Questions

In gathering this book to a conclusion, I am moved to ask: What comes next? During these past few years I have been privileged to become a minor part of a diverse learning community, and to spend time in the company of fearless, inspiring educators. I am not sure if anything written here can adequately convey the depth and complexity of the teaching and learning that I observed and participated in enacting (yes, to the smallest extent permissible, I recognize myself as an participant in those enactments). Perhaps an honorable way to exit the stage is to project the research farther. Based on the learning described thus far, several questions and ideas for future study are resonating:

Typology

Regarding the typology of Ways and Challenges, how might it be useful in exploring teachers' learning in other learning ecologies? Are teachers in other schools encountering digital making and learning practices as the teachers in this school have? Further research might involve surveys drawn from the typology, perhaps expanding the ethnographic motivations of my work and making quantitative orderings of experience available to interpretation. Another way to investigate this might be as a social media exploration—what hashtags are relevant to enactments of digital making and learning practices in schools?

Materialities

Regarding the effects of digital materiality, how evident is decentered embodiment in teachers' experience? As a finding of the study, the construct itself (that is, digital materiality and its affordances, especially decentered embodiment), feels layered onto my interpretations of observations and inter-views. That is, no participant talked about "decentered embodiment." This is due at least in part to *materiality* being overlooked as an actant. But how might digital materiality be described in a way that makes it available to teachers as a tool? Was my encounter with Amanda and her practice an anomaly? In what ways are similar practices emerging in other schools? An exploration of these questions might resemble this study, perhaps in the sense of being a situated residency with an exploratory, ethnographic disposition, though certainly the particulars would vary. I wonder, for example, how an action research project might address these issues.

Spatial Complexity

How does holding pedagogy as a topological diagram influence practice? This question points to an extension of the study that has emerged from writing this book, suggested by the unexpected resonance that the Möbius strip anal-ogy has had on my imagination. As described in Chapter 2, the Möbius strip appeared early in the construction of the digital making and learning assem-blage, when Resnick's spirals of iteration and Gee's and Ito's fluid boundary crossings overlapped and juxtaposed their respective making and learning trajectories. For these researchers, and for many who have been inspired by their work, ideas about how teaching and learning gets done are presented in their spatial maps—spiral, affinity space, HoMaGo. In struggling to articu-late what I had encountered at the school, and wondering how digital mate-riality might be entangled with that difficulty, the strip became a map for my own approach—this was unexpected. That is, as a visual artist with an affinity for holding pictures (drawings, paintings, photographs, and all manner of mark-making visualizations) as evidence of a cognitive + affective entan-glement *with* the world, I consider myself predisposed to engage maps and diagrams on multiple levels, but I had not felt them as relational assemblages in themselves. I am struck by the incongruity of this: how odd that I had not felt this.

My point here is that spatial complexity, especially as a heuristic, is under-theorized in pedagogy, perhaps particularly in teacher education. Fenwick et al. (2011) suggested as much in their survey of sociomaterialism, and Sørensen (2009) argued that spatial metaphors were crucial for coming to grips with the materiality of learning. But in reading their works, I was per-plexed, especially by Sørensen's exploration of spatial formations that change shape until they can "be characterized as a spatial imaginary" (p. 177). Her insistence on this point of methodology has stayed with me, however, and her definition of the "materiality of learning…as the *achieved ability of a growth in knowledge to connect to other particular entities*" (p. 177, original emphasis) resonates strongly with my experience in this study (particularly her notion of knowing as connecting). Gradually, over the course of these 2 years, I have become aware of the potential for spatial imaginaries to influence practice as materialities in themselves. For example, the image of desks in rows exerts a force on our imaginations as both a warning about how not to teach and as a hint about how to reshape teaching and learning. No rows; circles! But can moving the furniture around truly reform schooling? In this sense, diagrams not only map obstacles, they constrain options, just like stepladders bind us to the higher shelves. In teacher education, would unpacking these spatial dynamics help schools enact more empowering and emancipatory pedagogies?

In this, I am reminded of Lakoff and Johnson's (1980) claims that metaphors both reveal and conceal experience, and their observations about the difficulty of recognizing our indebtedness to what is hidden in the process of understanding what is known. They illustrate this with what they call *conduit metaphors*, pointing out that understanding sentences such as *I gave you that idea* or *It's difficult to put my ideas into words* position *ideas* as *objects* and *containers*, and equate *communication* with *sending*. Further, they argue that keeping these complex analogies simultaneously available in the background but suppressed in the foreground is a requirement of communicating effectively, especially if the speakers hold different worldviews. For example, employing a conduit metaphor depends on the binary opposition of objectivity/subjectivity: *Ideas* are *objects* that we, as *subjects*, externalize and *send* to other *subjects*. But this configuration of space, this relationship of knower to known, depends on holding ourselves outside space and time, separate from the world—a proposition that seems normal enough to those of us steeped in Western science and literate ways of knowing. But as I've suggested at so many places in this book (for instance, with the stepladder analogy), that picture of the world might also be held as a relational construct that becomes enacted by our use of a particular tool—in this case, the tool of written language. Are we isolated as individual subjects, surrounded by the objects of our environment, like a letter is surrounded by an envelope? Or are we entangled knots of emergence interwoven within a tidal flux of a world-makes-world recursivity? And why stop with just these two (apparently) oppositional spatialities? In a particularly disruptive proposition based on the idea of suppression, Lakoff and Johnson argue that "metaphorical imagination," the ability to examine and manipulate rich conceptual relationships, "is a crucial skill in creating rapport and communicating the nature of unshared experience" (p. 231). In other words, they are saying, communicating effectively requires that we understand that we don't know what we're talking about.

This paradox reminds me of Elisabeth Kasl's (Kasl & Yorks, 2012) eyes-closed experience with clay, and the *knowing without thinking* that connected her to an "epistemology [that was] vastly different from her usual way of knowing" (p. 512). It also reminds me of Bamberger and Schön's (1983) open-ended cognitive objects (musical tunes) that were experienced as a meandering flow of paying attention to the "unexpected insights [that] evolve in the work of making" (p. 73). These concordances and overlaps with what I've described as material learning lead me to the speculation that even language, as a material, relies on affordances and assemblages that reprise the material gestures that precede linguistic sense making, like the gestures of the very young child described by Vygotsky (1978). Could it be that literacy itself is pre- or extra-linguistic? How might the proposition that text is a material affect teaching practices in makerspaces?

In this respect, Sørensen (2009) agreed with Lakoff and Johnson (1980) about the necessity of learning to manipulate metaphors, though her notions of spatialization and materiality contrast with their mostly cognitive and linguistic ideas. Following Sørensen, I would ask if diagrams of spatial imaginaries might inform *potential* enactments of teaching, as Mol (2002) suggests, by keeping options open. To what extent might alternative topologies open new practices? After all, we already use shapes to order all kinds of experience: Pyramids explain food; boxes explain constraints; trees explain families. And in terms of mapping knowing as an action, the rhizome (Deleuze & Guattari, 1987) and the fungus (Engeström, 2008) are just two of the spatialities we find in the literature. How might any of these be applied to the education of teachers?

Metaphor

And finally, regarding the making of metaphors, to what extent might this skill matter to teaching in the digital age? This question has floated in the background from the beginning—Papert's soap-sculpture math, Resnick's spiral, Burton's material voices, my own career in photography and digital art—but its emergence as a component of teachers' learning in makerspaces and FabLabs is a surprise. As an intellectual field, the study of metaphor has a rich history, with multiple stakeholders who agree with and contradict each other about metaphor's centrality or irrelevance (Fauconnier & Turner, 2002; Lakoff & Johnson, 1980; Latour, 2013; Latour & Woolgar, 1979; Law, 2004; Sørensen, 2009; Wheelahan, 2012). In teacher education, the application of metaphor (and metaphorical narrative) is addressed as background inspiration for understanding the place of education in culture, as in Maxine Greene's (1995) magnificent oeuvre, or in Jerome Bruner's (1987) reappraisals of cognitive dynamics, but it is rarely held as a material that teachers must handle in order to enact practice. Exceptions exist, of course (for example, Egan's [2008, 2010] blueprint for teacher education based on storytelling and metaphor making), but the literature as a whole is largely silent about how to teach educators to recognize, make, and apply metaphors in their teaching.

A similar situation pervades mainstream maker education: The literature is silent on making as a metaphor for knowing. As an example of what's missing in many K–12 makerspaces, see Colin Angevine's (2015a, 2015b) work in a Philadelphia high school, where students crochet scarves with Morse code and make sound waves into touchable objects. In prompts that expand the relational potential of making activities, Angevine invites students to map material (as substance) onto affect (as materiality). On the other side of the country, Natalie Freed (2014), a K–12 computer science teacher in Seattle, makes internet-enabled objects that respond to the rhythms of the world. Regarding her *Tide Book*, a handmade paper book containing pastel drawings embedded with LEDs and Wi-Fi connectivity, she writes: "When it was finally receiving live tide data it felt like the book suddenly came alive and became connected to the world—not in the social media, always-connected kind of way, but as though there was a thread tying it to a real thing far away" (n.p.). In these examples, material metaphors enact an explicit relationship with the world that expands and extends narrative imagination. Examples like these, however—where metaphor is invoked as a materiality, or relational assemblage, and where playing with the specific affordances of particular configurations of matter, endurance, relevance and affect is the desired outcome—are extremely rare, at least as far as I've been able to determine.

This absence requires an explanation and a corrective. As I have discussed, enacting new practices in cultural ecologies (whether or not they're conceived as new paradigms) requires new configurations of learning. In the case of learning to teach with the tools and materials of digital networks, I would argue that getting a handle on the complex, oscillating trajectories that decentered embodiment precipitates requires a particularly adept skill at mapping the abstract onto the concrete, the insensible onto the sensible. This has been supported by descriptions of storytelling and metaphor making throughout this book, and by recognizing that the participant with the richest sense of metaphor also enacted the most complex relationship with the ethos of digital making and learning, even though she had barely begun to investigate its tools. That is to say, Amanda's fearless embrace of ways of knowing that she did not understand and was skeptical toward prompted her to articulate and enact a practice that entangled deep curiosity and dynamic impatience. These are characteristics that good teachers want for all their students. Did living and breathing these dynamics affect the way Amanda brought them to presence with her students? I didn't assess student learning in this project, but I cannot pretend to think that Amanda's students didn't benefit from her embodied passion for learning and knowing. On this point, in itself, a further study is warranted.

Particularly fascinating to me, however, is coming to realize how much of Amanda's practice reprised digital materiality's paradoxical affordances of decentered agency and amplified embodiment. She depended on students' conversations with documents; and she danced in the classroom to encourage them to construct embodied metaphors. I want to know how Amanda came to this particular trajectory in the world. Interviews, observations, and casual conversations were filled with hints about aspects of her upbringing, personality, and prior experience, but I am not convinced that I know the answer to this question. Tinkering in her father's furniture shop as a child, participating in making-infused workshops, earning a doctorate in church history, talking to the text, relentless curiosity, dancing: What are the critical components here? Or, have we not yet touched the periphery of how she does what she does? My suspicion is that her skill in making and using metaphor is fundamental to the practice enacted around her. This reprises the emergence of the inquiry, as described in the introductory chapter of this book. And yet I am skeptical. While not a resolution, perhaps this suggests a different route: Instead of following actors through the entangled mess of their practices, why not take a journey fueled by the feeling of knowing? How might teaching with the materiality of metaphor, as an enacted encounter, prepare teachers for decentered but embodied practices?

Conclusion

One last aspect of Amanda's practice must be highlighted: her passionate expertise for the study of history. While the role of expertise in maker education has been an implicit part of the story, I want to be explicit about it in these concluding thoughts. At the end of Chapter 2 I pointed out that the literature of maker education is mostly silent about how students acquire the deep knowledge they need in order to make complex projects come to life in FabLabs and makerspaces. In Chapter 7 I illustrated the contact point I called Lack of Expertise with Aidan's comment that "you don't really know how anything works all the way through, [so] you don't have the fluency or the expertise to help [students] deal with their frustrations." In Chapter 8 I profiled Thomas's exhaustion in his engineering class, where his students had "no idea what they were going to do," which meant he would be "making eleven projects." And throughout the book, I've referred to the "make it up as we go along" strategy that the school administration and multiple teachers referred to: their reliance on Kieran, the only teacher with any formal training in the new tools and materials in the FabLabs and makerspaces, to show them what to do. Broadly speaking, this attitude about expertise—a skepticism or nonchalance about who has it; where it comes from; even its relevance—is consistent across maker education. Ironically, the reluctance to robustly theorize expertise reprises a characteristic of our educational systems more generally: Deep learning as an educational good is under threat in contemporary schooling, often sinking beneath testing and jobs training on school agendas.

Other fields of practice have noticed similar ambiguities toward expertise. In medicine, Mol (2002) argues that the predominant metaphors ordering practice are markets and demographics (that is, patients are either customers or statistics). This paucity of alternatives constrains our ability to imagine other options for achieving the good that we expect from medical care. One reason for this is that professional expertise has become devalued in the age of Google's endless catalog of symptoms and treatments, where fast answers are cheap and easy to pull from a vast ocean of trivia.

I would point to this dynamic in the conversation about schooling, which might partly explain the divisive mistrust over standards and accountability, and even suggest why expertise is undertheorized in maker education. That is, by positioning itself as the antidote for what ills schools, maker education offers the anti-expertise, anticanon, alternative of social learning, do-it-yourself learning, and self-interested learning. But in doing so, it aligns squarely with normative schooling's misalignment of deep knowing with high scores on external exams. But achievement cannot be reduced to higher test scores, in spite of how often these things are conflated in the press and in policy statements. And while I've never heard a maker educator suggest as much, the disciplined study required to learn coding or sewing looks something like the disciplined study that learning history or English literature requires. Could the logic of resemblance be animating maker education's ambivalence toward expertise? How come we don't see kids studying in makerspaces or FabLabs? What affordances does this absence conceal?

For Amanda, expertise makes available a "reward of pleasure and play, [an] experience [of] scholarship as freedom and joy." And this joy is resonant in her teaching. For her, expertise is complex; it includes content—"stuff I'm teaching that I could ask you to write an essay about and expect you to furnish it out of stuff from your head"—as just one part of a feeling of knowing. She said that "good high school teaching includes some cognitive content, stuff educated people ought to know because…it is going to make them into better, more reflective citizens." And she is confident in her own skills and capacity to argue that the relationship of grit, determination, and perseverance with materials (in her case, the material of history) is a precondition of imagination and curiosity. She said, "You can't ask kids to think creatively until they have some content, right, because they can't manipulate it until they know it." This is not the perspective of teachers who disavow canons, or teaching with explicitly instructional tactics—the ones we might recall from the worksheets handed to us by teachers walking up and down those rows of desks we remember from childhood.

That might be putting it too simplistically, but distrust of instructionism (Papert, 1980a) resonates with advocates of maker education's learn-by-doing evangelism. This again begs the question, though, of whether "old-fashioned" individual study has any place at all in schooling. At the risk of looping right back to the very beginning of the conversation, we must again entertain this clash of paradigms. How does knowledge come to presence in a given ecology? Is it in the head, or in the community? Should we attend to it as a verb or as a noun? Right. We're back at the central conundrum. Perhaps we never left, even after traipsing through so many makerspaces and media labs. This might be the ultimate affordance of our literacy—clearly defined opposites that are hard to hold but impossible to put down.

In Amanda's choreography of knowing, there is a private mind, but it is thoroughly knit through with the expectations and responsibilities of relationships. For her, the reason for studying the "factual material" of history is to make a "better, more reflective citizen." It's why good teaching "includes some cognitive content stuff educated people ought to know." And it's why the feeling of knowing matters. Amanda's passion is for facilitating, coaching, mentoring, and cajoling her students to "become more thoughtful, more insightful, a little bit more self-aware of themselves as interpreters." She said, "I care about content, but the whole point of learning about 5th-century or 6th-century Athens is because it informs what we do now."

The complexity of this interwoven learning and knowing that co-emerges with doing and becoming human is rarely talked about in schools. Its absence is due in part to our devotion to superficial measurements of contingent outcomes, such as high-stakes testing and curriculum as job training. And although these goals are not without merit—it's good to have a job, after all—these things have as much to do with deep expertise, innovation, and creativity as splashing on the surface of the water has to do with long-distance swimming. One might lead to the other, but there is no necessity of such. Simply, while related, splashing and swimming are different ways of being in the world.

What I have learned from Amanda leads me to speculate that maker education is facing a conundrum that might undermine its existence. That is, while economic and policy leaders explicitly desire the kind of learning that leads to innovation, and while educational scholars have theorized its attainability through constructionist, situated, and connected pedagogies of inventing and making, our approaches to learning and the ecologies in which we find ourselves are often misaligned. One challenge is that the tools and materials that invite us to imagine a new culture and new ethos of learning— the new materialities of digital networks, laser cutters, 3D printers, microelectronics, computer programming, and the huge variety of craft materials we find in makerspaces and media labs—are too slippery and complex to be held seriously and playfully without a significant investment of skill, perseverance, grit, time, and, it must be said, money. Our schools, however, can rarely sustain these requirements, and without them, the sustained engagement that might lead to innovation is reduced to tinkering, a favorite and highly valued word in maker education. But tinkering is too often like splashing on the surface of the water, especially when deep learning and material expertise have been forfeited.

Another challenge is that digital making and learning scholarship has attended almost exclusively to children and youth learning. That is, until very recently, there has been little conversation about the challenges faced by adult learners, or by teachers who are attracted to the promise of engaged and passionate students but who do not understand how to fit making into what they have been hired to do. In fact, as I've speculated here, one aspect of that challenge might be that these teachers, and their teacher educators in teachers colleges, can't articulate their misgivings and doubts. And without doubt, there are few openings for new practice.

Following Amanda's example, I would argue that innovations in pedagogy require a different kind of time, space, and dialogue, and a different grappling with materiality than either schools or teacher education programs are currently configured to address. That is, schools—both private preparatory schools and over-regulated public schools—are liable to stakeholders and agendas that originate from far outside their boundaries. And teacher education and certification programs often answer to those same agendas. In both cases, existing practice prevents making-infused pedagogy from gaining the traction it needs to survive. And yet, this slippage into obscurity, which has been the fate of earlier pedagogical reform movements, might be avoidable.

By my reading, after nearly 3 years of closely attending to the dozen teaching practices I've profiled in this book, I would argue that for teachers to enact pedagogies infused with interest-driven, connected making and learning, they require the time and space to explore a different way of knowing—a material knowing, an overlapping pinboard kind of knowing, an unscripted knowing that leads with materials and attends to inquiry and serendipity. This is where innovation comes from. But to do this, teachers need to collaborate with coaches and facilitators who have the experience and expertise to explicitly guide their endeavors—a claim, I realize, that implies transgressing the borders between instructionism and constructionism, and between socially centered learning and developmentalism.

As this study has been an ethnographic exploration of broad issues in maker education, my findings here are not generalizable, but I would argue that maker teachers everywhere are encountering similar challenges. What comes next for any individual practice, however, is irreducibly complex, and might be describable only in language that opens to a different kind of presence. This difference might be hinted at within the digital making and learning framework-assemblage developed here, or in the typology of contact points that helped me explore the practices gathered in this book, or in the conundrum of the Möbius strip that continues to puzzle my understanding of pedagogical space. But these questions remain for further testing.

In the meantime, in spite of the gaps and misstatements in this narrative, the outright errors, the idiosyncrasies of interpretation, and the particularities of my dispositions and personal history, I hope something in this book will be useful for teachers and teacher educators who want to engage with making-infused, project-based learning and knowing. My fear is that how we attain trajectories that aspire to innovation and make-to-surprise serendipity, with or without the tools of digital making and learning, has not been adequately addressed. For example, I'm painfully aware that in this book I've barely even nodded in the direction of the uneven and irregular patchwork of education policy in this country, and haven't acknowledged the extreme challenges that schools face because of it—for example, as described and analyzed by Darling-Hammond (2010) and Ravitch (2013), among others. Nevertheless, my hope is that the good of attending to the questions that launched this study is in their invitation to a more robust conversation between teachers, scholars, researchers, administrators, and students about the purpose and value of materiality in learning, and about the necessity of enacting our paradigms as open and emergent.

So many of us are now devoted to project-based, making-infused learning and knowing that I find myself entertaining unreasonable hopes: Perhaps we are indeed on the threshold of a new ethos and new culture of learning! More soberly, of course, I would argue that the conversation and iteration never end, and that the goal must be a commitment to ourselves and to each other to keep striving for more empowered and emancipatory knowing and learning in schools.

REFERENCES

Agency by Design. (2015). *Maker-centered learning and the development of self: Preliminary findings of the Agency by Design Project.* Cambridge, MA: Project Zero, Harvard Graduate School of Education.

Andrews, M., Squire, C., & Tamboukou, M. (Eds.). (2013). *Doing narrative research* (2nd ed.) [Kindle version]. Thousand Oaks, CA: Sage.

Angevine, C. (2015a). Making metaphors [Web log comment]. Retrieved from http://maker space.friendscentral.org/2015/01/08/making-metaphors/

Angevine, C. (2015b). Significant objects [Web log comment]. Retrieved from http://maker space.friendscentral.org/2015/09/27/significant-objects/

Atkinson, D. (2011). *Art, equality and learning: Pedagogies against the state.* Boston, MA: Sense.

Atwell, N. (1987). *In the middle: Writing, reading, and learning with adolescents.* Portsmouth, NH: Boynton/Cook; Heinemann.

Baldacchino, J. (2014). *John Dewey: Liberty and the pedagogy of disposition.* New York, NY: Springer.

Bamberger, J., & Schön, D. A. (1983). Learning as reflective conversation with materials: Notes from work in progress. *Art Education, 36*(2), 68–73.

Barrett, E., & Bolt, B. (Eds.). (2013). *Carnal knowledge: Towards a 'new materialism' through the arts.* London, UK: I. B. Tauris.

Barron, B. (2004). Learning ecologies for technological fluency: Gender and experience differences. *Journal of Educational Computing Research, 31*(1), 1–36.

Bennett, J. (2010). *Vibrant matter: A political ecology of things*. Durham, NC: Duke University Press.

Best, S., & Kellner, D. (2001). *The postmodern adventure: Science, technology, and cultural studies at the third millennium*. New York, NY: Guilford Press.

Biesta, J. J. G. (2010). *Good education in an age of measurement: Ethics, politics, democracy*. Boulder, CO: Paradigm.

Blikstein, P. (2013). Digital fabrication and "making" in education: The democratization of invention. In J. Walter-Herrmann & C. Büching (Eds.), *Fablab: Of machines, makers and inventors* (pp. 203–222). Bielefeld, Germany: Transcript Verlag.

Blok, A., & Jensen, T. E. (2011). *Bruno Latour: Hybrid thoughts in a hybrid world*. London, UK: Routledge.

Bolt, B. (2007). Material thinking and the agency of matter. *Studies in Material Thinking, 1*(1). Retrieved from https://www.materialthinking.org/papers/37

Bolt, B. (2010). The magic is in the handling. In B. Bolt & E. Barrett (Eds.), *Practice as research: Approaches to creative arts enquiry* (pp. 27–34). London, UK: I.B. Tauris.

Bolt, B. (2011). *Heidegger reframed: Interpreting key thinkers for the arts*. London, UK: I. B. Tauris.

Bolt, B. (2013). Introduction. In E. Barrett & B. Bolt (Eds.), *Carnal knowledge: Towards a 'new materialism' through the arts* (pp. 1–13). London, UK: I.B. Tauris.

Braidotti, R. (2010). The politics of "life itself" and new ways of dying. In D. Coole & S. Frost (Eds.), *New materialisms: Ontology, agency, and politics* (pp. 201–218). Durham, NC: Duke University Press.

Braidotti, R. (2013). *The posthuman*. Cambridge, UK: Polity.

Britzman, D. P. (1995). "The question of belief": Writing poststructural ethnography. *International Journal of Qualitative Studies in Education, 8*(3), 229–238.

Brown, J. S., & Adler, R. P. (2008). Minds on fire. *Educause Review, 43*(1), 16–32.

Bruner, J. (1987). *Actual minds, possible worlds*. Cambridge, MA: Harvard University Press.

Bruner, J. (1994). Life as narrative. In A. H. Dyson & C. Genishi (Eds.), *The need for story: Cultural diversity in classroom and community* (pp. 28–37). Urbana, IL: National Council of Teachers of English.

Buechley, L., Peppler, K., Eisenberg, M., & Kafai, Y. (2013). *Textile messages: Dispatches from the world of e-textiles and education*. New literacies and digital epistemologies. New York, NY: Peter Lang.

Buechley, L., Qiu, K., & Boer, S. D. (2013). *Sew electric: A collection of DIY projects that combine fabric, electronics and programming*. Cambridge, MA: HLT Press.

Burton, J. M. (1980). Developing minds: Beginnings of artistic language. *School Arts, 80*(1), 6–12.

Burton, J. M. (1991). Some basic considerations about "basic art." *Art Education, 44*(4), 34–41.

Burton, J. M. (2000). The configuration of meaning: Learner-centered art education revisited. *Studies in Art Education, 41*(4), 330–345.

Burton, J. M. (2009). Creative intelligence, creative practice: Lowenfeld redux. *Studies in Art Education, 50*(4), 323–337.

Cabral, M. & Justice, S. (2013). *Material learning: Digital 3d with young children*. FabLearn 13: Digital Fabrication in Education, Stanford University. Palo Alto, CA.

Carter, P. (2004). *Material thinking: The theory and practice of creative research*. Melbourne, Australia: Melbourne University Publishing.

Carter, P. (2010). Interest: The ethics of invention. In E. Barrett & B. Bolt (Eds.), *Practice as research approaches to creative arts enquiry* (pp. 15–25). London, UK: I. B. Tauris.

Chase, S. E. (2011). Narrative inquiry: Still a field in the making. In N. K. Denzin & Y. S. Lincoln (Eds.), *The Sage handbook of qualitative research* (4th ed., pp. 421–434). Thousand Oaks, CA: Sage.

Clark, A. (1997). *Being there: Putting brain, body, and world together again*. Cambridge, MA: MIT Press.

Clark, A. (2011). *Supersizing the mind: Embodiment, action, and cognitive extension*. Oxford, UK: Oxford University Press.

Connolly, W. E. (2010). Materialities of experience. In D. Coole & S. Frost (Eds.), *New materialisms: Ontology, agency, and politics* (pp. 198–225). Durham, NC: Duke University Press.

Coole, D., & Frost, S. (Eds.). (2010). *New materialisms: Ontology, agency, and politics*. Durham, NC: Duke University Press.

Creswell, J. W. (2007). *Qualitative inquiry and research design: Choosing among five approaches* (2nd ed.). Thousand Oaks, CA: Sage.

Csikszentmihalyi, M. (1975). *Beyond boredom and anxiety: The experience of play in work and games* (2nd ed.). San Francisco, CA: Jossey-Bass.

Csikszentmihalyi, M. (2008). *Flow: The psychology of optimal experience*. New York, NY: Harper Perennial Modern Classics.

Daichendt, G. J. (2010). *Artist-teacher: A philosophy for creating and teaching*. Bristol, UK: Intellect.

Damasio, A. R. (1994). *Descartes' error: Emotion, reason, and the human brain*. New York, NY: Putnam.

Damasio, A. R. (1999). *The feeling of what happens: Body and emotion in the making of consciousness*. New York, NY: Harcourt Brace.

Darling-Hammond, L. (2006). *Powerful teacher education: Lessons from exemplary programs* [Kindle version]. San Francisco, CA: Jossey-Bass.

Darling-Hammond, L. (2010). *The flat world and education: How America's commitment to equity will determine our future*. New York, NY: Teachers College Press.

Darling-Hammond, L. (2013). *Getting teacher evaluation right: What really matters for effectiveness and improvement* [Kindle version]. New York, NY: Teachers College Press.

Davidson, C. N. (2011). *Now you see it: How technology and brain science will transform schools and business for the 21st century* [Kindle version]. New York, NY: Viking.

Deleuze, G., & Guattari, F. (1987). *A thousand plateaus: Capitalism and schizophrenia*. Minneapolis, MN: University of Minnesota Press.

Dewey, J. (1997). *Democracy and education: An introduction to the philosophy of education*. New York, NY: Free Press. (Original work published 1916).

Dijk, T. A. V. (1997). *Discourse as social interaction*. Discourse studies: A multidisciplinary introduction. Thousand Oaks, CA: Sage.

Doctorow, C. (2014). *Information doesn't want to be free: Laws for the Internet age*. San Francisco, CA: McSweeney's.

Efland, A. (1990). *A history of art education: Intellectual and social currents in teaching the visual arts.* New York, NY: Teachers College Press.

Egan, K. (1997). *The educated mind: How cognitive tools shape our understanding.* Chicago, IL: University of Chicago Press.

Egan, K. (2002). *Getting it wrong from the beginning: Our progressivist inheritance from Herbert Spencer, John Dewey, and Jean Piaget.* New Haven, CT: Yale University Press.

Egan, K. (2008). *The future of education: Reimagining our schools from the ground up.* New Haven, CT: Yale University Press.

Egan, K. (2010). *Learning in depth: A simple innovation that can transform schooling.* Chicago, IL: University of Chicago Press.

Eisner, E. W. (1985). *The educational imagination: On the design and evaluation of school programs* (2nd ed.). New York, NY: Macmillan.

Engeström, Y. (2008). *From teams to knots: Activity-theoretical studies of collaboration and learning at work* [Kindle version]. New York, NY: Cambridge University Press.

Esterly, D. (2012). *The lost carving: A journey to the heart of making.* New York, NY: Penguin Books.

Fauconnier, G., & Turner, M. (2002). *The way we think: Conceptual blending and the mind's hidden complexities.* New York, NY: Basic Books.

Fenwick, T. J. (2000). Expanding conceptions of experiential learning: A review of the five contemporary perspectives on cognition. *Adult Education Quarterly, 50*(4), 243–272.

Fenwick, T., & Edwards, R. (2011). Considering materiality in educational policy: Messy objects and multiple reals. *Educational Theory, 61*(6), 709–726.

Fenwick, T., & Edwards, R. (Eds.). (2012). *Researching education through actor-network theory.* Malden, MA: Wiley.

Fenwick, T., Edwards, R., & Sawchuk, P. (2011). *Emerging approaches to educational research: Tracing the sociomaterial.* London, UK: Routledge.

Feynman, R. P. (1999). *The pleasure of finding things out: The best short works of Richard Feynman.* Cambridge, MA: Perseus.

Fleming, L. (2015). *Worlds of making: Best practices for establishing a makerspace for your school.* Thousand Oaks, CA: Corwin.

Flores, C. (in press). *Making science.* Torrance, CA: Making Modern Knowledge Press.

Foley, J. M. (2012). *Oral tradition and the Internet: Pathways of the mind.* Champaign, IL: University of Illinois Press.

Freed, N. (2014). Tide book [Web log comment]. Retrieved from http://www.nataliefreed.com/tide-book/

Freire, P. (2000). *Pedagogy of the oppressed* (20th anniversary ed.). New York, NY: Continuum. (Original work published 1970).

Galloway, A. R., & Thacker, E. (2007). *The exploit: A theory of networks.* Minneapolis, MN: University of Minnesota Press.

Garoian, C. (2011). Art as pedagogy as art. In R. Hickman (Ed.), *The art and craft of pedagogy: Portraits of effective teachers* (pp. ix-xii). New York, NY: Continuum.

Gee, J. P. (1999). *An introduction to discourse analysis: Theory and method.* London, UK: Routledge.

Gee, J. P. (2004). *Situated language and learning: A critique of traditional schooling.* London, UK: Routledge.

Gee, J. P. (2005). Semiotic social spaces and affinity spaces: From the age of mythology to today's schools. In D. Barton & K. Tusting (Eds.), *Beyond communities of practice: Language power and social context.* Learning in doing: Social, cognitive and computational perspectives. New York, NY: Cambridge University Press.

Gee, J. P. (2006). Oral discourse in a world of literacy. *Research in the Teaching of English, 41*(2), 153–159.

Gee, J. P. (2007). *What video games have to teach us about learning and literacy.* New York, NY: Palgrave Macmillan.

Gee, J. P. (2010a). *New digital media and learning as an emerging area and "worked examples" as one way forward.* Cambridge, MA: MIT Press.

Gee, J. P. (2010b). *How to do discourse analysis: A toolkit.* London, UK: Routledge.

Gee, J. P. (2013). *The anti-education era: Creating smarter students through digital learning.* New York, NY: Palgrave Macmillan.

Gee, J. P., & Hayes, E. R. (2011). *Language and learning in the digital age.* London, UK: Routledge.

Gershenfeld, N. (2007). *Fab: The coming revolution on your desktop—from personal computers to personal fabrication.* New York, NY: Basic Books.

Goldsmith, K. (2011). *Uncreative writing: Managing language in the digital age.* New York, NY: Columbia University Press.

Goldstein, D. (2014). *The teacher wars: A history of America's most embattled profession.* New York, NY: Anchor Books.

Goodwin, C., & Heritage, J. (1990). Conversation analysis. *Annual Review of Anthropology, 19,* 283–307.

Gravel, B., Tucker-Raymond, E., Kohberger, K., & Browne, K. (2015). *Literacy practices of experienced makers: Tools for navigating and understanding landscapes of possibility.* Proceedings from Fablearn '15, Palo Alto, CA.

Green, B., & Bigum, C. (1993). Aliens in the classroom. *Australian Journal of Education, 37*(2), 119–141.

Green, E. (2015). *Building a better teacher: How teaching works (and how to teach it to everyone.* New York, NY: W.W. Norton.

Greene, M. (1995). *Releasing the imagination: Essays on education, the arts, and social change.* San Francisco, CA: Jossey-Bass.

Halverson, E. R., & Sheridan, K. (2014). The maker movement in education. *Harvard Educational Review, 84*(4), 495–504.

Hansen, M. B. N. (2004). *New philosophy for new media.* Cambridge, MA: MIT Press.

Hansen, M. B. N. (2005). *Bodies in code: Interfaces with digital media.* London, UK: Routledge.

Hansen, M. B. N. (2015). *Feed-forward: On the future of twenty-first-century media.* Chicago, IL: University of Chicago Press.

Hayles, N. K. (1999). *How we became posthuman: Virtual bodies in cybernetics, literature, and informatics* [Kindle version]. Chicago, IL: University of Chicago Press.

Hayles, N. K. (2012). *How we think: Digital media and contemporary technogenesis* [Kindle version]. Chicago, IL: University of Chicago Press.

Heidegger, M. (1977). *The question concerning technology, and other essays* (W. Lovitt, Trans.). New York, NY: Garland.

Hetland, L., Winner, E., Veenema, S., & Sheridan, K. M. (2013). *Studio thinking 2: The real benefits of visual arts education* [Kindle version]. New York, NY: Teachers College Press.

Hickman, R. (2010). *Why we make art and why it is taught.* Bristol, UK: Intellect.

Hickman, R. (2011). *The art and craft of pedagogy: Portraits of effective teachers.* Continuum studies in educational research. New York, NY: Continuum International.

Hockney, D. (2006). *Secret knowledge: Rediscovering the lost techniques of the old masters.* New York, NY: Penguin Viking Studio.

Honey, M., & Kanter, D. E. (Eds.). (2013). *Design, make, play: Growing the next generation of STEM innovators* [Kindle version]. New York, NY: Routledge.

Ingold, T. (2013). *Making: Anthropology, archaeology, art and architecture* [Kindle version]. London, UK & New York, NY: Routledge.

Irvine, W. B. (2014). *Aha!: The moments of insight that shape our world.* New York, NY: Oxford University Press.

Isaacson, W. (2011). *Steve Jobs.* New York, NY: Simon & Schuster.

Ito, M. (2010). *Hanging out, messing around, and geeking out: Kids living and learning with new media.* John D. and Catherine T. MacArthur Foundation reports on digital media and learning. Cambridge, MA: MIT Press.

Ito, M., Gutierrez, K., Livingstone, S., Penuel, B., Rhodes, J., Salen, K....Watkins, S. C. (2013). *Connected learning: An agenda for research and design.* Digital Media and Learning Research Hub.

Ito, M., Horst, H. A., Bittanti, M., Boyd, D., Stephenson, B. H., Lange, P. G.,...Robinson, L. (2009). *Living and learning with new media: Summary of findings from the digital youth project.* John D. and Catherine T. MacArthur Foundation reports on digital media and learning. Cambridge, MA: MIT Press.

Ito, M., Okabe, D., & Tsuji, I. (2012). *Fandom unbound: Otaku culture in a connected world.* New Haven, CT: Yale University Press.

jagodzinski, j. (2005). Virtual reality's differential perception: On the significance of Deleuze (and Lacan) for the future of visual art education in a machinic age. *Visual Arts Research, 31*(1), 129–144.

jagodzinski, j., & Wallin, J. (2013). *Arts-based research: A critique and a proposal.* Boston, MA: Sense.

Jenkins, H. (2006). *Convergence culture: Where old and new media collide.* New York, NY: NYU Press.

Jenkins, H., Clinton, K., Purushotma, R., Robison, A. J., & Weigel, M. (2009). *Confronting the challenges of participatory culture: Media education for the 21st century.* Chicago, IL: MacArthur Foundation.

Kafai, Y. B., Peppler, K. A., & Chapman, R. N. (2009). *The Computer Clubhouse: Constructionism and creativity in youth communities.* Technology, education—connections series. New York, NY: Teachers College Press.

Kafai, Y. B., & Resnick, M. (1996). *Constructionism in practice: Designing, thinking, and learning in a digital world.* Mahwah, NJ: Erlbaum.

Kasl, E., & Yorks, L. (2012). Learning to be what we know: The pivotal role of presentational knowing in transformative learning. In E. W. Taylor & P. C. Associates (Eds.), *The handbook of transformative learning* (pp. 503–519). San Francisco, CA: Jossey-Bass.

Kasworm, C. E., Rose, A. D., & Ross-Gordon, J. M. (Eds.). (2010). *Handbook of adult and continuing education.* Thousand Oaks, CA: Sage.

Kegan, R. (1998). *In over our heads: The mental demands of modern life.* Cambridge, MA: Harvard University Press.

Kelly, T. M. (2013). *Teaching history in the digital age.* Ann Arbor, MI: University of Michigan Press.

Kennedy, P. (2016). *Inventology: How we dream up things that change the world.* New York, NY: Eamon Dolan/Houghton Mifflin Harcourt.

Kirp, D. L. (2013). *Improbable scholars: The rebirth of a great American school system and a strategy for America's schools* [Kindle version]. New York, NY: Oxford University Press.

Kittler, F. A. (1999). *Gramophone, film, typewriter* (G. Winthrop-Young & M. Wutz, Trans.). Stanford, CA: Stanford University Press.

Koyama, J. P. (2009). Localizing No Child Left Behind: Supplemental education services (SES) in New York City. In F. Vavrus & L. Bartlett (Eds.), *Critical approaches to comparative education: Vertical case studies from Africa, Europe, the Middle East, and the Americas* (pp. 22–37). New York, NY: Palgrave Macmillan.

Kroger, J. (2006). *Identity development: Adolescence through adulthood* (2nd ed.). Thousand Oaks, CA: Sage.

Kuhn, T. (1970). *The structure of scientific revolutions* (2nd ed.). Chicago, IL: University of Chicago Press.

Lakoff, G., & Johnson, M. (1980). *Metaphors we live by.* Chicago, IL: University of Chicago Press.

Lankshear, C., Gee, J. P., Knobel, M., & Searle, C. (1997). *Changing literacies.* Changing education. New York, NY: Open University Press.

Lankshear, C., & Knobel, M. (2011). *New literacies everyday practices and social learning* (3rd ed.). Maidenhead, UK: Open University Press.

Lankshear, C., & Knobel, M. (Eds.). (2013). *A new literacies reader: Educational perspectives.* New York, NY: Peter Lang.

Latour, B. (1987). *Science in action: How to follow scientists and engineers through society.* Cambridge, MA: Harvard University Press.

Latour, B. (1993). *We have never been modern.* New York, NY: Harvester Wheatsheaf.

Latour, B. (1996). *Aramis, or, the love of technology.* Cambridge, MA: Harvard University Press.

Latour, B. (2005). *Reassembling the social: An introduction to actor-network-theory.* Oxford, UK: Oxford University Press.

Latour, B. (2013). *An inquiry into modes of existence: An anthropology of the moderns.* Cambridge, MA: Harvard University Press.

Latour, B., & Woolgar, S. (1979). *Laboratory life: The construction of scientific facts.* Beverly Hills, CA: Sage.

Lave, J., & Wenger, E. (1991). *Situated learning: Legitimate peripheral participation*. Cambridge, UK: Cambridge University Press.

Law, J. (2002). *Aircraft stories: Decentering the object in technoscience*. Science and cultural theory [Kindle version]. Durham, NC: Duke University Press.

Law, J. (2004). *After method: Mess in social science research*. London, UK: Routledge.

Leonardi, P. M. (2010). Digital materiality? How artifacts without matter, matter. *First Monday*, *15*(6). Retrieved from http://dx.doi.org/10.5210/fm.v15i6.3036

Lowenfeld, V. (1957). *Creative and mental growth* (3rd ed.). New York, NY: Macmillan. (Original work published 1947).

Lyytinen, K., Yoo, Y., & Boland, R. J., Jr. (2016). Digital product innovation within four classes of innovation networks. *Information Systems Journal*, *26*(1), 47–75.

Malone, M. (1997). *Worlds of talk: The presentation of self in everyday conversation*. Cambridge, UK: Polity Press.

Markoff, J. (2015, October 9). An error leads to a new way to draw, and erase, computing circuits. *The New York Times*. Retrieved from http://www.nytimes.com/2015/10/10/science/an-error-leads-to-a-new-way-to-draw-and-erase-computing-circuits.html?_r=0

Martin, L. (2015). Promise of the maker movement for education. *Journal of Pre-College Engineering Education Research (J-PEER)*, *5*(1).

Martinez, S. L., & Stager, G. S. (2013). *Invent to learn: Making, tinkering, and engineering in the classroom*. Manchester, NH: Constructing Modern Knowledge Press.

Maxwell, J. A. (2004). *Qualitative research design: An interactive approach* (2nd ed.). Thousand Oaks, CA: Sage.

Maynard, P. (1997). *The engine of visualization: Thinking through photography*. Ithaca, NY: Cornell University Press.

Merriam, S. B., Caffarella, R. S., & Baumgartner, L. M. (2007). *Learning in adulthood: A comprehensive guide* (3rd ed.). San Francisco, CA: Wiley.

Miller, J. L. (2004). *Sounds of silence breaking: Women, autobiography, curriculum*. New York, NY: Peter Lang.

Mitchell, W. J. T. (2005). *What do pictures want? The lives and loves of images*. Chicago, IL: University of Chicago Press.

Mol, A. (2002). *The body multiple: Ontology in medical practice*. Durham, NC: Duke University Press.

Mulcahy, D. (2011). Assembling the 'accomplished' teacher: The performativity and politics of professional teaching standards. *Educational Philosophy and Theory*, *43*, 94–113.

Mumford, L. (2010). *Technics and civilization* (Reprint ed.). Chicago, IL: University of Chicago Press.

Nespor, J. (2002). Networks and contexts of reform. *Journal of Educational Change*, *3*(3), 365–382.

Orlikowski, W. J. (1992). The duality of technology: Rethinking the concept of technology in organizations. *Organization Science*, *3*(3), 427–398.

Orlikowski, W. J., & Scott, S. V. (2008). Chapter 10: Sociomateriality: Challenging the separation of technology, work and organization. *Academy of Management Annals*, *2*(1), 433–474.

Papert, S. (1980a). *Constructionism vs. instructionism.* Retrieved from http://www.papert.org/articles/const_inst/const_inst1.html

Papert, S. (1980b). *Mindstorms: Children, computers, and powerful ideas.* New York, NY: Basic Books.

Papert, S. (1993). *The children's machine: Rethinking school in the age of the computer.* New York, NY: Basic Books.

Papert, S. (2001). *Project-based learning.* Retrieved from http://www.edutopia.org/seymour-papert-project-based-learning

Papert, S., & Freire, P. (1980). *The future of school.* Retrieved from http://www.papert.org/articles/freire/freirePart1.html

Papert, S., & Harel, I. (1991). *Constructionism.* New York, NY: Ablex.

Peppler, K. A. (2010). Media arts: Arts education for a digital age. *Teachers College Record, 112*(8), 2118–2153.

Peppler, K. A. (2013). *New opportunities for interest-driven arts learning in a digital age.* New York, NY: Wallace Foundation.

Peppler, K., Santo, R., Gresalfi, M., & Tekinbas, K. S. (2014). *Script changers: Digital storytelling with Scratch.* John D. and Catherine T. MacArthur Foundation reports on digital media and learning. Cambridge, MA: MIT Press.

Ravitch, D. (2013). *Reign of error: The hoax of the privatization movement and the danger to America's public schools* [Kindle version]. New York, NY: Knopf.

Resnick, M. (2002). Rethinking learning in the digital age. In G. S. Kirkman, P. K. Cornelius, J. D. Sachs, & K. Schwab (Eds.), *The Global Information Technology Report 2001–2002: Readiness for the networked world* (pp. 32–37). New York, NY: Oxford University Press.

Resnick, M. (2008, December–January). Sowing the seeds for a more creative society. *Learning and Leading with Technology,* 18–22.

Resnick, M., Rusk, N., & Cooke, S. (1998). The computer clubhouse: Technological fluency in the inner city. In D. Schön, B. Sanyal, & W. Mitchell (Eds.), *High technology and low-income communities: Prospects for the positive use of advanced information technology* (pp. 263–286). Cambridge, MA: MIT Press.

Richardson, L. (2000). Writing: A method of inquiry. In N. K. Denzin & Y. S. Lincoln (Eds.), *Handbook of qualitative research* (2nd ed., pp. 923–948). Thousand Oaks, CA: Sage.

Richardson, L. (2002). Writing sociology. *Cultural studies, critical methodologies, 2*(3), 414–422.

Riessman, C. K. (2008). *Narrative methods for the human sciences* [Kindle version]. Thousand Oaks, CA: Sage.

Rodriquez, V., & Fitzpatrick, M. (2014). *The teaching brain: An evolutionary trait at the heart of education.* New York, NY & London, UK: The New Press.

Rubin, H. J., & Rubin, I. S. (2005). *Qualitative interviewing: The art of hearing data* (2nd ed.). Thousand Oaks, CA: Sage.

Rusk, N., Resnick, M., & Cooke, S. (2009). Origins and guiding principles of the Computer Clubhouse. In Y. B. Kafai, K. A. Peppler, & R. N. Chapman (Eds.), *The Computer Clubhouse: Constructionism and creativity in youth communities* (pp. 17–25). New York, NY: Teachers College Press.

Schwartz, D. L., & Arena, D. (2013). *Measuring what matters most: Choice-based assessments for the digital age*. John D. and Catherine T. MacArthur Foundation reports on digital media and learning. Cambridge, MA: MIT Press.

Sheridan, K., Halverson, E. R., Litts, B., Brahms, L., Jacobs-Priebe, L., & Owens, T. (2014). Learning in the making: A comparative case study of three makerspaces. *Harvard Educational Review*, 84(4), 505–531.

Shirky, C. (2011). *Cognitive surplus: How technology makes consumers into collaborators* [Kindle version]. New York, NY: Penguin Books.

Sørensen, E. (2009). *The materiality of learning*. New York, NY: Cambridge University Press.

Smith, A., West-Puckett, S., Cantrill, C., & Zamora, M. (2016). Remix as professional learning: Educators' iterative literacy practice in CLMOOC. *Education Sciences*, 6(1).

Stager, G. (2014, September 16). Making vs. school "reform": Schooling vs. making (table). Retrieved from http://inventtolearn.com/table/

Stiegler, B. (1998). *Technics and time*, volume 1: *The fault of Epimetheus* (R. Beardsworth & G. Collins, Trans.). Palo Alto, CA: Stanford University Press.

Strathern, M. (2005). *Partial connections* (updated ed.). Walnut Creek, CA: AltaMira Press.

Sullivan, G. (2010). *Art practice as research: Inquiry in visual arts* (2nd ed.). Thousand Oaks, CA: Sage.

Sweeny, R. (2013). Ten ways of making. *Art Education*, 66(2), 4–5.

Thomas, D., & Brown, J. S. (2011). *A new culture of learning: Cultivating the imagination for a world of constant change*. Las Vegas, NV: CreateSpace Independent Publishing Platform.

Vygotsky, L. S. (1978). *Mind in society: The development of higher psychological processes*. Cambridge, MA: Harvard University Press.

Walkerdine, V. (2007). *Children, gender, video games: Towards a relational approach to multimedia*. Basingstoke, UK: Palgrave Macmillan.

Walter-Herrmann, J., & Büching, C. (Eds.). (2013). *Fablab: Of machines, makers and inventors*. Bielefield, Germany: Transcript Verlag.

Wheelahan, L. (2012). *Why knowledge matters in curriculum: A social realist argument*. New studies in critical realism and education. London, UK: Routledge.

Wilson, F. R. (1999). *The hand: How its use shapes the brain, language, and human culture*. New York, NY: Vintage.

Yin, R. K. (2009). *Case study research: Design and methods* (4th ed.). Applied social research methods. Thousand Oaks, CA: Sage.

Yorks, L., & Kasl, E. (2002). Towards a theory and practice for whole person learning: Reconceptualizing experience and the role of affect. *Adult Education Quarterly*, 52(3), 176–192.

INDEX

Colin Lankshear & Michele Knobel

General Editors

New literacies emerge and evolve apace as people from all
walks of life engage with new technologies, shifting values
and institutional change, and increasingly assume 'postmodern' orientations toward their everyday worlds. Despite many
efforts to take account of such changes, educational institutions largely remain out of touch with the range of new
ways of making and sharing meanings that increasingly medi-
ate and shape the lives of the young people they teach and
the futures they face. This series aims to explore some key
dimensions of the changes occurring within social practices
of literacy and the educational challenges they present,
with a view to informing educational practice in helpful
ways. It asks what are new literacies, how do they impact on
life in schools, homes, communities, workplaces, sites of
leisure, and other key settings of human cultural engagement, and what significance do new literacies have for how
people learn and how they understand and construct knowledge. It aims to challenge established and 'official' ways
of framing literacy, and to ask what it means for literacies
to be powerful, effective, and enabling under current and
foreseeable conditions. Collectively, the works in this series will help to reorient literacy debates and literacy
education agendas.

For further information about the series and submitting
manuscripts, please contact:

Michele Knobel & Colin Lankshear
Montclair State University
Dept. of Education and Human Services
3173 University Hall
Montclair, NJ 07043
michele@coatepec.net

To order other books in this series, please contact our
Customer Service Department at:
(800) 770-LANG (within the U.S.)
(212) 647-7706 (outside the U.S.)
(212) 647-7707 FAX

Or browse online by series at:
www.peterlang.com